Robert Robertson is a composer and filmmaker. He has an MFA in Film Production from the Mel Hoppenheim School of Cinema, Montreal. His music/films include *Oserake and the River that Walks*, *Doors of the Spirits* and *I'm Back*, and he has composed the operas *The Kingdom*, *The Cathars*, and *Enoedickes*. He has been influenced by Eisenstein's ideas since 1977, and this book is the result of his doctoral research at King's College London, UK.

INTERNATIONAL LIBRARY OF CULTURAL STUDIES

EISENSTEIN ON THE AUDIOVISUAL

The Montage of Music, Image and Sound in Cinema

Robert Robertson

TAURIS ACADEMIC STUDIES
an imprint of
I.B.Tauris Publishers
LONDON • NEW YORK

791. 430233092 ROB

Reprinted in 2010 by Tauris Academic Studies,
An imprint of I.B.Tauris & Co Ltd
6 Salem Road, London W2 4BU
175 Fifth Avenue, New York NY 10010
www.ibtauris.com

Distributed in the United States and Canada exclusively by Palgrave Macmillan
175 Fifth Avenue, New York NY 10010

First Published in 2009 by Tauris Academic Studies
Copyright © Robert Robertson, 2009

International Library of Cultural Studies 5

ISBN 978 1 84511 839 6

A full CIP record for this book is available from the British Library
A full CIP record is available from the Library of Congress

Library of Congress Catalog card: available

Printed and bound in the UK by CPI Antony Rowe.
Typeset by Oxford Publishing Services, Oxford

TO CLAUDETTE

Contents

List of Illustrations

Acknowledgements

My research for this book would have been impossible without the generous and enthusiastic support of the David Lean Foundation. I shall always be grateful to them for this crucial help.

I would like to thank the following who have been of great assistance in this project:

Professor Richard Taylor, for his invaluable help and advice, for encouraging the publication of my first book on Eisenstein's ideas on audiovisual cinema, for his permission to cite from his edition of *Eisenstein's Selected Works*;

Professor Peter Rist, who prompted me to submit extracts from my work on Eisenstein to *Offscreen*, the online cinema journal;

Dr Donato Totaro, Founding Editor of *Offscreen*, who has supported the publication of my articles on Eisenstein and the audiovisual in his journal;

Professor David Rodowick, who enthusiastically encouraged my research on Eisenstein and the audiovisual at King's College, London;

Rasna Dhillon, my editor at I.B.Tauris, who has helped to simplify for me the intricate process of publishing a book;

Professor Herbert Eagle, who generously gave me a copy of the out-of-print edition of Eisenstein's book *Nonindifferent Nature*;

Professor Julian Graffy, who enabled my access to the DVD collection at the Slavic and East European Studies Library at University College London.

I would also like to thank the helpful librarians at the Maughan Library, the library at University College London (including the Slavic and East European Studies Library), the library at Senate House, London University, and the British Library.

As a composer and filmmaker, my research was not going to be undertaken outside a practical context. For this reason I would like to give special thanks to my fellow artists and friends, the poet Spike Hawkins, and the playwright Seamus Finnegan, for reading my text and for their tremendous enthusiasm and support. Another friend and a fellow composer, the late Christopher Bodman, also provided me with much-needed support in the early stages. In addition I have received valuable encouragement from fellow artist filmmakers Nick Collins, Dennis Dracup, Chris Lynn, Derek Ogbourne, and the writer Susana Medina, who kindly checked my translation of extracts from a poem by St John of the Cross.

My final and special thanks go to my wife Claudette, who has supported me unconditionally in the adventure of this book, from its inception to its conclusion. Her help with various computer programmes was vital, and she provided me with boundless moral support. We work as a team; separately we may falter, but together we can achieve anything.

Preface

When we draw, Paul Klee suggests that we take a line for a walk.

In my work I have adapted his suggestion: I take an idea for a walk.

This book is for those who write, compose, photograph, paint, draw, sculpt, build, choreograph, film; for all who think as a result of doing.

This book is for those who, largely free from imposed preconceptions, enjoy taking their ideas for a walk.

Robert Robertson

Introduction

> The process of assimilating material, i.e. making it 'one's own',
> happens at the moment when, coming into contact with reality, it
> begins to set itself out according to a grid of outlines and sketches
> of the same special structure as that in which one's consciousness
> was formed.[1]

Eisenstein's work is multi-facetted and encyclopaedic in its scope, like that
of other intensely creative artists such as J. S. Bach, James Joyce and
Vsevolod Meyerhold. If we decide to study a facet of Eisenstein's output,
we soon find that this facet inter-reflects with other facets, which in turn
relate organically to other aspects of his achievements.

Fortunately, like Bach, and to a certain extent Meyerhold, Eisenstein
had a gift for pedagogy and in his case, an overwhelming need to explain
to others *what* he was doing and *why* he did what he did. This need led to
his extensive writings about film, in particular about his own work and the
experiences that led to the development of his ideas. His preoccupation
with the expressive possibilities of the sound film, and his search for ways
of structuring it, meant that he wrote more about film as an audiovisual
medium than any other filmmaker.

However, there is a problem with a large proportion of his writings, a
problem of which Eisenstein was very much aware. When he was
writing the introduction to his autobiographical texts in 1944, he
admitted that 'beginning a page, or a section or a phrase, I have no idea
where it will take me as it develops.' This lack of a prepared structure
resulted in texts which have the character of an inner monologue, a
stream of consciousness resulting in a fusing magma of ideas. He
explains how this writing style leads him to 'whole new tracts of utterly
unexpected territory whose existence I never dreamed of, much that is
completely new.' He reaches these new territories of thought by the
technique of unexpected juxtaposition: 'but for juxtaposition – the
separate and uncoordinated facts and impressions had neither the right
nor the grounds to claim their place here!' Eisenstein's serious heart
attack on 2 February 1946 contributed to a strengthening realisation of
his own mortality, and consequently to a speeding up of his highly

associative stream of consciousness style of writing: 'on a good day I can manage up to thirty-four pages of manuscript (this is in the region of one printer's sheet) at one sitting.' This speed of composition and consequent lack of structure contributes to a feeling of improvisatory brilliance which energises his text. However, this kind of writing may cause problems of clarity: Eisenstein had planned to write a textbook. As early as 1927, he wrote about his aim to combine 'autobiography and practical examples (to) make a high-flown theoretical abstraction concrete.'[2] This idea was not an unusual one at this time. Konstantin Stanislavsky had written *My Life in Art* (published in London in 1925), Meyerhold had written *On Theatre* (published in St Petersburg in 1913), and Walter Gropius had commissioned a series of strongly individual artist's textbooks under his Bauhaus School imprint.[3]

So my primary aim in this research is to broaden and clarify our understanding of Eisenstein's ideas, specifically focusing on his thinking about cinema as an audiovisual medium. I am aiming to answer this question: how does Eisenstein contribute to our understanding of cinema as an *audiovisual* medium?

By the term 'audiovisual' I mean the interaction of music, sound and film. This definition is a generalised one, as Eisenstein is more specific when he uses the term 'audiovisual', depending on his context.[4] I believe that these contemporary contexts are vital to an understanding of Eisenstein's ideas on audiovisual cinema.

My other aim is to provide the beginnings of a study of Eisenstein's ideas on audiovisual cinema. Eisenstein was a polymath: he was trained as an architect and civil engineer, he was also a theatre director, actor, graphic artist, film theorist, film director, writer and teacher. In addition he was influenced by a bewildering range of artists, philosophers, scientists, writers, poets, even composers. Where, and from what perspective does one even begin to examine Eisenstein's ideas on audiovisual cinema?

Since 1977, when I came across Yon Barna's biography of the director, I have read everything I could find by Eisenstein which has been translated into French and English.[5] Several key ideas emerged from my thinking about his writings, amongst them are audiovisual counterpoint, organic unity, nonindifferent nature, and synaesthesia. These four ideas form the chapters and the basic thematic structure of this text, which is part of my continuing research on Eisenstein's ideas on audiovisual cinema.

I shall now outline one of Eisenstein's key ideas: the 'montage of attractions', and compare it to the ideas on montage of his contemporaries, Dziga Vertov and Vsevolod Pudovkin. In my continuing research I shall examine in depth Eisenstein's concept of 'dialectical montage' and how he developed it from his 'montage of attractions' idea, and then extended its application to his approach to audiovisual montage.

The montage of attractions

It is remarkable how much of Eisenstein's early article about his new approach to theatre, *The Montage of Attractions*, relates to his future work in cinema. In 1923 this article was published in the journal *Lef*, edited by the poet and playwright Vladimir Mayakovsky. In it Eisenstein states that what he terms the 'basic material' of theatre 'derives from the audience', and he gives his definition of what he calls 'the montage of attractions:'

> *any aggressive moment in theatre, i.e. any element of it that subjects the audience to emotional or psychological influence, verified by experience and mathematically calculated to produce specific emotional shocks in the spectator in their proper order within the whole. These shocks provide the only oppor-tunity of perceiving the ideological aspect of what is being shown, the final ideological conclusion.*[6]

In this approach the audience is raw material which is processed by the theatre, like a factory which moulds the basic audience material into the correct ideological shape or product. The image of the artist-engineer which underlies this definition is characteristically Constructivist, as is the idea of mathematically calculating the emotional or psychological shocks to which the audience will be subjected, once these shocks have been verified by experience. Just over a year later, in 1924, in his article *The Montage of Filmed Attractions*, Eisenstein states that theatre 'is linked to cinema by a common (identical) *basic* material – the audience – and by a common purpose – influencing this audience in the desired direction through a series of calculated pressures on its psyche.'[7]

The idea of an 'emotional or psychological influence, verified by experience' is one that Eisenstein explored further in his study of reflexology, in particular Vladimir M. Bekhterev and Ivan P. Pavlov, and the latter's work on conditioning and the conditioned reflex. Eisenstein's research on audience response studies and other psychological matters (like the phenomenon of synaesthesia) was carried out in close collaboration with Lev Vygotsky and Alexander Romanovich Luria, the pioneer Soviet neuro-psychologists, in the 1930s. Like them he was fascinated by the idea of how ideas could be transferred to an audience just through cinematic means.[8]

In his 1923 article, Eisenstein mentions the popular entertainments which were the source of his montage of attractions idea: the circus and the music-hall. He underlines the importance of form in these performance genres, which rely for their success on well-structured programmes. His concern with the structure of a show leads him to describing an attraction as being a 'molecular (that is compound) unit', which is also an 'independent and primary element.' Eisenstein sees the attraction as being a 'unit of the *effectiveness* of theatre and of *theatre as a whole.*' The relation of the 'molecular unit' to the whole demonstrates his interest in organic unity.

Eisenstein also mentions another form of popular theatre, the Grand Guignol, to differentiate it from a genre he wants to avoid: the bourgeois theatre with its 'unravelling of psychological problems.' He is drawn to popular theatre because of the emotional and psychological shocks it provokes in the audience by representing acts of extreme violence on stage. He used this kind of explicit violence the following year in his first feature film, *The Strike*, when he shows a tiny baby deliberately dropped from a high balcony. Eisenstein concludes his film with the graphic slaughter of a bull, which he inter-cuts with the massacre of a crowd of workers by soldiers representing the ruling class.[9]

He also mentions the influence of the mystery play in relation to the 'compound' nature of his attraction. In his attraction, Eisenstein saw the emotional shock to the audience not as a simple and straightforward emotion, but one which is full of psychological ambiguity. To illustrate this emotional dynamism he mentions the torture scenes from mystery plays, where 'religious pathos gives way to sadistic satisfaction.' Eisenstein went on to research various forms of religious experience, especially in the Catholic tradition, and what he called 'pathos', a form of emotional ecstasy. On his visits to France (in 1929 and 1930) he spent much of his time visiting Catholic holy places, gathering information which was to prove of considerable value when he was shooting his film of Mexico in 1931. In this country he found the combinations of different religions, the mixtures of Mesoamerican and Catholic faiths as well as various combinations of religious pathos and sadism, which are described in the chapter, *Nonindifferent Nature.*[10]

In Eisenstein's montage of attractions idea, each attraction is arbitrarily chosen and independent of the work. In this way he achieves an 'effective structure' for the show as a whole, as well as an efficient means of expressing an idea: 'a specific final thematic effect', an 'essential' ideological theme. An example of his approach to montage is his image of a serape, with its violently contrasting coloured stripes, which he used as an overall structure for his film *Que viva Mexico!* For Eisenstein, this serape is 'the symbol of Mexico'. The different stripes of this garment are analogous to the contrasting episodes ('attractions') in his planned film: 'different in character, different in people, different in animals, trees and flowers.' He intended these contrasting attractions to be 'held together by the unity of the weave' of the serape. For *Que viva Mexico!* he planned 'a rhythmic and musical construction' which would have been part of this unifying weave of the montage of attractions, for what would have been his first audiovisual film.[11]

Published in the same issue as Eisenstein's article *The Montage of Attractions*, was an article entitled *The Cine-Eyes. A Revolution*, by a very different proponent of montage construction, Dziga Vertov. His text, in a layout designed by the Constructivist artist Aleksandr Rodchenko, implies a shouted delivery, as if by a speaker at a large revolutionary rally of party workers. Its tone resembles Mayakovsky's declamations of his poems, to be performed to big audiences, not for reading silently to oneself under the light of a lamp in a bourgeois living-room. Mayakovsky was a close friend of Vertov, and they both shared a passion for revolutionary statements in the form of slogans: Mayakovsky in his agitprop posters and poems, and Vertov in his texts about his type of documentary cinema. This sloganising revolutionary fervour does appear at times in texts by Eisenstein from this period; he was also a passionate adherent of the Revolution, but his background was very different: Eisenstein made a transition from the theatre medium to working in film, whereas Vertov never worked in theatre.[12]

A close contemporary of Eisenstein, Denis Arkadievich Kaufman was born in Bialystock in 1896. He changed his name to the dynamic sounding Dziga Vertov in 1918, when he became involved in making newsreels in Moscow. He had studied psychology at the Psycho-Neurological Institute in Petrograd, where he had set up a 'Laboratory of Hearing.' There he experimented with the use of early recording techniques to capture 'the exterior world of sound.' He cut up recorded sounds and arranged them in musical rhythms, and worked with language, making 'literary-musical montages of words.' His interest in sound was also musical: he had studied the piano and violin in his home town, before his studies and research in Petrograd. Vertov's background was thus a combination of musical and scientific influences, and his special interest in the perception of sound and vision led him naturally to filmmaking. In 1918 he began working at the Moscow Film Committee, and there he developed what he called his 'Cine-Eye' method for making documentary films.[13]

Vertov, like Eisenstein, also wanted to avoid the bourgeois genre of six-act theatre productions, which had become in cinema what he called 'six-reel psycho-dramas.' He wanted a *revolution through newsreel film.* He believed that his camera was superior to the human eye. Vertov's camera has a life of its own, it 'gropes in the chaos of visual events for a path for its own movement or oscillation and experiments, stretches time, dismembers movements, or it does the opposite, absorbing time unto itself, swallowing the years and thus schematising the lengthy processes that are inaccessible to the normal eye.' This Constructivist apotheosis of the machine, of the new technology of the cine-camera, is an example of the artist-engineer who transforms the material of everyday life through an industrial process, to produce art to ideologically influence the newly liberated working class. This idea is parallel to Eisenstein's own new and industrial approach to theatre, described above. Nevertheless there is a divergence of approach between these two filmmakers: Vertov never had to deal with a theatre audience.[14]

Eisenstein actually observed the way in which theatrical audiences react to performances, and he understood their capacity to empathise with what is happening on the stage. At a performance at the Moscow Art Theatre, he had been highly amused at the way an entire audience hummed the waltz a couple on the stage was dancing and singing.[15] Vertov was more concerned with motion, rather than emotion, with showing the audience what the Constructivist camera could do technically, rather than getting the audience to empathise with what was happening on the screen:

> I am the Cine-Eye. I am the mechanical eye.
> I the machine show you the world as only I can see it.
> I emancipate myself henceforth and forever from human
>   immobility.
> *I am in constant motion.*[16]

Vertov, the Constructivist, is keen to impress his audience with the power of the new cinema technology, and this is his ideology. Eisenstein, also a Constructivist, but with a background in theatre, uses his audience as raw material, and uses the new cinema technology to transmit his ideology through his audience's empathy with what is happening in the film they are watching.

Vertov, the Constructivist, is influenced by Lev Kuleshov's early montage experiments: he revels in the ability of his new medium to create imaginary spaces, to create a room by showing twelve walls filmed in different parts of the world. Just like Kuleshov experimented with inventing an ideal filmed woman from parts of different women, Vertov proposes a new Soviet 'Adam':

I am the Cine-Eye.
I take the strongest and most agile hands from one man,
the fastest and best proportioned legs from another,
the most handsome and expressive head from a third
and through montage I create a new, perfect man. ...[17]

As part of his montage method, Vertov is keen on the idea of a montage breakdown which uses his 'mechanical eye' to create a 'dislocation' of the audience's normal view of a staged event like a boxing match or a ballet. His aim is to impose on the audience his own view of these performances, to avoid what he calls the *'series of incoherent impressions that are different for every member of the audience.'* Eisenstein, with his experience of theatre, knows that audiences' impressions are far from incoherent, especially when the performance is effective, and the audience empathises, as one person, with what is happening on the stage. In his montage breakdowns he parallels the reaction of someone to an event, rather than using Vertov's method of depicting the action from his own, the Cine-Eye's point of view, which Eisenstein believes results in 'illusory depictions.'[18] And where in Vertov's montage method is an equivalent of Eisenstein's idea of a practical overall conception, relating each element in the work to the whole film? Vertov asks 'How can we construct our impressions of a day into an effective whole in a visual exercise?' His answer is to build *'by intervals to an accumulated whole through the great skill of montage'*. Vertov explained what he meant by 'intervals' in an earlier article, *We: A Version of a Manifesto*, published in 1922, in the journal *Kino-Fot*. He uses a Constructivist image of a machine to explain this term: 'the material – the elements of the art of movement – is composed of the *intervals* (the transitions from one movement to another) and by no means the movements themselves. It is they (the intervals) that draw the action to a kinetic conclusion.'[19]

Eisenstein makes use of a similar idea in his concept of the 'montage of attractions', except that it is based on a theatre model. He sees his montage as being separate, not from the mechanical process of editing, but from *'any thematic connection with the actors.'* This separation of the 'attraction' from the work enables an audience to link one part of the work with another, to compare a later part with an earlier section. This 'historical' dimension within a work is not a feature of Vertov's 'intervals', which exist only in the present moment. His audiences are passive witnesses to a mechanical process, whereas Eisenstein moulds his audience by using a series of emotional and psychological shocks. This set of attractions is held together by an overall concept: the part is in the whole, the units of attraction combine to make the work itself an attraction, to produce for the audience '*the final ideological conclusion*'. In Vertov's case the ideological conclusion remains the same; like the poetry of Mayakovsky, it is largely anchored in the Constructivist present tense. The historical dimension which is nearly always there in Eisenstein's work, in both his filmmaking and in his film theory, is what makes his 'montage of attractions' concept possible and different from Vertov's montage of 'intervals'.[20]

Another close contemporary of Eisenstein and Vertov, the film director and film theorist Vsevolod I. Pudovkin, was born in 1893. Like Vertov, he had a scientific background, studying physics and chemistry at Moscow University. He was a front line soldier from 1914–15 in the First World War, and was wounded and captured; he escaped and returned to Moscow in 1918. After working as a chemist in a factory he enrolled at the new State film school in Moscow, and studied in Lev Kuleshov's workshop. From an early stage his work in film involved him both as a director and an actor. He acted in two of Kuleshov's films, the satire *The Exraordinary Adventures of Mr West in the Land of the Bolsheviks* (1924) and *The Death Ray* (1925). He directed the short film, *Chess Fever* (1925), and a documentary about Pavlov, *Mechanism of the Brain* (1926). He then directed his three best known feature films, also acting in the first two: *Mother* (1926), *The End of St Petersburg* (1927), and *Storm Over Asia* (1928).[21]

Pudovkin also published texts on film technique and film acting. His writing style is very lucid and calm. Unlike Vertov, with his declamations and slogans, Pudovkin conveys his theory with textbook-like clarity and confidence. The process of making a film is presented in an orderly manner: 'first is worked out the action of the scenario, the action is then worked out into sequences, the sequences into scenes, and these constructed by editing from the pieces, each corresponding to a camera angle.' He provides a generalised solution to a generalised problem. Pudovkin, unlike Eisenstein, does not give a specific problem which he works through to find a specific solution.[22] His approach to a definition of film editing is equally concise: editing 'is a method that controls the 'psychological guidance' of the spectator.' This is a statement with which both Eisenstein and Vertov would agree.[23]

In his list of various kinds of film editing, Pudovkin gives his reader five types of montage, which he collectively terms 'relational editing.' First is editing by contrast, and as an example he gives the representation of a glutton contrasted with the representation of a starving man. Then he mentions editing using 'parallelism', in which two simultaneous actions are inter-cut. As an example of this technique he describes the everyday actions of a factory owner, which are inter-cut with the hanging of one of his employees. Thirdly, to illustrate relational editing using the technique of 'symbolism' he cites Eisenstein's use of images of a bull being slaughtered, which he inter-cuts with the massacre of the workers at the end of *The Strike*. For his fourth technique of film editing, 'simultaneity', he gives another example from a well known film: D. W. Griffith's representation of two actions, which are intercut with increasing speed until they reach a climax, at the end of his filmed epic *Intolerance*. The fifth editing technique Pudovkin calls 'leitmotif.' Here he refers to the reiteration of a theme, for example the repetition of the same shot to emphasise a statement.

This five-point approach to film editing is a combination of the montage methods of Griffith, Eisenstein, and Kuleshov. In his text *Beyond the Shot*, published in 1929, Eisenstein mentions Kuleshov's 'brick by brick' montage method, calling it disparagingly the 'old school of film-making.' To illustrate his point he quotes from Kuleshov's book *The Art of Cinema*, published in Moscow in 1929: 'If you have an idea-phrase, a particle of the story, a link in the whole dramaturgical chain, then that idea is expressed and built up from shot-signs, just like bricks.' Kuleshov's idea of the 'dramaturgical chain' of the 'idea-phrase' which is built up from 'shot-signs, just like bricks', underlies Pudovkin's montage method in which a scenario is broken down into sequences, scenes and camera set-ups which provide shots from a certain angle. For Eisenstein this montage breakdown, 'brick by brick', is a method which risks becoming a dead formula, instead of a dynamic montage which works not by a process of addition, but a process of collision.[24] There is nothing static or formulaic about Eisenstein's approach to writing about montage. Vertov is also dynamic, but he knows in advance what he is going to write about. Eisenstein's writing, with its convoluted subordinate clauses, completely lacks Pudovkin's didactic clarity:

> *Our present approach radically alters our opportunities in the principles of creating an 'effective structure' (the show as a whole) instead of a static 'reflection' of a particular event dictated by the theme, and our opportunities for resolving it through an effect that is logically implicit in that event, and this gives rise to a new concept: a free montage with arbitrarily chosen independent (of both the PARTICULAR composition and any thematic connection with the actors) effects (attractions) but with the precise aim of a specific final thematic effect – montage of attractions.*[25]

Pudovkin and Vertov are notating their pre-existing thoughts, whereas

Eisenstein's writing style is one in continual transition; his thought is developing as he writes.

A note on source texts

The characteristics of an extensive range of Eisenstein's writings – their chaotic, multi-lingual and magma-like quality – make them exciting and full of creative and associative possibilities for the artist. However these same characteristics are also what make his writings bristle with difficulties for the film historian, who is correctly anxious to make the presentation of Eisenstein's own thinking as close as possible to what is known of the director's original intentions.

In order for me to attempt to capture as closely as possible the spirit of Eisenstein's writings on audiovisual cinema, as well as to try to give a sense of the artistic and cultural contexts from which his ideas grew and developed, I have relied as much as possible on texts translated from primary sources. My main source has been the four volumes of the English edition of Eisenstein's writings. This edition, under the direction of Richard Taylor, the leading authority on Soviet cinema, is internationally known as being the closest to what can be called a definitive collection of Eisenstein's writings in English translation. The proximity of the scholars to the Eisenstein papers in the State Archives of Literature and Arts in Moscow (TsGALI), its detailed and scholarly accounts of the primary sources and their presentation, the care which has been taken with the translations, have all contributed to its status. This edition has also benefited from the support and encouragement of Jay Leyda and close collaboration with Naum Kleiman, the Eisenstein scholar of international standing.[26]

The first volume, published in 1988, comprises a selection of important writings from 1922 to 1934, arranged in chronological order. The second volume, published in 1991 and entitled *Towards a Theory of Montage*, mostly drops the chronological approach. Richard Taylor explains why: Eisenstein's writings on montage from the 1930s and the 1940s are very extensive and at times fragmentary, unfinished, and interwoven from different periods.[27] Eisenstein wrote *Mise en scène*, the first volume of his work *On Direction*, in the early 1930s. Before he could begin the second volume, *Mise en cadre*, Eisenstein started filming *Bezhin Meadow* in 1935. In 1937, his work on this film was stopped by the authorities, and he resumed the writing of several texts on montage including the extensive *Montage 1937*. After his work on directing *Alexander Nevsky*, in 1938 Eisenstein wrote *Montage 1938*, which was based on materials for *Montage 1937*. *Montage 1938* is followed by *Vertical Montage* (originally entitled *Montage 1939*). *Montage 1937* was first published in the journal *Iskusstvo kino* in 1939; in 1940 and 1941, *Vertical Montage* appeared in two parts in the same journal. In 1940 Eisenstein wrote texts he entitled *Montage 1940*. Taylor explains that these texts were revised as *Once Again on the Structure of Things*, which Eisenstein later included in his book *Nonindifferent Nature*. Other texts from 1940 became part of his writings on colour.

The third volume, published in 1995, returns to a chronological presentation of Eisenstein's writings, from 1934 to 1947. This volume's collection features texts which have a strongly political dimension, and which reflect the turbulence of the times in which they were written: the period of Stalin's tightening grip on power, the terror of his purges, and the Second World War. Some texts are transcripts, for example of conference speeches (from the 1935 conference of Soviet film-workers), and of a meeting held by Stalin in February 1947, with Molotov and Zhdanov, Eisenstein and Cherkasov, about the second part of *Ivan the Terrible*. In addition we get a sense of Eisenstein as a lecturer (about music and colour in *Ivan the Terrible*, in 1947), and of his pedagogical aims in his teaching programme for his Direction course at the State Institute for Cinema in 1936.

The fourth volume, published in 1995, comprises an extensive collection of Eisenstein's autobiographical writings, the complex and meandering history of which is lucidly described in the *Foreword*, by Naum Kleiman. Written mostly during the director's convalescence from his major heart attack in 1946, none of these writings were published in Eisenstein's lifetime.[28]

In addition I have made use of Jay Leyda's own translations of Eisenstein's writings: *The Film Sense* (1942) and *Film Form* (1949). Leyda was a former student of the director, and he worked closely with Eisenstein on these collections, though *Film Form* was published after Eisenstein's death. *The Film Sense* is largely based on Eisenstein's text *Vertical Montage*, and Leyda has included some very useful primary material, and illustrations, not available elsewhere in English. I have also referred to Leyda's *Eisenstein at Work* (1985), as well as his *Eisenstein on Disney* (1988), for the same reason.

The *Notes of a Film Director* collection of Eisenstein's writings (edited by R. Yurenev, and published by the Foreign Languages Publishing House in 1958) was useful for texts I could not find anywhere else in English translation. An example is the translation of Eisenstein's last text, on which he was working just before he died in February 1948: his unfinished letter to Lev Kuleshov, about colour film. Another example is his text P-R-K-F-V, about his collaboration with the composer.

For the same reason of availability, I referred to Herbert Marshall's edition of Eisenstein's book *Nonindifferent Nature* (1987). Marshall's work lacks scholarly precision and concern with chronology, but his edition of *Nonindifferent Nature* is the only one available in English, though it remains out of print. However it benefits from an introduction by Herbert Eagle, which provides a short account of the genesis of *Nonindifferent Nature*. Naum Kleiman refers to this edition in passing in *The History of Eisenstein's Memoirs*, his account of the scholarly work relating to the preparation of Volume 4 of the Eisenstein edition in English.[29] Interestingly, he does not mention at all Herbert Marshall's edition of Eisenstein's memoirs, *Immoral Memories* (1985). However, I have made an occasional use of this edition, again because I could not find certain texts by Eisenstein available elsewhere in English.

Another source text is Marie Seton's long and at times extremely subjective book: *Sergei M. Eisenstein, A Biography* (1952). On the few occasions I have referred to it, I have given details of the source of her information, or provided an additional and alternative source. In two cases, I feel that her descriptions of Eisenstein's activities in London and Chicago do tally with the type of research activities he describes himself as undertaking.[30]

Anne Nesbet, in her study of Eisenstein's thought, *Savage Junctures: Eisenstein and the Shape of Thinking*, mentions Eisenstein's concept of writing a book of his ideas on film which he imagines would be in the shape of a sphere: 'for everything I do touches everything else: the only form capable of satisfying this condition is a sphere: from any meridian transition is possible to any other meridian.'[31] This structure is analogous to the one I describe at the beginning of this introduction, where I mention the inter-reflecting facets of Eisenstein's thought. I hope that these patterns of his ideas will emerge throughout my text, as it is being read and thought about.

1
Audiovisual Counterpoint

... audiovisual counterpoint, the sine qua non of audiovisual cinema.[1]

Fugue

Eisenstein used counterpoint, and in particular fugue, to find a way of structuring what in 1946 he termed 'audiovisual cinema'. Counterpoint is the simultaneous and contrasting combination of two or more melodic lines or voices, held together by common motifs and harmonies. Fugue is a complex form which makes use of counterpoint in a wide variety of ways, as shown in my diagram of the basic structure of a fugue for three voices (Fig.1). 'Audiovisual cinema' is Eisenstein's concept of how the sound film should work in terms of an interaction of music, sound and film as a unified form. For Eisenstein fugue was an important formal technique for 'audiovisual cinema'. So how can we explain Eisenstein's passionate interest in fugue?

Eisenstein, music and synthetic art

In his *Memoirs*, in the *'The Knot that Binds' (A Chapter on the Divorce of Pop and Mom)*, Eisenstein recalls that after the departure of his mother, when he was eleven years old, 'the piano went too, and I was released from my music lessons which I had just started having'. A few sentences later he explains that 'I do not play the piano; only the radio or the wind-up gramophone.' So his 'playing' of music was to be limited to listening to the performances of others, and his grounding as a practitioner would hardly have gone beyond the earliest stages. In his text *The Dollar Princesss*, Eisenstein confesses that he never had a musical ear. On most occasions he couldn't recall a tune in order to sing it to himself. But at an early age, after attending Offenbach's operetta, *The Tales of Hoffmann*, he could sing the melody from *The Barcarolle* over and over. He was also able to hear internally (but not sing) a waltz tune from another operetta, *The Dollar Princess*, which he first heard in Riga at the age of about twelve. His first encounter with opera was an amateur dramatic production, also in Riga, of

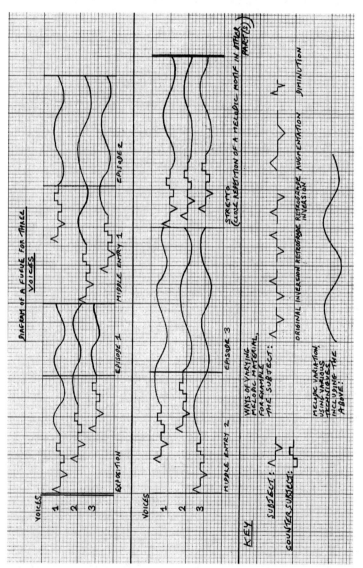

Fig.1 Schematic diagram of a fugue.

Tchaikovsky's *Eugene Onegin*. He also had childhood memories of other operas, operettas and plays: he mentions *Hansel and Gretel, Götz von Berlichingen, Wallenstein's Death, Der Freischütz, Madame sans gène, Around the World in Eighty Days, Feuerzauberei*. Along with the circus (where he liked clowns the best), these were his first experiences of audiovisual performances.[2]

Though not mentioned in an audiovisual context, but regarding colour in cinema, Eisenstein remembers his first experiences of colour films: a Méliès underwater scene, and later, between 1910 and 1912, short educational films and episodes from the *Fantômas* and *Vampire* series. These films would have been accompanied by music, so they can also be counted as being amongst his early experiences of audiovisual work. Lastly, another significant audiovisual influence, demonstrated in the scenes set in the cathedral in *Ivan the Terrible*, would have been the young Eisenstein's experiences of the services of the Russian Orthodox Church.[3]

However, in order to find the origins of Eisenstein's preoccupation with fugue we need to expand the frame and to examine in greater detail a later period of artistic activity, in which there was much experimentation in the combination of visual and aural means of expression, beyond the tradition of Western opera. In some cases this 'Synthetic art' involved influences from the Far East. For example, in 1914 Eisenstein's mentor, the theatre director Vsevolod Meyerhold, directed a double bill of plays by the Russian poet Aleksandr Blok, comprising *The Unknown Woman* and *The Fairground Booth*, in a production which was influenced by Japanese theatre. The Kabuki and Noh traditions were particularly of interest to both Meyerhold and Eisenstein because of their highly audiovisual nature. Performances in these Japanese theatre traditions involve a tight unity of movement, colour, music and text.[4]

Other artists from this period shared a background in both music and the visual arts, which is reflected in their work. In the cases of Viking Eggeling and Hans Richter, this background is combined with a passion for musically inflected painting from China and Japan. In the summer of 1922, Eisenstein joined Foregger's performance group FEKS (Factory of the Eccentric Actor). There he met Grigori Kozintsev, who later became a fellow film director.[5] Kozintsev, in his book about his film of *King Lear*, mentions how he often went with Eisenstein to productions of the Kabuki Theatre, when it visited Moscow in August 1928. He describes how 'Synthetic art, which was so much talked about in the first years of the revolution, was before our very eyes.'[6]

In the period referred to by Kozintsev, in continental Europe there were many experiments relating to the synthesis of light, sound, colour and music. In his text *Vertical Montage*, written and published in 1940, Eisenstein analyses one of the earliest examples of 'Synthetic art', Kandinsky's *The Yellow Sound*.[7] The Russian-born painter, a pioneer of abstract art and co-founder of the Blaue Reiter group of artists, published *The Yellow Sound* in the *Blaue Reiter Almanach* in 1912.[8] This work features an almost abstract plot involving actors wearing costumes which are in various symbolic colours. Kandinsky effects an intricate interaction of music, stage lighting and action to attempt a total synthesis of music, light and colour. Eisenstein notes that Kandinsky calls this work a 'stage composition'. He quotes extensive extracts from it, but he writes dismissively of its concentration on form at the expense of content. However, it is Kandinsky's idea of a performed synthesis of colour and sound which caught the filmmaker's attention. He describes Kandinsky's 'vague perceptions of the interplay of colours understood as music, of the interplay of music understood as colours'.[9] Here Eisenstein is definitely more interested in the principle of sound and colour interaction mani-fested in 'synthetic' art, rather than in its actual realisation in Kandinsky's 'stage composition'. We shall see the far-reaching consequences of his approach.

It is this interplay between music and colour which was to inspire a significant number of artists during the 1910s and the 1920s, quite a few of whom were also preoccupied with fugue, for example the painter-musicians Adolf Hoelzel, Paul Klee and Lyonel Feininger.[10] By examining the 'synthetic' work of these painters, we can see how the idea of a visual fugue became a feature of the experimental art world of this period. This artistic climate, which Eisenstein experienced on his trips to Germany, France and Switzerland from 1926 to 1930, would inform his own theory and practice of audiovisual cinema.

Painters and fugue

An early mention of fugue in the context of a painting can be found in the work of Adolph Hoelzel, a painter who experimented with abstraction even before Kandinsky.[11] He was also a musician (a violinist) and an admirer of J. S. Bach. He developed his own colour theory, using musical terms to describe his systems of colour circles. He explained his borrowing of musical terminology by saying that musicians often used terms from painting for similar purposes. In 1916 he painted *Fugue on a Resurrection Theme*, an abstract painting with a rhythmic use of angular forms, evoking the closed forms of stained glass windows.[12] The dominant shape in this painting is the triangle, which appears in a wide variety of types and positions. This variety of a recognisable shape corresponds to the immediately recognisable melodic motif, the subject of a fugue, which appears in various forms throughout a fugal composition. This formal technique produces an organic unity in which each part of the work is related to the whole, whether it is a painting or a piece of music.

Paul Klee, who joined the *Blaue Reiter* group of artists in 1912, was born into a musical family. He was also fascinated by fugue and polyphony. His father was a music teacher and his mother a singer; he became an accomplished violinist. Even after developing as a visual artist, he continued to play the violin throughout his life, occasionally in public concerts. Admiring Bach and Mozart above all other composers, Klee felt that classical music had entered a decline after the eighteenth century. He believed that 'music was now primarily a reproductive activity; it no longer offered the creativity present at the time of the great masters.' It was this belief which led him to become a visual artist, although he was frequently inspired by musical structures. Klee's ambition, as stated in his diary in 1918, was to master painting to the extent that the composers of the past he admired had mastered music. His aim was to achieve in painting the clear structures and variations of themes which he found in the form of the fugue.[13]

Klee was also influenced by the brightly coloured Cubist paintings of Robert Delaunay, and he appreciated them in musical terms. Delaunay had been an invited participant in the exhibitions organised by the *Blaue Reiter* group, and his work had been reproduced in the *Blaue Reiter Almanach*. In the French painter's work, Klee detected a temporal quality, resulting in a visual representation akin to a fugue: 'Delaunay strove to shift the accent in art onto the time element, after the fashion of a fugue, by choosing formats that could not be encompassed in one glance.'[14] This association of a painting with the fugue is an important idea which was developed by the artists Hans Richter and Viking Eggeling. They (and later, Eisenstein) were to make a similar connection between the traditions of Chinese and Japanese scroll painting and the fugue.

For Klee, the temporal aspects of a painting had a greater *spatial* quality than was possible in music. He called this type of art 'polyphonic painting'. This involved a significant correspondence between the space in a picture and the passage of time. 'Polyphonic painting' could be realised in various formats, horizontal or vertical, but they all had in common the characteristic that they could not be grasped in a single instantaneous glance. Klee's use of the term 'polyphony' also implies that in this synthetic form of art more than one 'voice' appears simultaneously – these voices are shown in visual and spatial terms, and they are analogous to melodic lines in a musical score.[15]

Klee's watercolour *Fugue in Red* (1921) is a good example of 'polyphonic painting'. Here the repetition of various shapes evokes the visual equivalents of canonic imitations, where the echoing of melodic motifs are expressed by the close repetition of shapes in the painting. Melodic inversion, the turning upside down of melodic patterns, is shown in shapes which are reversed in an analogous way, like the triangles in the middle and in the bottom right of the painting. Invertible counterpoint, whereby melodic material can be placed alternatively both above and below another melodic line, is found in combinations of shapes which are spatially arranged in the same way, like the rectangles at the bottom left below the vase-like shape, which appear above a similar shape on the right in the picture. What Klee achieves in such 'polyphonic painting' is similar to musical notation, a visual representation of a musical structure, where the space from left to right in the picture corresponds to the passage of time in a piece of music.[16]

During the early period of his teaching at the Bauhaus, Klee would experiment with such fugal structures in his paintings in an attempt to solve problems of visual composition by borrowing elements of this musical form. Other artists at the Bauhaus experimented with possible structural relations between fugues and the visual arts. Heinrich Neugeboren, for example, worked in a more literal manner than Klee. He made a sculptural transcription in steel of four bars from a fugue by Bach in his *Plastic Depiction of Measures 52–55* of the *Eb minor Fugue* by J. S. Bach (1928). His intention was to clarify the spatial and temporal aspects of this extract from a fugue. This sculpture clearly delineates a counterpoint of three melodic lines. Reading the sculpture from left to right like a music score, one can see a canonic imitation (like a *stretto*) between the three voices, beginning with the lowest one. This echoing pattern is finished by the middle of the sculpture, and it also occurs with an inversion of the second part of the motif at the 'end' of the sculpture on the right. This echoing pattern also begins in the lowest voice. The vertical aspects of the sculpture correspond to the vertical harmonic nature of the fugue. These vertical aspects support the melodic outlines of the motifs. By using his sculpture to 'analyse' this extract from a Bach fugue, Neugeboren could not only hear more distinctly what was happening in the music at this point, but he could also see its spatial and temporal aspects more clearly than with traditional music notation. In this intention he echoes Klee's belief that the temporal aspects of a painting could be shown to have a greater spatial presence than was possible in music. Neugeboren has thus moved beyond Klee's idea of 'polyphonic painting' to make a three dimensional 'polyphonic sculpture'.[17]

With Klee at the Bauhaus was another musician-painter, Lyonel Feininger, who composed fugues for organ which were performed in Germany and Switzerland between 1921 and 1926. Like Hoelzel and Klee he had a strong musical background. Like them he also had a special affection and admiration for the music of J. S. Bach. Music was so important to him that he stated, 'Without music I cannot see myself as a painter.' However, he professed not to be interested in expressing music in terms of painting, acknowledging that many artists had attempted to do this. Instead he confirmed his interest in polyphony, which when 'paired with delight in mechanical construction, went far to shape my creative bias'.[18] This statement is comparable to Eisenstein's fascination with the polyphonic nature of the building of a pontoon bridge, which he witnessed as a young trainee engineer during the First World War. In *Nonindifferent Nature* he described the coordinated efforts of each student engineer, which 'merge into a single general production, and taken all together, are combined in an amazing orchestra counterpoint experience of the process of collective work and creation'.[19]

It was inevitable that some of these painters with a strong musical background should become involved in making the first experimental films. It was a short but daring step to shift from making abstract visual art structured by musical forms, to adding an actual temporal dimension thereby making these images move in abstract films.

Hans Richter and Viking Eggeling: from abstract art to abstract film

In Zürich in 1919, Klee met Viking Eggeling, who, together with Hans Richter pioneered abstract film.[20] Richter's first meeting with Eggeling also took place in Zürich, in 1918, thanks to the Dada poet Tristan Tzara.[21] During the First World War, Zürich was not only the cradle of Dada but it was also a focal point for other artists like Ferruccio Busoni and James Joyce, both of whom lived in Zürich at this time and were to have an indirect but key role in the invention of audiovisual counterpoint.

Within three years of their first meeting, Richter and Eggeling made their first abstract films, which owe as much to their background as visual artists as to the influence on them of musical composition. Both artists grew up in families where music was important. Richter's mother played the piano and there was much music-making in his household. Later in life he confirmed that he had always had since childhood a great passion for music. Eggeling's father ran the music shop in the Swedish artist's home town and was also a clarinettist and composer for military band. According to Richter, Eggeling from childhood was surrounded by music.

In order to gain some understanding of how abstract film came into being, and how music was involved in this process, we need to look at what both Richter and Eggeling brought to their collaboration. Following this path we shall find some surprising connections between the ideas and methods Richter and Eggeling used to make the transition to film using musical techniques, and Eisenstein's investigations into ways of combining music with film.[22]

In 1916 Richter became a key member of the original Dada group of artists in Zürich who set up the Cabaret Voltaire in a nightclub where they performed sketches, poetry and music and exhibited works of art. He made extensive use of chance methods in his work, which was almost abstract. Richter explains that to the Dadaists 'chance appeared (to us) as a magical procedure by which one could transcend the barriers of causality and of conscious volition, and by which the inner eye and ear became more acute, so that new sequences of thoughts and experience made their appearance.' In Richter's explanation the Dadaists' chance procedures can already be seen. They were associated by them with the idea of a transcendence into new possibilities of thought and experience, as well as with a heightened inner audiovisual sense.[23]

At that time Richter also felt the overwhelming presence of Cubism, and its resultant fragmentation of the image – the Dada group, as mentioned earlier, showed the influential French artist Robert Delaunay's work in their art shows.[24] However, another side of Richter's personality was drawn to highly ordered structures, which he associated with music. He used techniques derived from music to control what he called 'the heap of fragments inherited from the Cubists'. By 1917 he felt that 'a structural principle was needed to save the new freedom of this unlimited-form-and-color-world from anarchy.' He found that the music of J. S. Bach was a great help in this respect. Using Bach's contrapuntal techniques he realised that in various places on his canvas he could repeat a theme and vary it to a greater or lesser extent, in this way combining order and structure with the other more chance-derived and abstract nature of his work.[25]

In the attempt to find some sort of equilibrium in the forms he used in his drawings, Richter's passion for music led him to the idea of meeting with the Italian German composer Ferruccio Busoni. Also living in Zürich, Busoni was famous as a piano virtuoso, conductor, composer, and specialist in the music of J. S. Bach. In the evenings he would hold court by a fountain outside Zürich railway station. Richter sought his advice about how he could obtain a sense of equilibrium and counter-equilibrium between the black ink marks and the white paper in his drawings, a difficulty he believed was analogous to a musical problem. Busoni advised him to study counterpoint, in particular the preludes and fugues Bach wrote for his wife, Anna Magdalena. At the piano Richter studied these pieces: 'the up and down, the movements and counter-movements all leading to a definite unity.' This is how Richter came to use techniques derived from counterpoint, to move from the almost chance-created and nearly abstract series of black and white *Heads* (for example the *Heads* of Jean Arp from 1916) to a musical and total abstraction of forms.[26] To avoid a sense of chaos in his work, Richter sought an order which would function as its dialectical opposite. However, this would be a living organic order which would permit the mind to be present and to operate in free flow. He saw musical counterpoint not only as a technical means, but also as an actual philosophy, one which would afford him a clearer perspective of the interaction of motives and forms. He believed that this approach would enable him to completely let go of the figurative in the form of objects (like his *Heads*) so that he could work with free abstract forms on a surface. He would make these forms interact with each other, moving them together, as well as one against the other. He saw this realisation of forms in both musical and visual terms.[27] So his use of a visual version of counterpoint enabled him to find a firm structure for his abstractions, very much in the way that Klee had solved analogous compositional problems in his own painting, also by using fugal structures.

By using these contrapuntal formal techniques Richter realised that he could 'articulate only by contrasts and could establish relations only by analogies'.[28] For him, counterpoint involved not only the principle of contrast – one melodic line contrasting simultaneously with another – but it also had a tremendous potential in terms of analogies. At the same time as Richter was seizing upon counterpoint as an answer to his formal problems with regard to order and indeterminacy, Eisenstein was a young engineer taking part in the making of a pontoon bridge over the Neva River, as mentioned earlier. He watched the impressive coordination of the lines of soldiers assembling the bridge, and years later he described his vivid impressions in terms of an amazing multi-linear orchestral and rhythmic counterpoint, whose operations created dynamic lines imprinted in space, showing the rhythms and duration of their flight.[29] Richter mentioned a similar experience, where he was also aware of the powerful potential of a musical analogy: 'I found rhythmical expression not only in music but also in the steadily repeated movements of workmen in the streets.'[30] This was a period of heightened interest in the interaction of the machine and human labour, manifesting itself in the Constructivist movement.[31] Consequently it is not surprising that both Richter and Eisenstein (and Feininger, as I mentioned earlier) shared an interest in the quasi-mechanical movements involved in collective manual labour. However, it is more interesting to note that these artists shared a sensitivity to the musical analogies of such activity, and that they realised the fundamental importance of the use of such analogies in the solving of their formal problems. The concept of musical analogy was to be a pivotal idea in the collaboration between Richter and Eggeling, and it was this concept and this collaboration which led to the birth of abstract film.

In 1916 Eggeling exhibited his work at the Cabaret Voltaire, the same year that Richter became a member of the Dada group. The Cabaret Voltaire was founded and organised by the poet Hugo Ball and his future wife, the singer Emmy Hennings. Ball was deeply impressed by Kandinsky's idea that there was a need for a synthesis of the arts, a new form of Wagner's *Gesamtkunstwerk*. This was one of the key ideas underlying the mixes of poetry, music, visual art and dance in the performances at the Cabaret Voltaire. Amidst the disaster of the First World War, in neutral and peaceful Zürich, The Dada group's activities were in part fuelled by a desire to create a new synthesis for a new beginning.[32]

Eggeling shared this idealism, and would also have been aware of Kandinsky's ideas about correspondences between the aural and the visual.[33] In the *Blaue Reiter Almanach* Kandinsky quotes Goethe's statement that 'in painting the knowledge of the thorough bass has been missing for a long time; a recognized theory of painting, as it exists in music, is lacking.' Kandinsky, in his essay 'On the Question of Form' in the *Almanach*, states that the rules of this 'thorough bass' would merely be 'the recognition of the inner effect of various methods and their combination'.[34] This idea gave Eggeling the impetus and the name for his systematic sequence of drawings of abstract motifs, the *Thorough-Bass of Painting*.[35] Goethe's idea of the 'thorough-bass' or *basso continuo* was derived from music, in particular the music of the Baroque era, the period of J. S. Bach. At this time the thorough-bass, the lowest line of melody in the music, was used to anchor harmonic structure – it provided the structural foundation for each composition. A musical analogy of this sort was appropriate for a period where artists were attempting to find a new way to structure their work, to completely re-think it from its foundations, from its 'thorough-bass'.

Like Richter, Eggeling met with Busoni during one of the evenings when the composer was available for discussions at the fountain by the railway station in Zürich.[36] In his composition classes Busoni would explore with his students what he believed was a fundamental musical technique and form: counterpoint and fugue.[37] This was a reflection of his passion for the music of J. S. Bach, whose works he studied, transcribed, edited and performed. After his meetings with Busoni, Eggeling developed his *Thorough-Bass of Painting* by adding to his drawings the concept of counterpoint, resulting in his *Horizontal-Vertical Orchestra* (1919).[38] The latter work began as a set of drawings based on combinations of forms from the repertoire of shapes and drawings in his *Thorough-Bass of Painting*. Eggeling then used these abstract motifs, which are related both in horizontal and in vertical terms like counterpoint, to make a ten minute film also titled *Horizontal-Vertical Orchestra*. By this time he had already met Hans Richter and they had started their collaboration.

As mentioned above, Eggeling was introduced to Richter in 1918, by one of the key poets and founders of the Cabaret Voltaire, Tristan Tzara. The poet had realised that they were both 'experimenting with similar ends in view'. When at their first meeting Eggeling showed Richter a drawing from his *Thorough-Bass of Painting*, Richter later recalled that for him the Swedish artist's repertoire of forms was a revelation. He realised that Eggeling had achieved a level of control of form which he had not yet found. He also saw that Eggeling's approach had room for the inclusion of the element of chance, which was so important to the Dadaist approach (Eggeling was also a member of the Dada group). In addition, Richter recognised that his *Thorough-Bass of Painting* had 'a level of visual organization comparable with counterpoint in music: a kind of controlled freedom or emancipated discipline'.[39] The combination of all these elements was what Richter had been seeking: what he called Eggeling's 'system' could solve the formal problems in his own work.[40] According to Richter this system involved the most elementary pictorial element, the line, and he was working on what

> he called its 'orchestration'. ... This was the interplay of relationships between lines which he had arranged (as I had done with positive and negative surfaces), in contrapuntal pairs of opposites, within an all-embracing system based on the mutual attraction and repulsion of paired forms. ... We were no longer interested in 'form' but in a principle governing relationships. Form could be placed in context only by its opposite, and could be brought to life only by the establishment of an inner relationship between the two opposites. This was the only way to create a unity, that is to say, an artistic whole. ... At the time we were convinced that we had set foot in completely unknown territory, with musical counterpoint as its only possible analogy.[41]

Richter realised that he and Eggeling were seeking passionately the same solution: they were both trying find the fundamental laws of expression. It dawned on Richter that he was only at an early and exploratory level, whereas Eggeling had already assembled an entire complex model.[42] His system was based on the 'orchestration' of line which involved a 'counter-point' of opposites, a simultaneous combination of opposite forms.

Here we see the importance of music for both artists. For Richter, music had provided him with his first awareness of something existing on a transcendent level, and he described how Eggeling 'like me … had arrived at his theory by way of music, and always explained it in musical terms'. Richter and Eggeling were not using music literally, but they were using the power of analogies derived from music to take them into 'completely unknown territory'. Both artists shared a preoccupation with the spiritual and philosophical implications of counterpoint. For Richter, counterpoint went beyond technique and it even took on the importance of a philosophy which influenced his approach to life.[43] This approach is comparable to the way Eisenstein took a musical structure like fugue and used it at first as a formal artistic solution, then extended it to apprehend an even broader range of experience and phenomena. But before turning to Eisenstein we need to see how Eggeling and Richter made the difficult transition from the still to the moving image.

Chinese and Japanese scrolls and counterpoint

In Richter's description of Eggeling's *Thorough-Bass of Painting* can be detected the influence of Far Eastern philosophy, namely Taoism. This is particularly clear when he mentions the 'contrapuntal pairs of opposites, within an all-embracing system based on the mutual attraction and repulsion of paired forms' and the concept of a unity of opposites. These ideas relate to the Chinese Taoist vision of the interaction of two directly opposing principles, the Yang and the Yin, which when brought together in various ways provide the basis for all phenomena.

Eggeling and Richter, inspired by Busoni's ideas about counterpoint, found that using the idea of counterpoint to structure their work led them to a horizontal expansion of their motifs. This approach resulted in a structure which was similar to that of a musical score, where the passage of time is symbolically presented in a movement from left to right. As both artists wished to remain in the sphere of the visual arts rather than become involved in the representation of music, it was a natural progression for them to look to a tradition of painting which has a strong temporal element. They found this tradition in Chinese and Japanese scrolls, painted by artists who were inspired by Taoist thought. These scrolls were a perfect synthesis of their Taoist-inspired vocabulary of abstract motifs in combination with the use of counterpoint, and especially fugue, as a means to structure the progression in time of the variations of their abstract motifs.

So, inspired by Chinese and Japanese scrolls, Richter and Eggeling set out the variations of their graphic themes on long scrolls, where 'the orchestration of all stages of form development is seen and felt simultaneously.' Eggeling made his *Horizontal-Vertical Orchestra* scroll in 1919, and Richter made his *Preludium* scroll in the same year, followed by other scrolls: *Fugue* (1920), *Rhythm 23*, *Fugue* (1923) and the sketches for *Rhythm 25*. The numbers in the titles of some of these scrolls are named after their year of composition. Richter explains how all his scrolls begin with a basic pattern whose forms are developed to the utmost extent, using every contrapuntal device at a variety of stages. This is close to the way a good fugue should work. For example, in his *Fugue* scroll from 1920, there are five sets of shapes laid out to be read from left to right, as in a musical score. The first two sets of interlocked motifs appear in retrograde form in the fourth and fifth sets on the left. The central set of motifs is a variation of the sets of shapes on either side of it. These interlocked shapes or motifs are analogous to the repeated melodic motifs in a fugue, which are spatially arranged on varying levels, as in the upper or lower voices in a fugue. The shapes interlock both horizontally and vertically as do motifs in fugal counterpoint. The motifs of the white 'F' shape and the black and white 'L' shape could be loosely connected with the analogy of the subject and countersubject melodic motifs in a fugue. However, this type of analysis should not be taken too far, as neither Richter nor Eggeling were aiming at the literal transcription mentioned earlier in Neugeboren's sculpture of four measures from a fugue by Bach. Richter and Eggeling's aim was to use the analogy of counterpoint and fugue to solve their formal problems, not to create one-to-one visual transcriptions of music. In this way they avoided the limitation that a tautology of forms would impose, and which would have resulted in alternative forms of music notation. The complexity of these problems would inevitably mean that their transition to film would not be a simple one. Richter describes this transition via a process of failure. His reasonable move from the easel format to the scroll had taken him out of a whole tradition of painting. After the completion of his first scroll in 1919, he realised that he had gone further than he had expected: he had never thought that the energy which had built up in this painting would demand a resolution in real movement.[44] This was a genuine surprise for both Richter and Eggeling. They had reached a point at which they realised that the only way forward was to create actual movement, but this was complicated by the abstract nature of their art.[45]

The transformations they operated on the counterpoint of forms were closer to a loose form of music notation than to any animation of a recognisable figurative image. They were not yet ready to produce the large amounts of repetition on a film strip which are needed to produce the illusion of a moving image. Also, their abstractions didn't have the obvious and foreseeable paths of movement of figurative animation, as they were to realise later when they encountered problems at the Universumfilm Aktiengesellschaft (UFA) animation studio in Berlin. In 1919 one of the Dada painters, Marcel Janco, tells how he came across Eggeling one night in the street in Zürich. Eggeling excitedly demonstated for him a large flip-book of images which he flicked through to create what Janco described as 'the illusion of a sequence of images miraculously superimposed on each other like at the cinema'.[46] This experiment shows how Eggeling was at a 'half-way' stage to film: there is an illusion of movement here, but it is through superimposition. The gradual change of images needed to avoid this effect of superimposition had not yet been achieved. Perhaps, given the abstract nature of the forms depicted, it had not yet been thought to be necessary. Another method Richter and Eggeling used in an attempt to transform their scroll paintings into films demonstrated a touching naivety, something which often accompanies real experimentation. Initially they had painted on very thin rubber sheets some shapes which they saw as being analogous to musical instruments. They then got Richter's brothers and sisters to pull the rubber sheets vertically or horizontally, thus stretching their drawings to produce a little motion, a result they found totally unconvincing. At this point they realised that film was the only way forward.[47]

Eggeling and Richter at UFA

Richter and Eggeling jointly wrote *Universal Language*, a pamphlet to raise money for their transition to film. By promoting this text and by canvassing various people, in 1920 Richter was able to gain access to UFA, the giant film company in Berlin.[48] They were permitted to use their animation studios as well as have the assistance of a technician to animate a part of their scrolls. However, their intentions collided with the practical concerns of the technician, who was evidently not used to animating abstract motifs. There was also another problem: it became rapidly clear that neither artist had thought about *how* movement takes place on a screen, in a film. They had just thought of animation in terms of a scroll of varying motifs, without the necessary gradual transitions between the varying positions of the images on their scrolls, which would create the necessary illusion of movement. Faced by the technician's reasonable but increasingly impatient questions, they realised that they had reached an *impasse*: he wished to know in what directions their images would go, how and when their motifs would disappear. Richter and Eggeling had not considered these questions. Richter tells how they had perhaps thought that their shapes would just move along together like the instruments playing in an orchestra, as in the music of Bach and Beethoven. They realised that this idea was not something they could communicate to the technician, so they made up a solution to this problem on the spot. The technician saw that this was what they were doing, and the resulting film, barely a minute long, was a great disappointment. Richter watched this film again and again and pondered as to what he should do next. Comparing it with his scroll he realised that he had to begin again with the very principles which had brought about their transition from easel painting to the scrolls, and to move instead directly to film.[49] So Richter realised that the solution for him did not lie in 'the orchestration of form which we had realized in our scrolls but the orchestration of time'.[50] This produced a completely different result from what Eggeling later achieved in his animated version of his scrolls, his *Diagonal Symphony*. Eggeling wished to retain his painstakingly elaborated vocabulary of forms, so with his companion Erna Niemeyer, he undertook the laborious task of animating this abstract 'universal language'.[51]

Richter, with his mercurial temperament, had found a radically different solution. He could more easily abandon a vocabulary of forms which he had not originated, so he made a mental leap from the articulation of Eggeling's forms to the articulation of time, in the space of the screen:

> Time, the fast the slow, the backwards the forwards – in space – all the articulation which you read in music – that was what really seemed the elementary problem. So I eliminated completely all forms. I used the simple projection screen, the movie screen, pressed it together, extended it again, horizontally, vertically, diagonally, and so forth. I took some parts and moved these parts against each other, concentrating only on different kinds of motion, of movement, and tried to articulate this.

Richter states that this was the underlying principle not only for *Rhythm 21*, his first film, but also for his later films.[52]

Music as a means of structuring film

Here one can begin to see the types of structural problems facing both Richter and Eisenstein. In the case of Richter his problem was to find (a) the transition from painting to the moving image: how to move from painting to film, (b) a way of structuring the moving image which he had derived from painting. He found his solution by referring to music, which he realised had elements in common with both painting and film. Music, with its associated elements (time and rhythm, musical instruments and orchestration) is what provided Richter with a means to understand his problem, as well as a solution to structure the new form of film he had developed, almost by accident. Music is sufficiently different to painting and film to avoid a tautology of form, but it is also sufficiently similar, thus providing useful structural principles, such as counterpoint and fugue. With Eisenstein this problem with form originated with sound film. He had found a way to structure film: dialectical montage. But now he had to find a way to structure audiovisual montage. Like Richter, he found the solution in music, in particular the structural principles of counterpoint, and in a form where the widest variety of contrapuntal techniques are used: the fugue.

For both artists a close examination of the articulation of time, and its associated element, rhythm, was what was needed. Richter has stated that:

> in this way, I very consciously...used my theme: the articulation of Time – not Form. In a way, that has been the underlying motif for all my films. I have always tried to articulate a kind of melody of movements found sometimes with animals, with human beings, with landscapes or whatever; but underneath is always the flow of rhythm – of an articulated time element.[53]

The idea of articulating 'a kind of melody of movements' is what brought Eisenstein later (in his memory of the repeated movements of the pontoon builders) to reinforce his idea of using the concept of counterpoint as a way of structuring film as an audiovisual medium. However, the connection between Eisenstein and Richter exists not only through the idea of using musical forms to structure film of various types: they actually met several times and even worked together on two short films.

Richter and Eisenstein

Richter met Eisenstein on a number of occasions in the late 1920s and 1930, in Berlin, Paris and London. In 1929, they were both invited to the Congress of Independent Film-makers at La Sarraz, Switzerland, where they collaborated on making a whimsical film of the conference, *The Storming of La Sarraz*. Later, in 1929 when they were both guests of the British Film Society in London, Richter directed *Everyday*, a short film in which Eisenstein acted the part of a London 'Bobby'.[54] Eisenstein saw a variety of recent experimental films at La Sarraz, including Richter's *Inflation* (1927), *Ghosts before Breakfast* (1928) and probably *Film Study* (1929). He also saw Eggeling's *Horizontal-Vertical Orchestra*, based on his *Thorough-Bass of Painting*, the drawings that he had shown Richter at their first meeting. In addition Eisenstein saw Walter Ruttmann's *Berlin, Symphony of a Big City* (1927).[55] This work, structured and edited along symphonic lines, was a portrait of a day in the life of Berlin. Ruttmann's 'city symphony' film was to come up in conversation when Eisenstein met with James Joyce in 1930.

Richter was tremendously impressed by what he described as Eisenstein's charming manner, his dignity, his great intelligence, and presence. He later was to remember him as the most interesting person he had ever met. There is a sketch portrait of Eisenstein by Richter which dates from this period. However, between them the learning process seems not to have been just a one-way street. At La Sarraz, Richter was amused by Eisenstein's intense curiosity, awakened by a film the like of which he had probably never seen before, his *Ghosts Before Breakfast*. He tells how Eisenstein asked him again and again what he had intended to express in his film. Apparently he had difficulty in believing that the theme of the film (which shows everyday objects rebelling against everyday routines) was the result of a combination of improvisations and a rhythmic idea. This was a painter's film, not one created by a writer.[56] Eisenstein's reaction to *Ghosts Before Breakfast* is not surprising, as he seems to have had little faith in Dadaism. Later, in his preface to the English edition of *The Film Sense*, published in the US in 1943, Eisenstein lists the multiple 'isms' in the arts of the inter-war years: Expressionism, Suprematism, Dadaism and Surrealism. For him these movements represented a simple but catastrophic flight to an early stage of art, one which was without image, without thought or formal considerations. They appeared at a point in the cyclical nature of culture and art which forms both an end and a beginning. He felt that no previous period in art had resulted in such a dead end, as at the start of this twentieth-century age of wars.[57]

We saw earlier how Eisenstein disliked what he considered to be the divorce of form from content in his analysis of Kandinsky's 'stage composition' *The Yellow Sound*, an analysis which not only appears in his article *Vertical Montage*, but also in *The Film Sense*.

Eisenstein's own listing of the films he remembers seeing at La Sarraz reflects his attitude towards abstraction and the avant-garde of the period. The short films of Cavalcanti and Man Ray he called 'abstract bagatelles' and the films by Richter, Ruttmann and Eggeling, 'experiments'. However, for Carl Dreyer's *The Passion of Joan of Arc*, a film with evident figurative content, he had unreserved admiration, describing it as a 'magnificent, tragic image'.[58]

At La Sarraz there is a fundamental difference between Richter and Eisenstein, between the abstract artist who makes short films and the director of feature films. In Richter's terms Eisenstein works like a writer directing the visual artist, while in Richter's case, 'the painter had directed the writer'. However, this different approach doesn't prevent Eisenstein from making use of ideas which both he and Richter have in common, in the same way that he takes what he needs from Kandinsky's work, though he is fundamentally not in sympathy with its results as he sees them.

The difference between both artists is also reflected in their drawings: Richter's output is often abstract, whereas Eisenstein's drawings are always figurative. In his later films influenced by Surrealism, Richter used abstract concepts to structure figurative elements, but in his early films, and when he made the transition from scroll painting to film, he used the abstract concept of counterpoint to structure abstract film. Eisenstein always worked figuratively in his films, using clear script and scenario-based narratives. However, he also used the abstract concept of counterpoint to structure the complexities of what he calls 'audiovisual cinema'.

In spite of their differences, it is clear that both artists were concerned about the potential *impasse* resulting from the influence of Cubism. Richter had needed to find a way to structure what he called 'the heap of fragments inherited from the Cubists'.[59] Eisenstein was equally concerned by what he called Cubist 'deformities' and the Cubists' capacity to destroy form. But like Richter he retained what he found interesting in Cubism. In an analysis of *The Strike* (1924), he singled out a scene which 'contained what I might call the first experiment with sound in all my work in the cinema'. In this scene (featuring an accordionist) he explains that he used 'Cubism's use of multi-level space, which was to some extent why I transferred it to cinema'. This may be why Eisenstein does not list Cubism in his list of the destructive 'isms' of the interwar years.[60]

It is remarkable that both artists found a solution to their formal problems by the use of counterpoint, and in particular fugue. Richter and Eggeling's meetings with the composer Busoni appear to have had a decisive effect in this respect. Eisenstein's idea of using counterpoint, and specifically fugue, came from an equally surprising origin: his meetings with a different sort of musician, James Joyce, in Paris in 1930. When Joyce was living in Zürich, he had also met with Busoni, and had attended his concerts.[61]

James Joyce and Eisenstein

In his Moscow apartment Eisenstein kept a photograph of James Joyce on his wall. In his writings he refers to Joyce much more frequently than to Richter; it is quickly evident that Joyce was a major influence on Eisenstein. For him Joyce was 'a veritable colossus, whose stature rises above fashions and the squalid *succès de scandale* caused by some too explicit pages in *Ulysses*.'[62] In 1928, between the completion of *October* and before resuming his work on *The General Line*, Eisenstein went to Gagri, a Black Sea resort, to rest. There he read and studied James Joyce's novel *Ulysses*.[63]

Surprising as it may seem, there is a direct relationship between the famous *Statement on Sound* and Eisenstein's reading of *Ulysses*. To trace this link we need to look again at the circumstances which produced this *Statement*. Published in the summer of 1928, the *Statement on Sound* was jointly signed by Eisenstein, Pudovkin and Alexandrov. It conveyed the anxiety of these filmmakers about the arrival of 'sound cinema', and the possibility that the use of sound in the new cinema would be 'along the line of least resistance', that sound would simply mimic what was happening on the screen. The Russian filmmakers knew that this sound/image mimicry would destroy their achievements with respect to montage, the principal means of influence and 'the indisputable axiom upon which world cinema culture rests'. Eisenstein in particular had pioneered the development of Soviet montage, and had witnessed the success of *The Battleship Potemkin* primarily because of its tremendous impact abroad. The solution to the problem of sound/image mimicry that the *Statement on Sound* provides is '*the contrapuntal use* of sound *vis-à-vis* the visual fragment of montage'.[64]

This emphasis on the counterpoint of sound and image originated from Eisenstein's enthusiasm when he discovered *Ulysses*. Joyce's use of the interior monologue in his novel dazzled Eisenstein with what he saw as its immense possibilities for cinema. This technique for showing the interior thoughts and feelings of characters in a continuous weave with external events would always be present in Eisenstein's work in the sound film, whether in projects which were realised, or which remained as scenarios and sketches. In 1928, the signatories of the *Statement on Sound* feared that 'in the USSR ... the practical implementation of sound cinema is not feasible in the near future.'[65] Consequently, Eisenstein realised that if he was unable at that time to experiment with interior monologue in the sound film, he would have to experiment with it in the form of text, specifically in his autobiography. This form of writing was to become an alternative outlet for his ideas and impressions when he would not be permitted to realise his film projects. In December 1928, Eisenstein wrote, largely in English, a 'stream of consciousness à la Joyce' which expresses his enthusiasm for Joyce's technique when the novelist describes Leopold Bloom, the hero of *Ulysses*: 'If I'll be quite disappointed in my art potence – I'll write my very scrupulous autobiography in that super-exact manner of Joyce's descriptions of Bloom. Putting all the associations that [cluster?] around the sentence or idea I am writing.'[66] In less than a year Eisenstein was to be able to meet Joyce face-to-face.

Eisenstein meets Joyce

In Paris, on 30 November 1929, Eisenstein had the first of several meetings with James Joyce. He later described the unusual and unforeseen circumstances of his visit – he hadn't expected to meet someone who was almost blind: Joyce disappeared to another room to autograph a copy of *Ulysses* for him, with an inscription that Eisenstein later found almost unreadable. At the end of their meeting he recalled Joyce blindly searching for his guest's overcoat. Embarrassed, Eisenstein later realised that he had metaphorically been blind to Joyce's near-blindness. He stated that the novelist's diminishing sight had correspondingly reduced his acuity of internal vision, which had been so much a feature of *Ulysses*, and which he had expressed through the marvellous technique of the inner monologues of his characters in the novel.[67] In another description he referred to this visit 'as "a ghost experience", because the room in which they met was so dark that both seemed shadows'.[68]

Though Eisenstein related the 'inner vision' of Joyce's *Ulysses* to the writer's problems with his sight, Joyce's semi-blindness must also have been a surprise for him, given the intense visual input provided throughout this novel:

> Bronze by gold, Miss Douce's head by Miss Kennedy's head, over the crossblind of the Ormond bar ... Miss Douce halfstood to see her skin askance in the barmirror gildedlettered where hock and claret glasses shimmered and in their midst a shell ... slow cool dim seagreen sliding depth of shadow.[69]

This section from *Ulysses*, the Sirens episode, with its cinematic interweaving of alcohol, song, and sensuality on a hot June day with the afternoon sun lighting up the glasses at the bar, particularly caught Eisenstein's imagination. Joyce's blend of the strongly visual with the musical, the melding of the 'bronze by gold' sirens with the 'oceangreen of shadow' and the marine references emerging from the song lyrics and the Homeric original, combine in a model of audiovisual counterpoint that

Eisenstein was seeking for the sound film.[70] Joyce was equally intrigued by Eisenstein's films and expressed a wish to see them. Eisenstein later wrote that the novelist was as interested in his (Eisenstein's) experimental techniques in cinema, as he was totally absorbed by Joyce's technical explorations in literature.[71]

Finnegans Wake

At the time of Eisenstein's visit, Joyce was already writing *Work in Progress*, later to become *Finnegans Wake*. He told Eisenstein that it was going to be a linguistic reflection of the birth of various languages emerging from their chaotic origins. His novel would be written in a fusing and poetic magma of words, of which Russian would form a part of this mix of tongues.[72]

In his book on Dada, Richter tells how he believes that Joyce developed his approach to prose style from Dadaist games 'with language, sound, words and associations of sound'.[73] Early forms of these multi-lingual experiments were in the form of 'simultaneist' poems, performed out loud at the Cabaret Voltaire. One of these, *The Admiral is Looking for a House to Let* (by Huelsenbeck, Janco and Tzara) was a poem simultaneously in German, French and English, performed by three poets as a counterpoint of words. Underneath the printed version of this simultaneous poem there is a *Note for the Bourgeois* by Tzara which explains that its creators wished to devise in poetry what the Cubists had achieved in painting. Tzara also draws an analogy between such poetry in its printed form and a musical score.[74] The Dadaists' impulses behind such poetry were to produce a language that went beyond narrow nationalisms, even to the extent of creating a new universal language.[75]

The multi-lingualism, the puns and other games with language, and the musical quality of Joyce's prose in *Finnegans Wake*, are certainly related to the Dadaist experiments, as they are also linked to Cubism's multiple and simultaneous perspectives.[76] For someone like Eisenstein, who admitted that he had used Cubist-derived techniques for an early audiovisual experiment in his film *The Strike*, Joyce's work in this respect would also have been of interest.[77] But again it is surprising what Eisenstein noticed in the extracts he heard from *Finnegans Wake*. Joyce played to Eisenstein a gramophone record of a reading he had made of an extract he called *Anna Livia Plurabelle*. As Eisenstein listened, he followed the text Joyce had read. It was printed in very large letters on a huge paper sheet, three feet wide.[78] These words had been greatly magnified from the published extract which had appeared in the literary magazine *Transition*, so that Joyce in making the recording could read his text in spite of his failing sight. For Eisenstein these gigantic words are a revelation: they are completely in keeping with the author. Their appearance formed a close parallel to Joyce's use of a metaphorical magnifying lens to explore the intricate and tiny labyrinths of the nature of language in literature. They formed a close analogy of the path of Joyce's meanderings through the internal emotional workings and the internal forms of the inner monologue.[79]

Finnegans Wake is the nocturnal counterpart to *Ulysses'* day, with Dublin's River Liffey at night transformed into Anna Livia Plurabelle, the river as a personification of a washerwoman. Joyce's publisher, Sylvia Beach, noted with amusement Joyce's recreation of the brogue of an Irish washerwoman, used when he read the part of Anna Livia Plurabelle. Here are two extracts from the recording that Eisenstein heard on his visit to Joyce:

> Tys Elvenland! Teems of times and happy returns. The seim anew. Ordovico or viricordo. Anna was, Livia is, Plurabelle's to be. Northmen's thing made southfolk's place but howmulty plurators made eachone in person? Latin me that, my trinity scholard, out of eure sanscreed into our eryan! Hircus Civis Eblanensis![80]

And its very musical ending:

> I feel as old as yonder elm. A tale told of Shaun or Shem? All Livia's daughtersons. Dark hawks hear us. Night! Night! My ho head halls. I feel as heavy as yonder stone. Tell me of John or Shaun? Who were Shem and Shaun the living sons or daughters of? Night now! Tell me, tell me, tell me, elm! Night night! Telmetale of stem or stone. Beside the rivering waters of, hitherandthithering waters of. Night![81]

Compared with *Ulysses* the writing here is far less visual. It is based much more on sound. Joyce's increasing blindness led inexorably to a work where the music of language, and the sonic interconnections between languages became dominant.

Both Joyce and Eisenstein were multilingual, so it is perhaps surprising that Eisenstein didn't really take to *Work in Progress*, once he had had a chance to study it more closely. Joyce's aims to 'reflect linguistically the birth of different languages from general chaos' to create 'a fusion of undifferentiated linguistic poetry' is comparable to the Dada poet Hugo Ball's aim to re-discover the original 'paradise language' before the Fall, to create a new universal language beyond the nationalisms which create wars.[82] This idea is not far from what the signatories to the *Statement on*

Sound wished to keep: the idea of cinema as a universal language, a form of sound film, structured by the *'contrapuntal method* (which) does not weaken *the international nature of cinema'*.[83]

But Eisenstein's attitude to abstraction and to Dadaism went against producing a universal language at the expense of a clear articulation of ideas. He likened *Work in Progress* to 'that mishmash cooked up in the kitchen of the subconscious and which passes through a person's mind when they are dozing or asleep'. In addition he described it as being 'an image of the decay and decadence of tomorrow's bourgeois literature'.[84]

The Sirens episode and fugue

Eisenstein was more interested in the visual, cinematic Joyce, which was interwoven with a strong musical element, like in the Sirens episode from *Ulysses*. In his text *The Springs of Happiness*, written mostly in 1946 and possibly later, he playfully counterpoints his observations about the Sirens episode with a description of the idyllic setting which accompanied the writing of his text about audiovisual counterpoint. He moves almost instantly from a description of scenes from his production of Wagner's opera *Die Walküre* at the Bolshoi theatre in 1940, to a decade earlier. He uses the pine trees he had used in the staging of Wagner's opera to make this temporal and thematic transition, in a cinematically rapid way, from Moscow to Finland to San Francisco. His text is both a statement about audiovisual counterpoint and a cinematic realisation in words about this subject, each line representing a highly mobile camera shot:

> I had identified the Valkyries with pine trees. Probably because I first heard their frenzied flight on someone's piano among the giant pines in the forests of Finland. The chords carried the warrior maidens off up to the crowns of the trees at Raivola Station. And I came to know the structure of leitmotif and counterpoint among the bases of even greater trees – the famous redwoods around San Francisco.[85]

As in Gagri two years earlier, Eisenstein had had a chance to rest for a week, concentrate on re-reading *Ulysses* and consider the problems of audiovisual counterpoint. To help him, he had a copy of Stuart Gilbert's commentary on *Ulysses* which had just been published, in 1930. Gilbert, who was one of the translators of the novel into French, was a friend of Joyce and so had access to the ideas and influences underlying *Ulysses*. In his introduction to the Sirens episode, he refers to the importance of music, both in the novel and in Joyce's life: 'all through *Ulysses* we find references to famous singers, to music and the fascination of music; the book itself is constructed on a musical pattern and has much of the formal intricacy of a fugue.'[86] Gilbert goes on to explain that Joyce himself had been known for his fine tenor voice, at a time when Italian-style tenors were extremely fashionable in Dublin in the early years of the twentieth century. So Joyce was a musician who, had he not opted for literature, could, according to Gilbert, have made a professional career as a singer.

Fugue and the sound film

Eisenstein notes that in Gilbert's chapter about the Sirens episode the references are not only to fugue, but also to other musical techniques which Joyce uses in a verbal form throughout this section in *Ulysses*. He explains how, having mastered 'visual counterpoint' (his previous work in montage) it 'was from … literature that I mastered the obvious tangibility of the technique of musical counterpoint'.[87]

This explanation is a key to understanding how Eisenstein uses counterpoint to structure audiovisual cinema. Though he would go on to study musical counterpoint by reading technical works about it by the Russian composer Taneyev and by the English musicologist Ebenezer Prout, it is by coming across it in literature, in a form where it was used to structure text, that he finds it of use: 'I needed the bare bones of counterpoint, separated from what was customary and usual – the world of sounds. In a form in which they could become the backbone of what was new, unprecedented.'[88] What is 'new, unprecedented' is Eisenstein's concept of audiovisual cinema. What the signatories to the *Statement on Sound* had feared and predicted would happen had taken place: *'talking pictures'* where sound and image were totally synchronised, leading to a cinema dominated by a theatrical aesthetic. What had still not happened was the use of sound 'as an independent variable combined with the visual image.' Though the *Statement on Sound* mentions 'a new orchestral counterpoint of visual and sound images' which would keep intact the achievements of Soviet cinema in the domain of montage, it was left to Eisenstein to determine exactly how the sound and image counterpoint was to be structured.[89] Through Joyce's use of counterpoint to structure an episode in *Ulysses*, Eisenstein had the idea of using this musical technique as the 'backbone' of audiovisual cinema, a way of structuring sound (and music) 'as an independent variable' in combination with the moving image.

More specifically, Joyce's Sirens episode is in the form of a fugue, and it was in this highly structured contrapuntal form that Eisenstein would find the solution to his formal problem in what he saw as the new art-form: the sound film. In fugue the horizontal element is totally married to the vertical, the melodic with the harmonic, multiple voices tonally united. This is a key aspect of fugue which Eisenstein learns from Gilbert's analysis, which specifies the presence of two to four parts in the episode, overlapping and interweaving through the same sentence, sometimes closely juxtaposed to heighten the vertical and harmonic aspect of this fugue. He also notes that Gilbert advises the reader to listen to this verbal fugue in harmonic (vertical) and in contrapuntal (horizontal) ways simultaneously.[90]

For Eisenstein this special and characteristically fugal combination reminds him of the 'counterpoint which I adored in the work on the pontoon bridge and the harmony of movements in space and in time'. He realises that his use of counterpoint and fugue as a structural principle 'enriched and expanded my films, giving them a breadth of expression' beyond what a simple familiarity with J. S. Bach's fugal practice, or Taneyev's theoretical writings about fugue would have provided alone.[91] This is one of the main reasons why the Sirens episode is an inspiration for Eisenstein: it successfully uses the structure of a fugue to marry two different art-forms, music and literature, to produce something which Gilbert explains is more than the sum of its parts, resulting in an intensification of meaning rather than a loss. In this way this process is an analogy of what Eisenstein had achieved in film before the arrival of sound: dialectical montage, the juxtaposition of two different images to create a sense which is beyond that of the two images which comprise it. This is something that Eisenstein was aiming for in the audiovisual combinations of the sound film: he had found a musical structure which could be used in the form of an analogy, as its polyphonic nature is an ideal fit for the polyphony of the combination of sound, music and film. And the use of the fugue structure in the combination of these elements also adds an intensity of expression which audiovisual cinema would not otherwise have, as sound would not dominate image, or vice-versa, at the expense of meaning. In this way he had found a means of expression equal to or perhaps more powerful in the effect of its structure than plain dialectical montage. As Richter had pointed out, fugue retains the dialectical 'movements and counter-movements all leading to a definite unity.'[92] Including a vertical harmonic unity, these techniques are fundamental in a dialectical approach to form.

There was another way in which the form of a fugue would be useful in the sound film. Eisenstein mentions that one of J. S. Bach's main points in his own teaching of fugue was the equal role of parts in the texture of the counterpoint – these were like voices of living people. If someone had nothing to contribute, then he or she would remain silent.[93] This approach provides an aspect of fugue which relates it to drama, thereby appealing to the humanistic and socially-conscious aspects of Eisenstein's work in cinema. It also relates to providing a clear narrative, without redundancy, and an expressive content which for him was always of central importance.

Fugue and urban simultaneity

Another aspect of the form of fugue is its simultaneity, the vertical combinations of its multiple voices, both in terms of its actual meaning and its possibilities for structural analogies. Gilbert tells us that in the Sirens episode, Joyce used a certain type of fugue, the *fuga per canonem*. This form involves the *stretto*, which is related to the form of a canon, a contrapuntal device in which each voice closely imitates a melodic motif just heard in another voice, or voices.[94] For Gilbert, Joyce's use of the *stretto* in the Sirens episode 'achieves the effect of simultaneity'.[95]

Simultaneity is a key idea here, as it is closely linked to the simultaneous angles of Cubism. In turn this concept is related to the simultaneities of the modern industrial city portrayed in films like Ruttmann's *Berlin, Symphony of a Big City* (1927), Fritz Lang's vertiginous urban perspectives in *Metropolis* (1927), Murnau's vision of the simultaneous activities of a huge city fairground in *Sunrise* (1927), and Vertov's portrait of modern city life in *The Man with the Movie Camera* (1929). Joyce, when questioned about the urban setting of *Ulysses*, explained that: 'cities are of primary interest nowadays. … This is the period of urban domination. The modern advance in techniques has made them so.'[96]

Joyce's use of the phenomenon of urban simultaneity takes a wide variety of forms throughout *Ulysses*. In the Sirens chapter, particularly in the very first section, it takes the form of what Gilbert calls an overture: an introductory piece of music containing 'fragments of the leading themes and refrains' which appear in a more comprehensible form and order in the main, fugal part of the chapter.[97] In terms of fugal form this section is like a prelude, as in the preludes and fugues of J. S. Bach. The compression of the phrases (and their layout on the page like in a poem) emphasise their musicality and also heighten the sense of simultaneity:

> Bronze by gold heard the hoofirons, steelyringing Imperthnthn thnthnthn.
> Chips, picking chips off rocky thumbnail, chips.
> Horrid! And gold flushed more.
> A husky fifenote blew.

Blew. Blue bloom is on the
Gold pinnacled hair.[98]

These phrases lose their epigrammatic obscurity, as the nature of their interlocked simultaneity becomes unravelled when the reader reads the next section of the chapter, the fugue.

The cinematic nature of this text, each line corresponding to a shot, is similar to Eisenstein's own cinematic texts, like the one quoted earlier featuring Finnish pine trees and American redwoods, where he uses these external elements to structure a meditation on audiovisual counterpoint. The above extract from the beginning of the Sirens episode takes place in Leopold Bloom's mind. It is a meditation, a contrapuntal merging of outside impressions and internal thoughts, an 'interior monologue'. In Joyce's novel, Bloom is the contemporary everyday incarnation of the Homeric hero Ulysses. And it is the stream of consciousness technique that Joyce uses to bring Leopold Bloom to life which caught Eisenstein's imagination with its immense possibilities for cinema.

Joyce: the interior monologue and audiovisual counterpoint

Ultimately, what Eisenstein found in Joyce was the possibility of a new means of expression in cinema, in particular the sound film, achieved through Joyce's counterpoint of everyday events interwoven with his characters' interior monologues: 'The interweaving of a recital of events with the interior monologue of the person who passes through these events, and with those, his passing through which the main character experiences as an event: that is what *Ulysses* consists of in terms of plot and thematic material.'[99]

Joyce's depiction of the counterpoint of the inner monologue with external events has had a key influence on literary form. This is why Eisenstein is fascinated by the minutiae of Joyce's descriptions, his use of the framework of a single day for *Ulysses*, as well as the Homeric foundation of his novel, and the way it is simultaneously structured like a dismembered human body.[100] In the chapter on organic unity we shall see how the relation of the part to the whole, the detail to the overall structure, was of paramount importance to Eisenstein. The melodic motifs which are stated at the beginning of a fugue are used to structure its entire edifice. This is one of its vital structural characteristics: each part of a fugue is consequently related to the complete fugue.

Eisenstein used Joyce's stream of consciousness technique as a model for his films, his scenarios and theoretical texts, and his work as a teacher of film. He turned this aspect of his enthusiasm for Joyce into exercises for his students: he 'made his students 'translate' Joyce's texts into 'film language', especially Leopold Bloom's interior monologues.'[101] Eisenstein was also struck by the remarkable conclusion to *Ulysses*, the long unpunctuated soliloquy of Bloom's wife, Molly. This is an interior monologue which features a simultaneous counterpoint of events and voices in Molly's mind as she hovers on the edge of sleep. Eisenstein called it a 'unique multivoice polyphony'.[102] In the following extract we can hear some of these voices interweaving through Molly's own voice:

> the last concert I sang at where its over a year ago when was it St Teresas hall Clarendon St little chits of missies they have now singing Kathleen Kearney and her like on account of father being in the army and my singing the absentminded beggar and wearing a brooch for lord Roberts when I had the map of it all and Poldy not Irish enough was it him managed it this time I wouldn't put it past him like he got me on to sing in the Stabat Mater by going around saying he was putting Lead Kindly Light to music[103]

Woven into these lines we hear Molly's voice singing, the 'missies' singing, Kathleen Kearney (possibly) saying that her father is in the army, and 'Poldy' Bloom telling people 'he was putting Lead Kindly Light to music.' This type of indirect polyphony is not unique: it is also found in J. S. Bach's *Sonatas* for solo violin, the second movements of which are fugues. Bach, using melodic, harmonic and rhythmic means, implies other unwritten melodies in counterpoint to the solo violin part: 'in these works [Bach] demonstrated his ability to create the illusion of a full harmonic and contrapuntal texture by means of multiple stops and single melodic lines which outline or suggest an interplay of independent voices.'[104] It is this complex associative polyphony which is characteristic of the interior monologue. After meeting Joyce, Eisenstein wrote, 'And how obvious it is that the raw material of sound film is not *dialogue. The true material of sound film is, of course, monologue.*'[105] Here Eisenstein suggests that dialogue is functional, it is in the province of the 'talkie', and it cannot directly express the larger internalised part of our lives. He believed that Joyce's internal monologue could be greatly expanded in the medium of cinema, and that it could be even more effective in this medium than what Joyce had achieved with it in literature.[106]

Though it is clear that Eisenstein had largely derived his interest in fugue from Joyce, there is another important influence involving fugue which helped him to address the problem of how to structure audiovisual cinema: the visual arts. Earlier we saw how artists like Hoelzel, Klee and

Feininger in the early twentieth century used fugue to structure art in which there was a high degree of abstraction. Then we saw how both Eggeling and Richter had found fugue useful to find a form for their abstractions which gradually developed into the first abstract films. Eisenstein's interaction with Richter at La Sarraz and their writings revealed attitudes to problems of form which they had in common, like their ambivalence with regard to the influence of Cubism, as well as the use of counterpoint as a way of structuring films. There were also substantial differences between them with respect to the value of abstraction and various contemporary movements, in particular Dadaism.

The extensive influence of the visual arts in Eisenstein's work is evident not only in his films and his drawings, but in his writings, where he mentions the work of artists from all periods as well as from non-Western traditions, as being a key source of inspiration. What we can now see is how the visual arts inspired Eisenstein in his struggle to find a form for the audiovisual film, and how this compares to Richter and Eggeling's struggles to structure their abstract films, described earlier. A good place to start is the influence of art from the Far East, in particular the tradition of Chinese and Japanese landscape scrolls.

Chinese and Japanese landscape painting and fugue

Like Eggeling and Richter, Eisenstein was inspired by Chinese and Japanese scroll paintings. We have seen how Richter developed his own scroll paintings using musical structures and titles, at times related to polyphony, for example *Fugue* (1920), and *Fugue 23*. Eggeling, in his *Horizontal-Vertical Orchestra* scroll (which he made into a film which Eisenstein saw at La Sarraz) also thought in terms of counterpoint. Richter points out that for Eggeling landscape was used as 'a test case in order to orchestrate form-groups against and with each other.'[107] This is a form of visual counterpoint, using the horizontal and vertical aspects characteristic both of contrapuntal music and of Chinese landscape scrolls. Eisenstein was struck by similar parallels, which he found in art historians' texts about Chinese and Japanese landscape painting. In these texts he noticed that the authors time and again used musical analogies to describe the effect of Chinese and Japanese landscape scrolls. For example they compare the scrolls to a score showing a polyphonic piece of music, both the notations of the landscape and of the music sharing simultaneous vertical and horizontal components.[108]

Eisenstein quotes an extract from Curt Glaser's book on the art of the Far East, published in 1922, where the author describes how Sesshiu (1420–1506), a Japanese painter inspired by the Chinese landscape tradition, repeats a very limited number of motifs and subjects of a similar shape, using a great number of tiny variations in his brushstrokes. In this way Sesshiu achieves variety amidst the unity of the restricted range of motifs he has painted. A single theme is addressed, which undergoes a large number of small variations, a structure which for Glaser inevitably brings to mind the way a fugue is composed. Then Eisenstein mentions that another art historian, Otto Fischer, goes further and describes Sesshiu's paintings as 'plastic' fugues comparable to J. S. Bach's fugues.[109]

The effectiveness of this musical analogy increases with the scroll painting, like the Japanese *makemono*, described by Ernst Diez in an introduction to Far Eastern art also published in 1922. Diez explains how this scroll painting genre cannot be grasped by a single glance, unlike most easel paintings in the Western European tradition. It can only be fully seen if there is time to see all of it as the scroll unfolds. This type of painting becomes a time-based form, like a piece of music. Consequently the way landscape is depicted in the *makemono* will necessarily follow formal rules which resemble compositional rules for a piece of music, which also unfolds its form in time. And the landscape elements depicted in the scroll will also have elements in common with the way music notation functions.[110]

This is the path which Richter and Eggeling had followed, from the repertoire of their 'universal language' drawings to the transfer of these into the form of scrolls. Then Eisenstein makes the link from scroll to film, much as Eggeling and Richter had done twenty-five years earlier, in 1920. In *Nonindifferent Nature* he describes the ancient Chinese picture scroll as being analogous to a ribbon without end, almost like a reel of film of a single panoramic shot of the landscape as it horizontally unwinds. Almost as soon as he has written this, he is aware that his scroll/film reel analogy can work in two ways. The first way is like a shot taken with the camera gliding on tracks, past a series of changing scenes and events. This method is similar to Richter and Eggeling's initial approach when attempting to transfer their scrolls in a literal manner into moving images. The second way is directly related to Eisenstein's realisation that not all of the picture can be wholly understood simultaneously by the eye. This perception has to happen sequentially: a single subject pours into the next subject, a fragment develops into the next fragment. This is the approach that made Richter realise that film works as a series of relationships in time (rather than just as a comparison of forms), a principle found in the single tracking shot. Eisenstein describes the second way as a set of shots in time, appearing to the eye as a flowing together of separate images, or even sequences.[111] This is a much more sophisticated and dynamic interpretation of the scroll/film analogy, and one which is truer to Eisenstein's own montage ideas.

Like Richter and Eggeling before him, Eisenstein found the common elements in both Chinese and Japanese scrolls and film useful, as well as the links between fugal form and the scrolls. However, the problem he wished to solve using these ideas was different. Richter and Eggeling were making the transition from still images which evoked movement, to actual moving images, whereas Eisenstein was already working with moving images, and he needed to find a way of adding the dimension of sound to what he had already achieved in film. As was made clear in the *Statement on Sound*, he didn't want to lose what he had achieved in film montage in the process of adding sound and music to film: 'sound used in this way will destroy the culture of montage, because every mere *addition* of sound to montage fragments increases their inertia as such and their independent significance.'[112] He found the way to fight such inertia in a dynamic form: the fugue. Fugue was also valuable as it provided Eisenstein with a form where there is a marriage between the instant and the successive, between the vertical and the horizontal, which is also something which is present in Chinese and Japanese scrolls.

Eisenstein uses the fugue analogy attached to the Chinese landscape scroll, which in turn is an analogy of the film strip containing convergent sequences, to find a concrete and practical solution to the problem of structuring film as an audiovisual medium. As we saw earlier, he took two media: music in the form of fugue and visual art in the form of the landscape scroll, to structure sound film. This method is analogous to his taking literature, in the form of Joyce's cinematic interior monologue and its implied polyphony (which is also at times fugal in nature), to achieve the same aim: to understand how to combine two different media, music/sound and film, in an effectively structured way.

Thus Eisenstein reaches his idea of vertical montage. He wishes to retain the horizontal juxtapositions of visual montage, and to add to these the vertical component of sound with image. The addition of sound to the image represents an instantaneous combination, but one which simultaneously takes place in a horizontal context. This assemblage represents a high degree of complexity, especially as there may be many voices or parts, interweaving in both the visual and auditory streams in the work. Eisenstein explains what happens in vertical montage: it can be seen in terms of two lines, each of which itself comprises an entire multi-part score. The finding of an audiovisual correspondence has to stem from a desire to match music and picture to a general sense of the imagery created by the work as a whole.[113] The idea of a multi-part score had been with Eisenstein for some time. In a text published in 1928, when his silent film *The Old and the New* was released, he wrote about a 'quality of polyphonic montage' with regard to the future sound film.[114] In his later text *Vertical Montage* (1940), which he adapted in *The Film Sense* (1943), he explains '*polyphonic* montage' as a simultaneous progression of many sets of lines, each keeping a separate compositional path, and each set making a contribution to the whole compositional development of the sequence. As an example he uses the montage structure of the 'procession' sequence from *The Old and the New*. He traces seven independent lines of development in this sequence: heat, changing close-ups, mounting ecstasy, faces of women singers, faces of male singers (he calls both these groups 'voices'), people who kneel (interwoven with bearers of icons, crosses and banners), and people grovelling in the dust. His audiovisual sense is present in the 'voices' of the male and female singers, and he uses the image of a coil of multicoloured yarn to give us an idea of the way these separately distinguishable lines of development run through and bind the whole sequence of shots. The coil of multicoloured yarn is an image for what he later describes as the 'general perception' or 'sensation' of the work as a whole.[115]

Eisenstein's concept of the general perception or sensation has two aspects. It is both the result of the polyphonic montage, as well as the intention, before the multiple lines of the audiovisual montage have been assembled. It is a key idea in the process of editing the sound film: to match music with the visual sequence, this general perception or sensation has to be a determining factor. Eisenstein goes on to explain that it is directly related to what he calls the '*imagery perception*' of both the visual and the musical aspects of the film. He doesn't give an explanation for this term, but writes that it needs constant modifications of each individual feature to retain the key overall effect. It is interesting that Eisenstein also applies the term '*imagery perception*' to the *music* for the film. He is using this term to refer to something which lies beyond the visual and the musical aspects of the film, to an audiovisual unity which exists over and above its visual and sound components. This idea leads us back to his concept of vertical montage and the related idea of 'overtonal' montage, which lie beyond the scope of this chapter and which will be examined later, in the chapter on synaesthesia.[116]

A new form for a new language

We saw earlier how Richter extended the idea of counterpoint beyond its use as an analogy to structure abstract film. For him it 'became more than a technique, it became a philosophy which was important for my general outlook in life.'[117] With Eisenstein, counterpoint, and more specifically fugue, also became extended beyond its technical use. He states that both fugue and the polyphonic principle give the fullest expression to one of the key fundamental principles at the basis of the 'phenomena of reality in general'. He then makes a specific reference to the principle of *'unity in variety'*, which he says is not only an aim to be achieved in works of art, but also a structural principle that is fundamental to diversity in natural phenomena.[118]

This ambitious idea recalls the aims underlying the Eggeling-Richter collaboration. Eggeling, when Richter met him, had made what Richter describes as 'a complete syntax of form-relationships' in his *Thorough-Bass of Painting*, derived from Kandinsky's quotation of Goethe's suggestion that a set of rules be devised that would be fundamental to painting. Eggeling's ambitious project involved 'thousands of exercises – to analyse and to understand all possible elementary relations of line and surface'. The main aim of their collaboration involved their belief in unity, which enabled them to realise that their graphic exercises in analysis were not just experimental in nature, but they actually formed the foundation for an innovative and universal language.[119] *Universal Language* was the name of the fund-raising pamphlet Eggeling and Richter wrote to finance their first abstract films. The idea of a universal language was also an important and similarly idealistic aim for the Dada poets. Their 'simultaneist' multi-lingual poems, and their experiments with sound poems which use onomatopoeia, assonance and alliteration were attempts to make 'universal' meaning. This universality was also one of the key aims of the signatories to the *Statement on Sound*: to retain the universality of 'silent' cinema in the sound film. Two fundamental aims are in evidence here. These artists, whether they worked with the moving image or with words, sought to find a universal language, and to find a way to structure it. At this point a new language needs a new form, whatever the medium of expression.

The influence of Cubism had produced the near abstract heads by Richter, and the multi-lingual poems and sound poems of the Dada poets. However both Richter and Eisenstein were concerned by the chaos implied in this work. Eisenstein called the Dada poems a 'retreat not merely to the nursery but to the cradle itself' and he was unconvinced by Joyce's *Work in Progress*, which probably had its roots in Dada poetry.[120] Richter and he were looking for structures which would provide an ideal ordering principle for their attempts at a universal language, but a principle which would allow what Richter called 'controlled freedom' and what Eisenstein referred to as 'unity in variety'.[121] Both of these concepts had their origin in Chinese philosophy – both artists had been influenced by Taoism, both mention the importance of the Yin/Yang principle in their work. Indeed, Eisenstein relates directly the Taoist system of oppositional pairings to what he calls '*the laws of montage combinations*'.[122]

During the first decades of the twentieth century, many artists were attempting a new form of what Richard Wagner called *Gesamtkunstwerk*, a complete unity of the arts, what was termed Synthetic art at the time. There arose the phenomenon of several artists who were also musicians, and who were looking for ways to structure what was largely abstract work. Because of its strong degree of abstraction, this painting had strong analogies with music, so it was not difficult for these painter musicians to use forms normally used in music to structure their paintings. What is striking about this phenomenon is the number of these artists who decided to use fugue to provide a form for their work. Eggeling and Richter went a step further and found that they were using fugue to structure what became the first abstract films. Both artists had been influenced by the Italian German composer Busoni, who believed that counterpoint and fugue were fundamental forms in music. In their transition from the still to the moving image, Eggeling and Richter also found the Tao-influenced Chinese and Japanese scroll paintings useful. Later Eisenstein was to be similarly influenced by these scroll paintings, as well as fugue, for his transition to the sound film. He wrote that it was through Joyce that he had discovered fugue as a means to structure audiovisual cinema. Joyce had also met with Busoni in Zürich, and he had attended his concerts. There may also have been a link here with Joyce's use of fugue in *Ulysses*.

The simultaneous perspectives of Cubism had influenced Joyce in literature, Richter in painting and Eisenstein in film. However the latter was never drawn to abstraction as an end-result in a work, and he distrusted it in Richter's work, and in Joyce's late work, *Finnegans Wake*. He had nevertheless to find a way to structure audiovisual cinema, to prevent it from becoming filmed theatre.[123] He was to achieve this through a process of abstraction, by understanding the abstract structures underlying the techniques of counterpoint and fugue, and using these as analogies, like Richter had done in his first abstract films, and Joyce in the Sirens episode from *Ulysses*. He was not interested in abstract film, but he did admire *Ulysses*. It was still a figurative novel, unlike Joyce's later and more abstract *Finnegans Wake*. Eisenstein realised that the use of counterpoint and fugue would help him, in the form of audiovisual counterpoint, to solve the formal problems involved in structuring any combination of music/sound and figurative film, and at the same time to create a new language: audiovisual cinema.

2
Organic Unity

... to develop one or other element of cinema is possible only through a thorough study of the basic phenomena of cinema. And the origin of each of these elements lies in the other arts.[1]

The concept of organic unity and the audiovisual was significant in the work of Vsevolod Meyerhold, and it also influenced Eisenstein's thinking about audiovisual cinema. In this context I define organic unity as a technique used to structure a work so that there is a direct relationship between each part of the work and its totality.

Meyerhold and Eisenstein: the interweaving of their lives and work

'I never loved, idolized, worshipped anyone as much as I did my teacher ... the greatest master of our theatre.'[2] In his autobiography, Eisenstein announces his teacher as if for an attraction in a revue: 'the divine! The incomparable! Mey-er-hold ... I was to worship him all my life.'[3] In turn Meyerhold, in 1936, towards the end of his career, wrote a dedication on a photograph of himself, which he gave to his former theatre student: 'I am proud of my pupil who has now become a master. I love the master who has now founded a school. I bow to this pupil and master, S. Eisenstein.'[4] In a lecture in the same year Meyerhold spoke of Eisenstein in a similar vein, showing the same ambivalence with regard to his former student's status: 'all Eisenstein's work has its origins in the laboratory where we once worked together as teacher and pupil. But our relationship was not so much the relationship of teacher and pupil as of two artists in revolt.'[5] Meyerhold's equivocal attitude to Eisenstein was rooted equally in his awareness of Eisenstein's exceptional talents, his awareness of his own talents and their contribution to Eisenstein's development.

In his text, *How I Became a Director*, written in 1945 for a collection of essays with the same title, Eisenstein tells of his first encounter with the work of Meyerhold, in 1917, at the Alexandrinsky Theatre in St Petersburg. Eisenstein, then aged 19, attended one of Meyerhold's most successful productions, his staging of Lermontov's play *Masquerade*. He described this experience as having been 'overwhelming and definitive' as it made him decide to abandon his engineering training and future career as an engineer and architect to work in the theatre.[6] This decision was made easier by the chaos of the 1917 Revolution, which had prompted the dissolution of the Institute of Engineering at which he had been studying. Eisenstein joined the Red Army as an engineer and assisted in the building of pontoon bridges and various fortifications as the Revolution turned into a civil war.[7] As 1919 drew to a close, a victory for the Communists was in sight and Eisenstein found himself involved in directing an amateur theatre group at a House of Culture near where he was based, at Velikie Luki.[8] Then he worked as a painter and scene designer on agitprop trains, eventually arriving in recently liberated Minsk in August 1920. It was here that he decided to learn Japanese, partly to be posted to Moscow, but mainly because he wished to travel to Japan to study Japanese theatre. Soon after Eisenstein arrived in Moscow to learn Japanese, he was appointed head of the scene design department at the Revolutionary workers' Proletkult Theatre in Moscow. He stopped his Japanese language studies to devote himself totally to theatre, and in 1921 he managed to meet Meyerhold for the first time at the final rehearsal for Mayakovsky's play *Mystery-Bouffe* in Moscow. Eisenstein then passed an audition to join Meyerhold's newly formed Directors' Workshops. As part of his audition he had to design a stage set for a chase scene. Eisenstein came up with a Constructivist idea which included six doors, a solution which Meyerhold was to borrow five years later for his famous production of Gogol's satirical play *The Government Inspector*.[9]

In his autobiography, Eisenstein recounts his sense of being entranced by Meyerhold's teaching. He described his lectures as 'mirages and dreams' during which it was impossible to write cogent notes.[10] From September 1921 to December 1922 Eisenstein experienced a spectacular period of study, during which he worked on his own as well as Meyerhold's productions. He also assisted Meyerhold in teaching and writing about Biomechanics. This study relied on a set of exercises in expressive movement, accompanied by music, which Meyerhold had developed and which he entrusted Eisenstein to explain and codify for instructional purposes, a task he probably realised was more suitable for his young student's temperament than his own. Amidst the activity of the Workshops and the productions, Eisenstein noticed that Meyerhold seemed to withhold the core of his ideas about theatre. One day Eisenstein asked him about this and was derisively rebuffed by his famous teacher. The young director immediately realised that Meyerhold had no intention of sharing his theatre technique secrets with his students. This intense period of activity was abruptly cut short when Eisenstein received a note from Zinaida Raikh, Meyerhold's wife and one of the professors in the Directors' Workshops, suggesting that he should leave Meyerhold, 'just as Meyerhold once left Stanislavsky.' She felt that Eisenstein had outgrown his teacher: 'when the pupil is not merely the equal to his teacher, but superior, then it is best for the pupil to leave.' Eisenstein ended his studies with Meyerhold forthwith.[11]

In spite of this break, their lives would continue to interweave. In 1923, to celebrate Meyerhold's twenty-five years in the theatre, Eisenstein directed his Proletkult Theatre in his production of Ostrovsky's *Enough Stupidity in Every Wise Man*, which featured his first film. This was a short filmed interlude called *Glumov's Diary*, which quoted one of Meyerhold's Biomechanical exercises. At the Proletkult Eisenstein taught Bio-mechanics, as well as directing the experimental theatre productions *Do You Hear, Moscow?!* and *Gas Masks*. In these he continued to explore the use of his circus-inspired concept of the 'montage of attractions', an account of which he published in 1923.[12] When Eisenstein parted company with the Proletkult Theatre in 1925 (in a dispute over the script for his first film *The Strike*), Meyerhold tried to get him to return to the theatre. He even offered Eisenstein a choice of projects to direct independently at the Meyerhold Theatre: *Hamlet*, *The Government Inspector*, or *Woe from Wit* by Griboyedov. However, at this time Eisenstein had already started filming *The Battleship Potemkin*.[13] The success abroad of this film led to Eisenstein being invited by Paramount to direct a sound film in Hollywood. A combination of US anti-Communist agitation and the fact that the young director had no intention of featuring Hollywood stars in his first sound film resulted in the failure of this plan. Instead, funded by the American socialist novelist Upton Sinclair, he went to Mexico to film *Que Viva Mexico!* another film project which in this case was tragically abandoned just before the filming had been completed. Eisenstein's return to the Soviet Union in 1932, after this double failure, was made worse by the increasingly repressive and totalitarian Communist system which was being led by Stalin. For a while he was not permitted to make films, so he was appointed head of the Film Directing Department at the State Institute of Cinematography. There he set up a complete four-year syllabus for forming film directors, which included the study of Biomechanics.

The 1930s were a dangerous time for both Meyerhold and Eisenstein, for other artists as well as countless others. Nevertheless, during this period Eisenstein would attend some of Meyerhold's rehearsals, for *The Prelude* (1933)[14] and probably for *The Lady of the Camellias* (1934). He would also meet with Meyerhold socially at his home in Leningrad. On several occasions there were press announcements that Eisenstein was going to

return to the theatre and direct various productions, but none of these
took place – Eisenstein had no intention of competing with his former
teacher in the theatre. Their last meeting probably took place after the
ceremony at which Eisenstein had been awarded the Order of Lenin for
his film *Alexander Nevsky*, in 1939.[15] Meyerhold was arrested in June 1939;
his wife, the actress Zinaida Raikh, was murdered a month later. He
endured seven months of interrogation and torture, during which he was
forced to confess to the false charges of spying for the British and
Japanese, and to having been a Trotskyist since 1923. He was shot in a
prison in Moscow in February 1940.[16]

The authorities then proceeded to eradicate Meyerhold's name from all
existing records, and no mention of him was even permitted. At
Meyerhold's stepdaughter's request, Eisenstein agreed to look after the
papers from his archive, which he hid at great risk in his dacha near
Moscow. According to Naum Kleiman, Eisenstein studied these papers,
and even took part of the Meyerhold archive with him when in 1941 he
was evacuated to Alma Ata to film *Ivan the Terrible*. Now that Meyerhold
was dead, Eisenstein was at last able to find out what the great theatre
director had been anxious to keep to himself, and at the same time rescue
a substantial part of his legacy.[17]

Meyerhold: his background and artistic development

By looking at Meyerhold's background and artistic development, one can
see how closely his own talents were related to Eisenstein's artistic
abilities, and consequently how his ideas influenced Eisenstein's thinking.
This influence is particularly noticeable with regard to the concept of
organic unity and how Meyerhold applied it to the audiovisual aspects of
his theatre. In turn, Eisenstein would use the concept of organic unity to
develop his practice and ideas on how to structure with maximum effect
the audiovisual aspects of the sound film.

Meyerhold was born into a wealthy middle-class German Lutheran
family in 1874 in Penza, a town about 350 miles southeast of Moscow.
The family spoke German at home, and like Eisenstein (whose father was
of German-Jewish origin) Meyerhold grew up in an environment where
the culture at home was somewhat different from the host culture.
Eisenstein grew up in a wealthy middle-class Russian-German family in
Riga.[18] Both Meyerhold and Eisenstein, partly as a means of escape from
their tyrannical fathers, spent many hours in their childhood and youth
reading books. Both loved the theatre and art.[19] However, with respect to
music, Meyerhold had a far more extensive education in his youth than
Eisenstein. His mother loved music and arranged musical evenings at

home, where members of the family and guests performed. Meyerhold learned to play both the piano and the violin from an early age. He had an ambition to become a virtuoso violinist, a dream which was only abandoned when, as a young student, he failed an audition to join the orchestra at Moscow University. In spite of this setback, Meyerhold's passion for music remained undiminished throughout his life. He regularly attended concerts, and associated with musicians.[20] In his work in the theatre, he collaborated with composers like Glazunov, Scriabin, Gnesin, Shebalin, Prokofiev and Shostakovich.[21]

Abandoning his law studies at Moscow University, Meyerhold entered the Moscow Philharmonic Society Drama School, where he studied under the famous Russian theatre director Nemirovich-Danchenko. In 1898 he graduated with distinction and was invited to join the Moscow Art Theatre, then being set up by Nemirovich-Danchenko and Stanislavsky. After acting with the company for four years, he outgrew his position (Nemirovich-Danchenko began to regard him as a disruptive influence) and left to direct a new theatre in Kherson in 1902. Over three seasons in the provinces he staged 165 plays, starting as a director very much under Stanislavsky's influence. However, he soon began to experiment with new forms of theatre, a practice he was to continue throughout his life. In these early years of the twentieth century, the Symbolist movement began to influence Russian theatre, and Meyerhold became one of its leading advocates, directing plays by Maeterlinck and trying out non-represen- tational stage techniques in his production of Przybyszewski's *Snow*. In 1905, Stanislavsky invited Meyerhold to lead his new experimental Theatre Studio, which was closed down after the 1905 Revolution, without there having been any performances in public. During its brief existence Meyer- hold continued his experiments, using music as an integral part of gesture, movement and pose, and devising a form of stylised declamation.[22]

In 1906 he read the German theatre director Georg Fuchs' book *The Theatre of the Future*, which led him to think of exploring other ways of using and extending the space of the stage, including the elimination of the stage curtain to remove the barrier between the spectator and the stage. He did this in several of his productions, notably Molière's *Don Juan* in 1910. In other productions he also removed the footlights and covered the orchestra pit, thereby extending the stage into the auditorium.[23] Earlier, Richard Wagner had covered the orchestra pit to bring his singers closer to the audience in his opera house at Bayreuth, which he had designed specifically for the performances of his music dramas.

In 1902, both Fuchs and Meyerhold had been inspired by the perform- ances of Otojiro Kawakami's company of actors, the first tour in the West by Japanese actors. Fuchs noted that their rhythmical movement was central to their tradition. For Meyerhold this experience of Japanese theatre was to become one of the main influences in his work, not only in terms of the use of stylised movement in the theatre, but also with regard to the prime importance of music in his productions.[24] At this point Meyerhold affirmed that music should determine the *mise-en-scène* and the action in a play. The visual elements of a production should be derived from the music and sound, and not the text of the play. Here Meyerhold was following the influence of Wagner. He was preparing for his production of Wagner's opera *Tristan and Isolde*, in 1909. At the same time, Meyerhold was reacting against the naturalist movement in theatre; he was aiming to make theatre more like Wagnerian opera. He compared the total control of all means of expression in Western opera to the Noh theatre tradition in Japan, where music also has a leading and unifying role.[25]

Up to the outbreak of the First World War, as well as directing plays featuring music and choreography, like d'Annunzio's *Pisanella*, he produced several operas. After *Tristan and Isolde* in 1909, he produced Mussorgsky's *Boris Godunov* in 1911, Gluck's *Orfeo* in the same year, *Elektra* by Richard Strauss in 1913, and Wolf-Ferrari's *Suzanne's Secret* in 1914.[26] In 1917 he produced Dargomyzhsky's opera *The Stone Guest*, then followed an 18-year break from operas, apart from an abandoned production of Wagner's *Rienzi* in 1921, due to the closure of the theatre in which it was being rehearsed.[27] He returned to opera when he produced Tchaikovsky's *The Queen of Spades* in 1935.[28] Meyerhold wrote that in this production he had aimed to allow his performers 'a contrapuntal rather than a metrically precise relationship' to the music, so that if they wished, they could act in contrast to the music; they could vary their responses to it, 'anticipating or lagging behind the score instead of simply keeping in unison.' He explained that this contrapuntal approach had been in complete contrast to his method in his 1909 production of *Tristan and Isolde*, where he had insisted that the performers' movements and gestures were to be synchronised with every aspect of the music 'with almost mathematical accuracy.'[29] Now we shall see how Meyerhold's experimental work, involving what could be termed the 'musicalisation' of theatre and under-taken in his break from producing operas, made his approach to combining acting with music much more organic.

The role of music in Meyerhold's theatre

In 1938, when talking to students, Meyerhold confirmed his belief in the fundamental importance of music to unify the various aspects of a theatre production into an organic whole:

Go to concerts more often. Music is the most perfect of the arts. When listening to a symphony, do not forget the theatre. The alternation of contrasts, rhythms, tempi, the main theme's relationship with secondary themes, all this is as necessary in the theatre as it is in music. The solution adopted for the composition of a piece of music can often help you to find the principles for the construction of a production.[30]

In the late 1930s, Meyerhold stated that he worked ten times more easily with an actor who loved music. He felt that actors should be made familiar with music at drama school, so that they would realise that music was not only useful to create atmosphere, but that it had a role as the most effective means of organising time in a theatre performance. He imagined the actor in performance as being figuratively in a 'duel' with time. It wasn't even necessary for the music to be heard, it just had to be *felt* by the actors. He dreamt of a production rehearsed with music and performed without music, with a rhythmically organised musical pace which had been internalised by each actor.[31]

Already in 1926 Meyerhold had encouraged his actors to perform and interact like instruments in an orchestra: 'here a flute, there a horn.' This approach relates to the musical technique of instrumentation and orchestration: the choice of which instruments to blend and contrast in a piece of music, and which instruments should play specific parts in the overall musical texture. Meyerhold believed that the secret of acting lay in the cohesive unity provided by the ensemble of actors, each one playing a part like instruments in the performance of music. To facilitate this technique each actor, prior to making their entrance, was to be aware of the level of tension created by the other actors, so that the 'musical' movement already in progress on the stage was not perturbed.[32] Meyerhold defined his productions in terms of a continuous state of progression, like music: 'if the acting is the melody, then the *mises-en-scène* are the harmony.'[33] He encouraged his actors 'to play modulations.'[34] His idea was to concentrate their attention on what had already been performed and on what they were to perform next. Here Meyerhold again turned to his extensive musical knowledge and experience to think of the theatre in terms of ideas relating in particular to rhythm and harmony. These elements would provide a sense of pace, a sense of rhythmic forward motion, a musical approach which could be usefully applied in theatre.

The theatre director as composer

In 1936, in a speech addressed to a theatre collective in Prague, Meyerhold took his musical analogy further.[35] He described the role of the director of a play as being a mediator between the playwright and the actors, like a conductor is a mediator between the composer and the orchestra. He also believed that his own role as a theatre director should be greatly extended and developed beyond this simple function of mediation, and he described his method of direction in musical terms, as being like that of a composer. On receiving the text of a play, before presenting the text to his actors, he would transform it into a production score. According to Meyerhold, a theatre director had the task of arranging the diverse elements of a play, delineating its individual characters and combining them so that each part of the production was related to its totality, thereby producing an organic unity in the work. For him the work of a theatre director took place in two stages: initially he worked alone on the play, he then worked in collaboration with the actors. Continuing his music analogy, he described the first stage as a *re-composition* of the playwright's text. Before his production in 1926 of Gogol's play *The Government Inspector*, he had taken ten years to recompose the text prior to starting the second stage of the directing process with the actors. Here Meyerhold was almost taking the place of the playwright, but his musical analogy for his role as director during this first stage of production was clearly that of the composer: 'in the same way that a composer when creating can hear how this or that instrument plays the different parts of his work, so the theatre director should, in the process of creating the concept of the totality of the play, have an idea which actor should express this or that element of this conception.'

Like a composer, Meyerhold would imagine the players interpreting each role, taking into consideration their vocal timbre, their physiological and psychological characteristics, their type (in terms of 'humours' – melancholic, sanguine or phlegmatic). From all these aspects he would choose 'which musical instrument (would) act in the orchestra of his production'.

Meyerhold described the second stage of the production process, his collaboration with the actors, as putting the flesh and skin on to the initial skeleton of the first stage, and watching the blood begin to flow in the veins of his production. In presenting the process of 'give and take' in his collaboration with the actors, he emphasised that he never strayed from his overall general concept of the work. He also confirmed that his role continued in this second stage to be that of a director-composer: 'If I arrive with a precise plan composed in advance, *I can only orchestrate my score with the actor, the living instrument of my work.*'[36]

So far, these ideas can be understood in terms of a poetic but useful analogy between Meyerhold's creative process and the practice of a composer. However his analogy was more direct and concrete. He explained that the pages of his production notes resembled musical staves, and that he used musical signs for his annotations – the laboratory of scientific research in his theatre was trying to find a way of translating his production notes into a form of notation that anyone could understand. Meyerhold's laboratory was described by one of his collaborators, Vladimir Soloviev, as a 'theatre laboratory whose aim was to scientifically research the entire history of theatre, in order to prepare materials which could be used by future theatre directors with their students'.[37]

Meyerhold even conceived theatre lighting in musical terms, using it to 'underscore' individual actor's lines, 'sometimes highlighting the text, sometimes shading it'. He believed that his lighting 'scores' would in time be read by theatregoers in the same way that musicians read musical scores. Concluding his speech, Meyerhold explained that the detailed and extensive use of musical methods in his theatre work was due to his musical background: his musical family, learning to play the piano from an early age and playing the violin for many years. He ended with this important statement: 'I wanted first of all to devote myself to music, then I abandoned it for the theatre. But I consider my musical education as the basis of my work as a theatre director.'[38]

Music and temporal proportion in Meyerhold's theatre

The concept of organic unity in a structure (one which shows evidence of a direct relationship between each part and the totality of a work) is necessarily related to the idea of proportion. Meyerhold also used a musical approach to deal with the problem of temporal proportion, one of his main concerns in the theatre. In the late 1930s he explained how his school of theatre dealt with this question. He imagined an episode in a play which had the following structure. Here is a diagram resembling a music score (Fig.2), to clarify what Meyerhold was describing. Each actor's voice is like an instrument in a piece of music: a dialogue between Voices 1 and 2 is followed by a monologue in Voice 3. Then a trio for Voices 1, 2 and 3 takes place followed by all the four voices appearing at once (a *tutti*), which concludes this episode. Meyerhold pointed out that the temporal proportions in this episode, 12:1:6:5, were what determined its compositional structure. Though he underlined that the actors needed to be aware of these proportions, this temporal limitation did not need to affect the improvisational side of the actor's craft in performing this episode. Meyerhold pointed out that good actors relished this 'stability in time' as a structure for their interpretative art.[39] Within these twelve minutes, his actors could introduce variations and

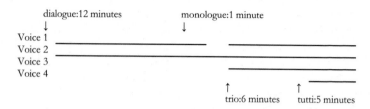

Fig.2 Score for an imaginary episode in a play, to illustrate
Meyerhold's ideas on temporal proportion in theatre.

nuances. They could try new ways of playing their part, looking for new details in it. This analogy is very close to the use of *tempo rubato* (literally translated as 'robbed time') where a musician performs a musical score using various slight fluctuations of tempo. These brief fluctuations of speed do not disrupt the overall organic proportions of a piece, as the tiny amount of extra time taken for playing one section of the piece is regained by playing a later section slightly more rapidly.

Meyerhold's example regarding the importance of temporal proportion may well have related to an unfortunate experience he had had with his production of Alexander Ostrovsky's play *The Forest* in 1924. At first his production comprised 33 episodes and lasted more than four hours, which resulted in the audience missing the last trams. His management pleaded with Meyerhold to make some cuts, so he abbreviated the production to 26 episodes. This resulted in a total performance time of three hours and twenty minutes. After a while the management complained that the production again lasted four hours. Meyerhold thought that the actors had replaced the scenes he had cut, but when he came to see his production again, he realised that they were simply extending the length of the 26 episodes by unconsciously slowing the pace of their performance. He tried reprimanding them but this did not work, so he had to arrange another rehearsal and he cut the production down to just sixteen episodes. This significant pruning produced a playing time of two and a half hours, which after a while grew again to four hours. At this point Meyerhold realised that the production was falling apart: the rhythms and temporal proportions within it had to be replaced by rehearsing it anew. As a result of this problem he realised that 'actors must be taught to be aware of time on the stage, as musicians are aware of it. A musically organized production isn't a production where music is being played or sung all the time behind the scenes, but rather a production with a precise rhythmic score, with precisely organized time.'[40]

From his experience with his production of *The Forest*, Meyerhold learned how to combat the elasticity of the passage of time in performance.

Each scene in a production must last its intended duration, otherwise the relationship of each part of the performance with the work's total duration would be lost; consequently the work's organic unity would also be destroyed. He tried to avoid this problem by making sure that the actors' subjective sense of time did not interfere with his intended duration for each scene, timed in minutes. This problem of the clash of subjective time with clock time was greatly aggravated in longer productions, like Meyerhold's *mise-en-scène* for *The Forest*, as small increases in duration rapidly added up to considerable extensions of clock time for the complete performance. The initial four-hour duration of *The Forest* seemed to have been anchored in the actors' psyche, no matter how many cuts were subsequently made by Meyerhold. This was why he saw the creation of a *mise-en-scène* as 'not at all a question of a static grouping, but a process ... there is also in it the time element, that is, rhythm and music.' In addition he mentioned what he called 'the plastic element ... the influence of time on space.'[41]

Opera and the 'tempodrama'
The idea of the influence of time on space can be seen in Meyerhold's production of Faiko's political farce *Bubus the Teacher* which he directed in 1925, a year after his production of *The Forest*. In *Bubus the Teacher* he used music throughout, very much as in the cinema of the period. For example, for the first act he used extracts and short pieces of piano music by Chopin and Liszt, arranged so that their tempi were continuously contrasted between fast and moderate speeds of playing. Meyerhold was particularly interested in using the piano to recreate in the theatre the strength of the audience's attention which he had noticed in the cinema. He also wanted to be able to control the slowing down of theatrical pace which occurred before a climactic moment.

His idea of using the performance of music in multiple styles (including an international selection of contemporary popular dances, like the fox-trot, the shimmy and the tango) throughout this production was derived from his experience of opera. As was mentioned earlier, before directing a production of *Tristan and Isolde* in 1909, he had studied Wagner's writings on his development of opera as a synthetic form which combined all the arts: the music drama. And in 1911 Meyerhold had directed a production of Mussorgsky's opera *Boris Godounov*, where he had noted the Russian pioneer composer's use of heightened speech in the composition of his recitatives.[42] These practical experiences of opera inevitably informed his intentions for *Bubus the Teacher*. In his introductory text for the production, Meyerhold called it a 'tempodrama', a new form of theatre that he proposed was to take the place of opera, which he considered obsolete.[43]

The 'theatrical symphony' and audiovisual counterpoint

Meyerhold's score for *Bubus the Teacher* also featured noises of various kinds, not least the clicking sounds of the bamboo curtain through which the actors appeared and disappeared. The variety of different means of expression used brings to mind an approach which was later to be termed 'total theatre'. Alexei Gvozdiev, a writer on theatre, wrote that it 'was organised by a very complex score where objects, light, sound, music, voice and words played the role of the different instruments in an orchestra. He [Meyerhold] was opening a path to the creation of a theatrical symphony.'[44] Musical structures were being used to bring together diverse elements into a dynamic and organic unity. For one of the key roles, Meyerhold hired an actor with a tenor voice whose vocal delivery was close to song. Even the nature of an actor's voice was chosen to make it an organic part of this production in which sound was used both as a means to structure the production, and as an expressive means in itself.

The music played as an accompaniment to silent films would parallel their content in terms of emotion and tempo. However, Meyerhold was keen that his actors perform *in counterpoint* with the music, not just following its mood and pace. There was to be a continual dialogue between music and action, one heightening the effect of the other by varying degrees of contrast. These contrasts were conceived by Meyerhold at the very start of his vision for the *mise-en-scène*; the visual elements were always intended to be in counterpoint with the music. For example, anguished music would be combined with a calm acting style, a tense scene would be offset by objectively repetitive and monotonous music. The music would be functioning as a 'co-construction' with the other elements of the production. In this way it would work like the orchestra in ancient Chinese theatre, the music of which was organically interlinked with the performances of the actors, rather than duplicating their impact.[45]

In his production of *The Lady of the Camellias* (1934), Meyerhold worked very closely with the composer Shebalin, and gave him in advance a complete breakdown of the precise musical tempi to be used in each part of the work, in addition to the number of bars, the metres to be used, the keys, the instruments, the placing of musical accents, and the musical styles contemporary with the action of the play. All these details had been worked out in rehearsals with the actors. It was almost as if Meyerhold just stopped short of composing the music himself for this production.

Once Shebalin's score was incorporated, Meyerhold made some adjustments, but he maintained the counterpoint between action and music, which sometimes involved extreme contrast between them. The music also comprised leitmotifs associated with the characters in the play.[46] These were developed organically, very much like Wagner's use of symphonic techniques in the development of his leitmotifs in his operas. However, the importance Meyerhold gives to dance and movement in his production also suggests a dramatic choreography, a danced play, or the type of film where music and action is closely counterpointed, as in Eisenstein's collaborations with Prokofiev, on *Alexander Nevsky* and *Ivan the Terrible*.

The Government Inspector

Meyerhold's production of this famous play by Nicolai Gogol provides an excellent example of the ways in which the director made use of the formal principle of organic unity, both within and across the media used in his production. Gogol's play is a satirical comedy. It shows how a young man is mistaken for a government inspector, travelling incognito. This error has a devastating effect on the officials and other inhabitants of a small Russian provincial town. The play has a far wider compass than this simple story would suggest. Towards the end of his life Gogol remarked that 'in *The Government Inspector* I tried to gather in one heap all that was bad in Russia. I wished to turn it all into ridicule.'[47] Meyerhold, who had been thinking about a production of Gogol's play since 1908, was determined to match the all-encompassing nature of Gogol's satirical vision of Russia. To do this, he incorporated elements from other writings by Gogol, including his novel *Dead Souls*, in which the writer used a travelling character, Chichikov, in his attempt to present a portrait of all Russia. Meyerhold spent fifteen months rehearsing and developing his production, which was first performed at his own theatre in 1926. A great success with the public and some of the critics, this production continued to be performed until 1938, when Meyerhold's theatre was closed down by the authorities.[48]

The creation of Meyerhold's production of *The Government Inspector* coincided with a period during which there was a lively debate in Moscow and Leningrad about theatre and cinema. By this time Eisenstein had left his work as a theatre director to commit himself fully to cinema: the international success of *The Battleship Potemkin* in 1926 confirmed his choice.[49] At this period he believed that theatre had died and only continued to exist through artistic inertia.[50] Yutkevich, Okhlopkov and several others who had also been Meyerhold's students went on to become film directors. After having already worked in the film medium (with *The Portrait of Dorian Gray* in 1915 and *A Strong Man* in 1917) Meyerhold had several film projects in mind at the time, including a film version of his production of Ostrovsky's *The Forest*. But he had no intention of leaving the theatre, and so it was natural that at this juncture he wished to show that cinema's powerful techniques could work equally well in his stage productions.[51]

In an article published in 1934, to celebrate Meyerhold's sixtieth birthday, Pudovkin pointed out that Russian film had its roots in theatre. Meyerhold had been a major influence for his (Pudovkin's) generation of film directors. He also mentions the importance of the fact that Eisenstein had been a student of Meyerhold: Eisenstein's mentor had taken theatre right to the edge of the territory belonging to cinema.[52] After having directed only two films (no other film projects were realised), Meyerhold's work in the theatre would always be inspired by some aspect of cinematic technique. For example, the general idea of Meyerhold's *mise-en-scène* for *The Government Inspector* was based on the use of a variety of theatre equivalents he had found for certain film techniques. He split the stage using several small mobile stages, thus affording rapid cinematic changes of scene, as well as concentrating the action within a limited space as on a film screen. He used spot lighting to highlight his actors, whom he placed at various levels, to create the multiplicity of viewpoints and viewing angles characteristic of cinema. He also used lighting and visual composition to create 'close-ups', thereby focusing the audience's attention on small changes of facial expression, and details of certain gestures. In an interview in 1926 he explained that 'we are trying not only to draw from our own experience, but also from the techniques of the greatest cinema actors.' In addition Meyerhold attempted a montage of 'shots' in scenes, using patterns of long shots, medium shots and close-ups.[53] However his visual ideas were not only from the realm of the cinema and film technique.

A key inspiration for Meyerhold for his choreography of the actors' gestures in his production of *The Government Inspector* was Albrecht Dürer's painting *Jesus Among the Doctors*. During rehearsals he showed reproductions of it to his actors. He was particularly fascinated by the expressive dance of hands in Dürer's painting. Meyerhold's deliberate use of restricted spaces for most of the scenes allowed the details of the position and movements of the actors' hands to create space in a different way, helped by the handling of all sorts of objects: glasses, pitchers, bottles, pipes, candles, pieces on a draught-board, which were highlighted by the strong vertical spotlights. The intimate scenes with few objects culminated in the 'freeze framed' crowd scene at the climax of the play. In this final moment, at a wedding ball, a police officer entered and announced the arrival of the *real* government inspector: everyone present was instantly 'frozen', holding a whole collection of objects which they'd been handling at that instant. The single objects had increased in number, and the actors holding them had become frozen into objects too. Meyerhold extended this organic growth of objects by adding some dummies in this final crowd scene, which had sporadically been evoked by the occasionally static positions taken up by some of the actors in earlier scenes.[54] Here he was using the principle of the 'part in the whole', the direct and organic relationship of the detail to the totality of the production.

Already in 1909, in a lecture, when he was working on his production of Wagner's *Tristan and Isolde*, Meyerhold quoted the Viennese writer of epigrams Peter Altenberg, when he referred to the Japanese love of synecdoche: 'to say a lot with a little – that's the secret. The task of the artist is to use the greatest riches with the most prudent economy. The Japanese have only to draw one blossoming twig to evoke an entire spring.'[55] Eisenstein demonstrated the method involved in a similar organic approach, in his diagram to illustrate the effectiveness of the cinematic framing used by Japanese children when they learnt to draw at school. He described this technique of drawing as 'hewing out a piece of actuality with the ax of the lens.' The selected details of a tree branch (Eisenstein referred to them as 'compositional units') when brought together made up the whole.[56] Where Eisenstein used a lens, Meyerhold used light: both used this direct proportion of the detail to the totality to achieve organic unity in their work.

The framing of Dürer's picture is also quite cinematic, like a high-angle close-up of a crowd. It looks as if Dürer used a long lens to flatten the perspective, to highlight the sense of Jesus caught in a highly claustrophobic space. This was just the type of claustrophobic space evoking a provincial town that Meyerhold wanted to show in his *mise-en-scène*, and which we can see in production photographs. His intention was to have his actors visually piled one on the other, like 'sardines in a tin'.[57]

Both Meyerhold and Eisenstein drew extensively from the fine arts in their work. Meyerhold amassed a huge personal collection of engravings, reproductions and art books, yet he envied Eisenstein's own apparently larger collection. Meyerhold mentioned inspiration and ideas he derived from amongst others, Perugino, Botticelli, Giotto, Holbein, Longhi, Callot, Rembrandt, El Greco, Manet, Renoir, Doré, Daumier, Hokusai, Rivera and Picasso.[58] With the possible exception of Perugino,

Eisenstein's list of painters who inspired him is identical, and in both cases other Japanese artists could be added. Eisenstein also mentioned Van Gogh,[59] Cézanne,[60] and various Chinese landscape painters, amongst yet other artists.[61] Both Meyerhold and Eisenstein made extensive use of their ability to transfer ideas from one medium to another. Meyerhold believed that 'music, painting and theatre are indissolubly connected. The laws of painting and those of music pass into theatre through the imagination of the theatre director.'[62] Eisenstein could have made the same statement, with regard to both theatre *and* cinema.

What is known of Meyerhold's production of *The Government Inspector* (1926) was made possible by the recording of rehearsals by his assistant Koreniev, covering the period from 18 October 1925 to 21 October 1926. This type of information is especially useful with regard to Meyerhold's musical approach to theatre, and its relation to the organic unity of his production. Piano music was used to accompany all the rehearsals. Meyerhold encouraged his pianist to supply for each rehearsal new sets of dances and songs from the first third of the nineteenth century. 'It's when we have new music each time that we shall find what we need' he explained. Using this creative process Meyerhold achieved a synthesis between music and action which corresponded exactly with his vision of Gogol's play, as well as corresponding closely to the ways in which music was used as an accompaniment to silent films. He decided to use two types of music: one was a Jewish provincial ensemble style, composed by Gnesin, and the other were dances and romances by Glinka, Varlamov and Dargomyzhsky. The Jewish music was intended to evoke the provincial character of the town in which the play was set, and the early Romantic music expressed the citizens' yearnings for the sophistication of the capital. At the wedding ball at the end of the play, the Jewish orchestra plays the Romantic dances, an ironic reference to the provincial pretentions of the event. Meyerhold added another type of music – a montage of various noises: the sounds of cries, roars, moans, whistles, various things being hit, bells, gurgling water, and silence. All sound, whether music or noise was thus directly related to the sense of space in the work (the narrow provincial space as opposed to the wider evocation of the distant capital) and the meaning and pace of the action on the stage.[63]

Meyerhold's approach to rehearsals for *The Government Inspector* was an organic one. The longest period was spent working on each scene as a separate unity. For the second part of the rehearsals Meyerhold concentrated on gradually unifying the separate self-contained scenes into a cohesive and organic whole. To achieve this unity he used musical means. He was very careful to choose the correct pace or tempo for each scene. The tempi he used were related to the actor's role, to sections in scenes, or to the whole of the scene. In this regard he worked very much like a composer, who gives precise instructions to musicians relating to tempo, including changes between different tempi, such as accelerations and gradually diminishing speed, or abrupt changes of pace. He orchestrated the voices of the actors, using the duet-type structures already inherent in Gogol's text. The intercalated dialogue of the Bobchinsky and Dobchinsky pair of characters naturally suggested duets, and other pairings of voices implied a duet where one line accompanied another. In one instance a girl's laughter accompanied and punctuated another character's monologue, in another a character sang a song at the same time as his wife, who sang out of tune.[64]

Meyerhold also used a choral principle throughout: there were choruses of civil servants, merchants, military officers, wedding guests. Some had a musical accompaniment, most used speech, and some just used mime, like the chorus in the final tableau. Each choral group was clearly made up of a group of individuals, whose personalities were each delineated in a comical or grotesque way. There were contrasts and echoes between a solo voice and the chorus, a powerful musical technique for creating a sense of forward movement. Using musical structures in this way, Meyerhold provided a vivid depiction of overlapping organic growth to describe what he was aiming to achieve in his *mise-en-scène*: 'a frightening continuity, a rope which winds round itself, where, without interruption, the elements generate each other.' Like a composer, he was also concerned with the vocal colouring, or timbre of the voices he used. For the choruses it was his deliberate intention to have the women's voices clearly heard in order to lighten the textures. He thought of the key male roles in terms of operatic registers: tenor, bass, *basso profundo*, to vary the vocal timbres and to heighten the personal traits of the characters the actors portrayed. Meyerhold extended this process of the 'musicalisation' of theatre by having his actors almost sing their words. When *The Government Inspector* was performed in Paris, the French theatre critics who didn't understand Russian found the musical delivery of Meyerhold's actors helped them to understand what was happening – one critic even described each phrase as a melody.[65]

In addition Meyerhold used a musical and organic approach to bind together the prolific growth of details characteristic of Gogol's work; he used a whole gamut of binary contrasts, found in sonata form. These contrasts not only operated in terms of music and sound, but they were also used visually, and emotionally. He juxtaposed his actors, 'a gallery of monsters', by contrasting their physical appearance – fat versus thin, tall versus short. He encouraged these strong contrasts: the space on the stage was either full or relatively empty, it was dynamic or static; the individual was continually contrasted with the group. These clearly articulated contrasts and oppositions formed motifs which reappeared throughout his production, in forms varied by different contexts, again an example of a technique used in sonata form. He also used the repetition of motifs on a smaller scale, in a shorter time-frame, employing devices involving voices repeating words in echo, as in the contrapuntal device of a canon. He used this canonic device for comical repetitions in the Bobchinsky and Dobchinsky duets, and when a choir would repeat a word or a phrase enunciated by a character functioning as a soloist in contrast to the choral group. Meyerhold even developed this type of contrapuntal imitation much further, in a scene where merchants gathered to complain to the government inspector about being bribed. Their list of grievances was articulated in the form of a spoken and whispered fugue, to the extent that the theatre specialist and musician, Emmanuel Kaplan, wrote that he was able to notate it on musical staves.[66]

The precision of timing involved in such episodes was also inspired by his experience of the performances of actors in touring Chinese and Japanese theatres. Meyerhold admired their ability to 'never be late, their performance is calculated in advance in seconds'.[67] He spoke scathingly of Russian theatre and the Russian actors' sense of timing, which he compared to the precision of the great Chinese actor Mei-Lan-Fang, whose performances he had seen and studied when his troupe had visited Moscow in 1935:

All our productions, including those with music, are put together in such a way that we do not have to make any of our actors understand the need to respect timing on the stage. We do not have a sense of timing. Fundamentally we do not know what saving time means. Mei-Lan-Fang counts in quarters of a second, and as for us, we count in minutes, not even taking seconds into account.[68]

Meyerhold felt that his actors' lack of a sense of precise timing could be remedied by a training in circus acrobatics. Here the performance of music was essential; the acrobats used it to time all their movements with great precision to avoid a disaster. When Meyerhold directed Mussorgsky's opera *Boris Godounov* in 1911, he was able to study at close hand Fyodor

Chaliapin's sense of timing in the leading role of Boris. He also admired the split-second timing of Black ensembles he had seen in Berlin in 1925, and in Moscow early in 1926. He described one dance where each performer began one second after the other and where all aspects of the performance were built on syncopation: 'we have to take lessons from them…it's monstrously difficult.'[69] These types of difficulties, involving an extraordinary control of the body, the voice and precision timing, forced Meyerhold to realise that his actors would need to be trained in a new way.

A new actor training for a new theatre

From the very beginning of his career as a director, Meyerhold was convinced of the 'impossibility of building a new theatre on old foundations.' He believed that a new theatre could only be achieved by a new type of training for actors.[70] Music was a significant part of this new training: in his early Theatre Studio experiments from 1908 to 1909, Meyerhold had the composer Mikhail Gnesin work with the actors towards 'the musical reading of drama'. For his classes Gnesin used conventional music notation to catch the melodic and rhythmic nuances of spoken Russian which he would then punctuate with chords on the piano. Scriabin, witnessing one of these classes, planned to use this technique of musicalising the spoken voice for a *Mystery* he was composing and which he planned to have performed in India.[71] Later, in 1912–1913, Meyerhold also invited a ballet dancer to teach dance, and two circus performers to teach acrobatics – both courses involving another type of unity of music and movement. In addition, he devised his own course on movement training.[72]

The total cultural and artistic reorganisation following the 1917 Revolution enabled Meyerhold to set up 'Courses in the Mastery of Stage Production', which were intended for the formation of future actors for his new type of theatre. As well as courses in gymnastics, juggling, acrobatics and stage movement, there were exercises in classical dance, rhythm in movement, the development of a sense of time, emotion and movement, and a list of recommended sports. Music was listed under 'Supplementary Subjects', comprising an elementary course, the playing of an instrument, rhythmic gymnastics, and singing classes, including *solfeggio*, choral singing, as well as solo and duet work. Drawing classes were also mentioned, including drawing from memory, drawing of 'position, pose, face, costume, plan, etc.' Lastly, under the title of 'Scientific-theoretical Subjects' were featured the basic principles of anatomy and physiology, theatre science, pantomime, dance, versification, and the psychology of emotions. There was also in this section the study of analogies between various art-forms, as well as the 'place of theatre as a synthesis of the arts among other arts.'[73] This topic was central to Meyerhold's whole enterprise in theatre: here he had a syllabus which comprised actor training from a multiple of perspectives, each one organically related to the other in terms of movement, music, physical and psychological training. This polyvalent education was intended to produce a new type of actor for a new type of theatre which consisted of an organic unity of various forms of art.

This new type of theatre would not remain fixed. Meyerhold continually experimented with it, so that it was an organic form, which would also grow and develop organically. For example, in his studio courses in 1921–23 (Eisenstein began his studies with Meyerhold in 1921) he added harmony and counterpoint to the music course. Then in the late 1920s, the history of music was added, as well as the rehearsal of actors to the accompaniment of the piano, to develop in the actor a sense of musical timing. Meyerhold's additions to his courses resulted from what he had learnt in the musical experiments he had carried out in previous productions, such as *Bubus the Teacher* in 1925, and *The Government Inspector*, premiered in 1926. In 1931, he described his vision of a new theatre in terms of the organically unified, streamlined architecture of a ship, a form which would involve a unity of 'the actor, light and music'.[74]

Traditional Chinese and Japanese theatre and Biomechanics

Meyerhold also studied Japanese theatre in depth, especially Kabuki. This interest began because of his passion for the fine arts. He loved Japanese prints and came across depictions of Kabuki theatre in Hokusaï's engravings. The experience of seeing a Kabuki troupe perform in Paris in 1928 proved to be a formative influence on his development of theatre. At the same time as recognising what he had already admired when he had seen Kawakami's Japanese theatre company in Moscow in 1902, the experience of the authentic Kabuki theatre he saw in Paris put everything in a new light for him. It also confirmed the validity of certain ideas which were taking shape in his mind.[75]

His study of the rhythmic and dance-like movements of the actors in traditional Chinese and Japanese theatre helped to form the sets of movement exercises he was planning for the training of his new type of actor. Another source was the precise movements which were the result of Frederick Winslow Taylor's time and motion studies of factory workers, part of what came to be known as 'Taylorism'. Meyerhold also used other movement vocabularies to develop the exercises: from the circus, the music hall, military drills, boxing, gymnastics and *commedia dell'arte*. These exercises he called Biomechanics, after a nineteenth-century scientific term for the study of the action of inner and outer forces on the living body. They became a fundamental part of the actor training courses in his directors' workshops, perhaps as early as 1918.[76]

Eisenstein and Biomechanics

When the young Eisenstein was admitted to these workshops in 1921, as well as being a gifted student in stage design, he also excelled in the Biomechanics and movement classes. He was appointed to teach Biomechanics to younger students, and early in 1922 Meyerhold asked him to write articles about these movement exercises and related movement research.[77] Later in the same year Eisenstein was appointed head of the theatre department of the revolutionary proletarian arts organisation, the Moscow Proletkult. During that summer in Petrograd he developed his own form of actor training, basing it on Meyerhold's model, including Biomechanics. The development of a detailed, almost scientific study of human movement was to preoccupy Eisenstein throughout his life. Much of what is known about Meyerhold's ideas and practice of Biomechanics is due to Eisenstein's research and teaching about movement training for actors.[78]

A particularly vivid and detailed account of this new actor training was provided by Eisenstein to his film directors' class at The State Institute of Cinematography in 1935. His students had just had their first training session in Biomechanics, so he was keen to teach them the ideas underlying this practical study of movement. After an unsatisfactory question-and-answer session about it, he explained that 'the most expressive, the most attractive movement is one which flows according to natural and organic norms'. As examples of these natural types of movement he mentioned children and wild animals, whose movements come across very effectively on the screen. Their 'organics of movement are not destroyed ... they don't have any distortions'. In the case of children they begin to cease moving 'harmonically' when, as they become adults, they are affected by various social pressures which cause them to move in a less organic manner. Eisenstein explained that 'in organic movement there is not a single expressive manifestation that does not involve the entire motor system as a whole.' He mentioned that this idea was derived from movement research in France in 1847, which resulted in the formula that 'an isolated movement is not organic'.[79]

The concept of organic unity which was found in natural forms was also applicable to expressive movement: the action of the entire body was involved 'in the very smallest individual gesture'. The idea underlying

Biomechanics was to use this principle to train actors to achieve a complete control and awareness of natural, organic movement, where 'each movement which is made is the result of movement by the body as a whole'. As an example Eisenstein referred to Chinese and Japanese theatre, where the actors have a 'special rhythmicality … that special culture of movement, the coordinated movement of all parts of the body'. Eisenstein pointed out that the knowledge of what comprised organic movements and how to master them would enable actors to be consciously aware of the types of movement distortions which were characteristic of certain individuals. This knowledge was for Eisenstein a key aspect not only of expressive movement in theatre, but also of the mechanics of instant communication between actor and audience. He noticed how audiences in their own manner reproduced the movements they saw on stage, how this was the mechanism which enabled theatre to work. He remembered how he was nearly thrown out of a theatre when, in a highly romantic scene, he had noticed how everyone in the audience was mimicking the humming of a waltz by the couple on the stage: he had burst out laughing at this comical phenomenon. The organic relationship between audience and actors was for him where the 'secret form' of the theatre lay.[80]

Meyerhold and organic unity in the theatre

This concern with a direct and organic relationship between audience and actors was mentioned by Meyerhold in his first book *On Theatre*, published in 1913, the first book by a Russian theatre director. In this collection of his articles and notes, which appeared in anthologies and journals between 1907 and 1910, Meyerhold expressed the three fundamental principles which laid the foundation for his future work in the theatre. His first principle delineated the key role of the theatre director as 'author' of the production. In practice, as was seen earlier in this chapter, for Meyerhold this role became akin to that of 'playwright/composer'. The second principle was 'the recognition of the stage and auditorium as a single organic whole and the audience as an active participant in the theatrical performance'. The recognition of this principle was what Eisenstein described twenty-three years later as the underlying 'secret form' of the theatre. The third principle affirmed the vital importance of movement in theatre.[81]

All three principles were applied in practice using an overall structural concept: organic unity. All movement was to be organically related, not only to other aspects of the production, but also within the body of the performer, as Eisenstein had explained to his students in 1935. As described above, Meyerhold used a wide variety of musical techniques and forms from his extensive knowledge and experience of music to ensure the organic unity of his highly fine-tuned productions. His experience of Chinese and Japanese theatre influenced his concept of the space of the stage: in these traditions there is an organic continuity of space between the actors and the audience, unhindered by a curtain. The musicians also perform on the stage, and in this way they do not clutter the space between the audience and the actors. The actors' declamatory style is frequently close to song. Meyerhold in *Bubus the Teacher* and *The Lady of the Camellias* had musicians perform on the stage. Already in 1910, in his production of Molière's *Don Juan* (which Eisenstein had seen as a child), he had made sure that the auditorium was fully lit, to unify the space between actors and audience; he also removed the curtain and the proscenium stage for the same reason.[82]

Meyerhold's influence on Eisenstein: other examples involving organic unity

Meyerhold's ideas and practice relating to organic unity in the theatre involved several instances of his direct and straightforward influence on Eisenstein, as for example with the practice of Biomechanics. However other instances of Meyerhold's influence on Eisenstein are more complex, as they comprise a synthesis of various ideas which the film director may well have borrowed from his mentor and colleague. An example of this synthesis is Eisenstein's only experience of producing an opera: Wagner's music drama *The Valkyries*, which was premiered at the Bolshoi Theatre in late 1940, a production commission which had resulted from the non-aggression pact Stalin had signed with the Nazis in 1939.

This production marked Eisenstein's return to the theatre, significantly following Meyerhold's arrest in June 1939.[83] Eisenstein wrote an article outlining his plans for his production, so that whatever would transpire in practice, a clear account of his initial intentions would survive. He intended to unify the various elements of Wagner's music drama by using space, sound and light. He planned to unify the stage space and the auditorium by extending across this space the most important part of his scene design, a huge symbolic tree, whose branches would extend under the roof of the auditorium. This would help to unify a space which was split in the Bolshoi Theatre by the orchestra pit. Like Meyerhold, Eisenstein planned not only to use space as a means of organically unifying a production, but also music and light. He stated his intention that the music for the *Ride of the Valkyries* should surround and envelop the audience by means of multiple speakers. These loudspeakers would be phased so that the sound would give the impression of riding backwards and forwards across and around the auditorium and its surrounding spaces.[84] This was a spatial sound technique that composers like Edgard Varèse and Karlheinz Stockhausen would later first achieve in concerts of their music, in the 1950s and 1960s. Bergan, in his biography of Eisenstein, mentions that this was an idea which anticipated the Dolby stereo 'surround-sound' in regular use in today's cinemas, and which Coppola used for the *Ride of the Valkyries* in *Apocalypse Now* (1979).[85] The third unifying technique involved the use of light. As an example, Eisenstein mentioned his idea of using golden rays shining from the stage into the auditorium at the end of Act One. At the same time as symbolising 'Siegmund and Sieglinde's rising celebration of love' this technique again unified the performance space with the auditorium.[86]

Eisenstein described a fourth method with which he aimed to achieve organic unity in his production. This involved the use of what he called 'plastic leitmotifs' which were mixed with the leitmotifs in the orchestral score. These 'plastic leitmotifs' were movement pattern equivalents to Wagner's use of leitmotifs: memorable melodic patterns which the composer associated with certain characters, significant objects and plot themes in his music dramas. Eisenstein intended 'the orchestration of plastic actions and movements' to be as strictly defined as the music.[87] Like Meyerhold he was using a musical model (in this case the orchestration of the Wagnerian leitmotif) to structure a means of expression in another medium, that of the performers' patterns of movement.

We saw earlier how Meyerhold believed that a musical form could be used to provide a solution to a formal problem encountered in the construction of a theatre production. Eisenstein adopted this musical approach to the structuring of a work when describing his formal intentions for the editing of an episode in his film *Bezhin Meadow*, when he was supervising the shooting of it in 1935. He saw the editing of this section as being 'handled in the same way a composer works on a fugue in four voices'. Two of the voices would relate to foreground material comprising 'figures and close-ups',[88] and background material, consisting of film for use as transparencies and back projection. The other two voices were to be sound and speech respectively. He was excited by 'the infinite number of combinations of these four voices'. By using this formal means, sound and vision became organically interchangeable elements which formed various types of audiovisual counterpoint, as well as sound on sound counterpoint. A rear-projection image would remain constant in the background, while 'the quarrelling, singing, shouting figures in the foreground change repeatedly.'[89] Alternative counterpoints would involve voices of figures in the foreground drowned out by the noise of the combine harvesters, and images of tractors accompanied by invisible voices.

The fugal nature of these types of counterpoint relates to the fugue having a main theme or 'subject' which is usually in the foreground, and the 'countersubject' which is the accompanying theme or background. The possibilities of combination mean that the importance of subject and countersubject can be reversed; foreground material can become background material. The combinatorial possibilities with a counterpoint of four voices using various types of thematic material in more than one medium can thus become hugely varied, yet they remain under the control of the fugal form, as was demonstrated in the chapter on audiovisual counterpoint.

Meyerhold's composerly approach to theatre was adopted by Eisenstein with respect to his work in film in other ways too. As was mentioned earlier, Meyerhold encouraged his actors to 'modulate', in order to provide a sense of forward motion as well as a connection between what had already been performed and what was to come. Eisenstein used a similar 'modulation' technique in parts of his scenario for *Sutter's Gold*, about the Californian gold rush, one of his Hollywood projects.

A section of the scenario features the great journey of Anna Sutter and her children to rejoin her husband who had left his family in Switzerland fifteen years earlier to settle in California. Now that he has become wealthy he wishes to see his wife and children again. Eisenstein shows how Mrs Sutter becomes more and more aware of her husband's fabulous wealth and fame through a musical repetition of Sutter's name, which increases in intensity and volume as she and her family approach California, and they come across more and more people who are talking about him. Then Eisenstein introduces a purely musical motif, which in itself develops and modulates like a Wagnerian leitmotif. This motif is a chord which is associated with Mrs Sutter's growing excitement as she gradually reaches her now illustrious husband's new home in California. The chord becomes a palpable manifestation of an emotion which would otherwise be invisible: 'and with the birth of her excitement there is born the first trembling sounds of a chord. A chord ever strengthening and its tone ever rising upwards, trembling and sobbing.' Here Eisenstein uses words to notate a musical sketch he can imagine but cannot write down in any other way. He then creates a song from the growing repetitions of Sutter's name: 'out of this chorus of exclamations is formed a song, a song without melody, but a song solemn and rhythmic.'[90]

Eisenstein is working like a composer, in a similar way to Meyerhold, when he was musicalising the spoken choruses he had created in his production of *The Government Inspector*. The Sutter chorus increases in size and strength and becomes more and more rhythmic, as the sound of the train's wheels begins to suggest the rhythm of Sutter's name. Eisenstein brings back the chord, and this time it takes on the rhythm of her heartbeat, suggesting a sonic and thematic connection to the binary rhythm of the Sutter leitmotif:

> the sobbing, long-drawn-out, crescendo chord, vibrating
> like her nerves, beating like her heart.
> Anna closes her eyes and, in a broken voice, pronounces
> the same and ever the same name –
> 'Johann …
> Sutter … Sutter …'

His name is then immediately picked up 'by a host of voices, singing, loudly and clearly, the song of Sutter and California'.[91] Eisenstein then describes various shots showing a sea voyage, and mentions the sounds of wind, waves and the ship, which in turn also become echoes of Sutter's name, then even the elements sing the song associated with him. The chord leitmotif returns in a more rapid and more frenzied form, evoking her inner turmoil as she collapses and has to be carried for the remainder of her long journey. As she reaches the gateway of the home of her husband, the chord reappears in a more fragile form, it 'rises higher and higher, mounts more pitifully and touchingly.' When she sees him, she is overpowered by her emotions, and the chord associated with her feelings falls apart as she collapses for the last time:

> A blow on the chord and the sobbing sound runs from
> its nadir to its apex and, reaching its highest timbre,
> shatters –
> The chord bursts shrill.
> And Anna falls back on the litter.
> Death is on her face.
> In the air sound the overtones of the shattered chord.[92]

In these last four short sentences Eisenstein uses two 'shots' of music to frame two visual shots, forming a unified audiovisual climax to a section where sound emerges organically from the images, then music emerges organically from the sounds, and sound, music and image are interwoven throughout. Additionally, each element of Eisenstein's audiovisual composition grows organically out of the content of the narrative.

Meyerhold was greatly concerned with the importance of notation for his theatre, as his aim was to have a notated score which would be as precise as music notation, and at the same time offer the possibilities of interpretation afforded to the performers by a musical score.[93] We saw earlier how he understood the role of the theatre director as being analogous to that of a composer. In a page from a notation of his production of *The Lady of the Camellias* (1934), each measure is one second long, and there are ten staves showings lines indicating the duration and direction of the movements of three performers. The spoken text is typed on various levels to indicate the style of vocal delivery for each line of speech. An explanatory diagram of the stage space is shown on the left side of the page, to make the spatial interactions clearer.

Eisenstein also used notation, but for a different purpose, as his work in film was evidently in a recorded form, unlike Meyerhold's theatre. Eisenstein used notation to explain how his montage of audiovisual counterpoint functioned, by analysing chosen extracts from his films. Notation was used for a pedagogical purpose and for his own research into audiovisual counterpoint. He used a combination of graphic and musical notations and still shots from an extract from *Alexander Nevsky* (from the sequence before 'The Battle on the Ice') to analyse his method of audiovisual counterpoint. Eisenstein's grid analysis of a section (Ivan at the coffin of Anastasia, from *Ivan the Terrible*) helped him to clarify his creative method after having worked with the complex audiovisual polyphonies in his second sound film (Fig.3).

Both the notations commissioned by Meyerhold in his theatre laboratories, and the analysis-notations carried out by Eisenstein shared a common almost scientific approach to theatre and film respectively. Their use of notation came out of an experiment-based culture in the arts during the 1910s and 1920s, which involved an attempt at an organic unification of the arts with science. For example, the work of both Meyerhold and Eisenstein on Biomechanics took place in the context of the work of Alexei Sidorov and the mathematician-philosopher Alexander Larionov in their study of movement in the Choreological Laboratory founded in Moscow in 1923, and the work of Rudolf von Laban in Switzerland in the 1920s, on the development of a scientific means of notating any type of movement.[94]

Meyerhold's interest in notation was also related to his preoccupation with proportion. He realised that temporal proportion was a key factor in creating a sense of organic unity for such a time-based form as theatre; the

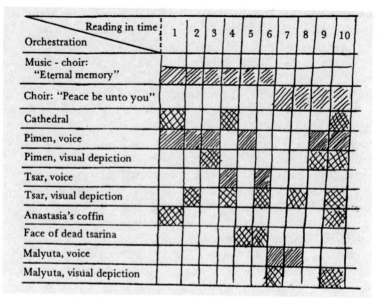

Orchestration \ Reading in time	1	2	3	4	5	6	7	8	9	10
Music - choir: "Eternal memory"	▨	▨	▨	▨	▨	▨				
Choir: "Peace be unto you"								▨	▨	▨
Cathedral	▨			▨						▨
Pimen, voice	▨	▨	▨		▨				▨	▨
Pimen, visual depiction			▨						▨	▨
Tsar, voice					▨		▨			
Tsar, visual depiction		▨		▨		▨		▨		
Anastasia's coffin	▨									▨
Face of dead tsarina						▨	▨			
Malyuta, voice							▨	▨		
Malyuta, visual depiction							▨		▨	

Fig.3 Eisenstein's polyphonic chart of the sequence
'Ivan at the Coffin of Anastasia'.

problems he had had with the rehearsals of Ostrovsky's *The Forest* (1924) bore this out. Eisenstein, in 1939, when examining how to achieve organic unity in a work, noticed how the five acts of *The Battleship Potemkin* were part of an organic structure along the lines of the golden mean, where the relationship of the smaller part to the larger part is the same as the larger is to the whole.

In fact Eisenstein pointed out that in a five-act structure it is possible to have a double golden mean, which in numerical terms is approximately in a proportion of 2:3, and 3:2. At the first point is a climax of stasis, corresponding to the appearance of the theme of the dead Vakulinchuk, at the end of Act 2. The other climax, a high point of maximum movement, occurs at the golden mean at the other end of the five-act structure, at the end of the third act, the 3:2 proportional point. Eisenstein concluded that the effectiveness of his film was partly due to the fact that *The Battleship Potemkin* followed the law of the structure of natural organic phenomena.[95] Interestingly, Meyerhold was less seduced by the form of the golden mean.[96] In 1936 he was addressing criticism of his experimental method and he mocked theatre directors who had found ready-made solutions for their work: 'forward nice and easy to the paradise of the golden mean!' ... Long live the golden mean!' Perhaps he knew that natural organic forms also followed other structures, not based on the principle of the golden mean. He concluded that 'in the true work of art, form and content are inseparable.'[97] This was the basis of his approach to organic unity.

Meyerhold's concern with the control of changes of pace in his musicalisation of theatre, what he called 'tempodrama', as practised in his production of *Bubus the Teacher* in 1925, was further developed by Eisenstein in the way he articulated the changes of pace in *The Battleship Potemkin*.[98] Eisenstein was particularly attracted to using total contrasts of pace, from extreme dynamism to total stasis, and vice-versa, rather than Meyerhold's gentler contrasts in tempo. He saw this technique of total contrast as being part of the organic development of the narrative in *The Battleship Potemkin*. He mentioned the tense stasis beneath the battleship's guns before the dynamism of the mutiny, the quiet scenes of mourning for Vakulinchuk before the 'theme of rage' in Part III, the violent streams of movement in the massacre on the Odessa Steps, after the fraternising between the crew and the inhabitants of Odessa, and other examples of extreme contrasts of pace from the film. In fact Eisenstein did not see these examples as contrasts, but as transitions 'to a distinct opposite'. This concept enabled him to achieve an organic unity between two opposite points of view. He explained that each transition to an opposite provides an image of the same theme, seen each time from an opposing angle, all the while growing ineluctably from it.[99]

However, Meyerhold did use a principle of extreme binary contrasts in his production of Gogol's *The Government Inspector* in 1926. These contrasts mostly involved the physical characteristics of actors, a full stage contrasted with a relatively empty one, as well as binary contrasts of dynamism and stasis, noise versus quiet. As was mentioned earlier, this binary formal principle enabled him to organically control the vast amount of material provided by Gogol. Meyerhold also exploited the use of simultaneous contrasts, especially with respect to music, where the mood of the acting would be set in direct opposition to the atmosphere suggested by the music, as in his production of *Bubus the Teacher*, in 1925.[100] His approach of having his actors perform in contrasting counterpoint with the music, not just in parallel with its mood and pace suggests a direct link to the mention of a similar, but filmic audiovisual counterpoint which is demanded in the *Statement on Sound* in 1928: '*the first experiments in sound must aim at a sharp discord with the visual images.*' This oppositional method of combining moving image and sound was intended to avoid the inertia resulting from 'every mere *addition* of sound to montage fragments'. And it was made clear that this audiovisual method should be contrapuntal in nature, to enable the sound film to have an exciting future: '*only the contrapuntal use* of sound *vis-à-vis* the visual fragment of montage will open up new possibilities for the development and perfection of montage.'[101]

In a lecture in 1918, following his experience of acting in and directing a film based on Przybyszewski's *Strong Man* and in *The Picture of Dorian Gray*, Meyerhold understood that 'an instinctive sense of time', what he termed 'an ear for time', was also of enormous importance for the cinema artist. Here again Meyerhold was thinking of theatre in a musical way; he believed that a sense of rhythm was also vital for a cinema artist, to the extent that 'the cameraman must study the rhythmical intervals of a passage and point out the slightest deflection from the agreed tempo.'[102] For Eisenstein, who was more concerned with editing than with acting, this musical approach was transferred to the montage stage of making a film. His ideas on the use of rhythm in the sound film will be studied in the chapter on audiovisual rhythm.

So far, the formal principle of organic unity has been analysed in terms of the following elements of theatre: movement, lighting, the space of the stage, the actors' delivery of the text, the use of music and sound to structure a production organically. However, for both Meyerhold and Eisenstein the principle of organic unity went beyond its application to the elements of theatre: they also applied it to the structuring of the relationship *between* the various expressive means used in performance. This point was made particularly clearly by Eisenstein in an article he wrote in 1928, after seeing Ichikawa Sadanji's visiting Kabuki Theatre troupe, which performed in Moscow and Leningrad. Eisenstein compared contemporary Soviet theatre with the Kabuki theatre: 'the sharpest distinction between Kabuki and our theatre is – if such an expression may be permitted – in a *monism* of *ensemble*.' He went on to describe the Moscow Art Theatre's technique of parallelism, 'the ensemble of a unified collective "re-experience"', as in conventional opera, where orchestra, chorus and soloists function along parallel lines. He explained how the Moscow Art 'synthetic' theatre at its worst exhibited the ludicrous collective animal imitations which were directly parallel to its human instigators. For Eisenstein, Japanese theatre showed 'another, extremely interesting form of ensemble – *the monistic ensemble*. Sound-movement-space-voice here do not accompany (nor even parallel) each other, but function *as elements of equal significance*.'[103]

Here Eisenstein used Spinoza's idea of 'monism', whereby all phenomena were derived from a single source, and each element was a different manifestation from the same origin, and therefore had equal significance. Consequently, for Eisenstein it was 'impossible to speak of "accompaniments" in Kabuki.' Later in the same article this concept is developed further, with regard to his approach to the sound film. Eisenstein reminded his readers about the joint *Statement* he had signed with Alexandrov and Pudovkin: 'in our "Statement" on the sound film we wrote of a contrapuntal method of combining visual and aural images. To possess this method one must develop in oneself a new *sense: the capacity of reducing visual and aural perceptions to a "common denominator."*'[104]

This 'common denominator' was what Eisenstein had also called a 'general perception'[105] or 'general sensation',[106] which was necessary to create organic unity in a work, and which in audiovisual terms unified images with music. He stated that the ability to reduce the visual and the aural perceptions to such a 'general perception' or 'common denominator' was 'possessed by Kabuki to perfection. And we, too – crossing in turn the successive Rubicons flowing between theatre and cinema and between cinema and sound-cinema – must also possess this. We can learn the mastery of this required new sense from the Japanese.'[107]

It is clear that Eisenstein, in crossing one Rubicon after another, was taking Meyerhold's organic unity approach with him, as well as the concept of counterpoint, also in part due to Meyerhold's ideas on theatre. However Eisenstein had also learnt something else from Meyerhold's ideas and practice, especially concerning theatre structured by using musical means. Meyerhold had used the idea of musical counterpoint to structure the interaction of his actors' voices in an organic way in his theatre. But he had also extended this technique to structure the interaction of the various expressive media he was using: light, movement, music and sound. He was using a 'cross-media' counterpoint which resulted in the organic unity of all the expressive means he was using. For both Meyerhold and Eisenstein, the experience of theatre from non-Western cultures, in this case the Chinese and Japanese traditions, had provided a practical proof that cross-media counterpoint could work. For Eisenstein this was a key part of his solution to the formal and expressive problems posed by audiovisual cinema.

Conclusion

Meyerhold was much more of a musician than Eisenstein. His thwarted career as a violinist resulted in his working in the theatre almost like a conductor and composer. Meyerhold's approach to organic unity was directly related to his experience and knowledge of music. This musical method was a great influence on Eisenstein's approach to the problem of audiovisual unity in the sound film. Along with music, an important influence on both artists was that of non-naturalistic theatre, in particular from the Chinese and Japanese theatre traditions. These types of theatre are more susceptible to combination with music, as the stylised acting is almost indistinguishable from dance, and in the case of both the Chinese opera and Kabuki theatre, acrobatic movement. In addition the delivery of the text approaches the stylisation of declamation and in some cases, song. In the Chinese theatre tradition, and in the Kabuki and Noh traditions, music is a vital component of the performance. The resultant combination of song, instrumental music and movement can be seen in action in Eisenstein's scenario for *Sutter's Gold*, where there is an organic relationship between all of these elements. He adopted this approach for *Que Viva Mexico!*, a film to which he planned to add a mix of traditional Mexican music styles.[108]

Naturalistic acting was never a major concern for Eisenstein, and Meyerhold was greatly criticised in the 1930s for not using it. Eisenstein had to have 'help' to have it included in *Alexander Nevsky*, along with the required Russian star actors.[109] Meyerhold's experience of both Mei-Lan-Fan's Chinese theatre troupe and Kabuki theatre helped him to find a non-Western solution to the problems posed by Wagner's rather static synthesis of the arts in his *Gesamtkunstwerk* concept. For Eisenstein this sense of synthesis in Chinese and Japanese theatre was also a powerful influence, and he became particularly interested in the work of Mei-Lan-Fan in 1935.[110] In his article *To the Magician of the Pear Orchard* (Mei-Lan-Fan's official Chinese theatre name) Eisenstein explained how this great performer's aim was to restore the synthesis of Chinese theatre in its most ancient forms, when dance and song were inseparable. Previously there had been a split in the performance tradition, whereby in the north of the country the vocal aspect of the performances was dominant, and in the south the drama became more visual. Now, Eisenstein explains, by his research into ancient Chinese stagecraft Mei-Lan-Fan had 'restored the actor's skill to its former synthetic quality'. He had 'resurrected the visual aspect of the spectacle, and its complex, recherché combination of movement with music and the luxury of ancient costumes'.[111]

Eisenstein castigated the forced naturalism of Western opera and the use of music in the narrative of the sound film, when it would be introduced with such phrases as '"Why don't you sing something?" or "Ah, here come the villagers – they are going to dance for the Count".' He felt that a much more organic way of combining music, theatre and dance could be achieved in operas which would be set in societies where music and dance were an integral part of everyday life, as in Georgia, Uzbekistan, Kazakhstan or the Ukraine. And he saw such a synthesis as having immeasurably greater potential in cinema.[112] This realisation was due to the influence of Meyerhold's non-naturalistic approach to theatre, which made an organic cross-media synthesis possible.

Eisenstein's experiences when shooting a film in Mexico gave him the opportunity to work directly with a society in which music, dance and theatre are an integral part of the everyday. His period in Mexico provided the stimulation for his ideas about what he called 'nonindifferent nature', a set of concepts which would help him develop significantly his approach to audiovisual cinema.

3
Nonindifferent Nature

The audiovisual image is the extreme limit of self-revelation outside the basic motivating themes and ideas of creative work.[1]

London, Chicago, New York

On his first visits to cities Eisenstein would choose a suitably malleable guide to show him round. In London, one of his guides was a contributor to the film magazine *Close-up*. Instead of visiting museums and the traditional tourist sites, Eisenstein decided that they should board a tram at the Embankment and travel on it to the end of the line and back. While his guide found this journey boring and meaningless, Eisenstein evidently found it most enjoyable and instructive. After this they travelled to Whitechapel and went on a pub crawl, during which the normally sober director drank several pints of beer and generally absorbed the lively East End conversations and atmosphere surrounding him.[2] Like his teacher Meyerhold, Eisenstein often preferred experiencing street life to visiting museums.[3] To his guides on his visit to Chicago he emphatically stated 'No museums!' He knew that a ride through a wealthy district was usually dull because there would be hardly anything going on in the streets, which is why he protested when he was taken to Chicago's Gold Coast district. He was similarly disappointed by the view from the *Chicago Tribune* Tower. What he wanted to experience was a living and breathing cityscape, so his guides took him to Chicago's street markets, its 'skid row', its Mexican and Black ghettoes. He enjoyed dancing at Navy Pier, eating popcorn and candy floss, and he preferred to eat at cafeterias rather than fancy restaurants. His curiosity about the criminal mind prompted him to contact a University of Chicago criminologist to guide him through the underworld clubs associated with Al Capone, in the Cicero district.[4] Eisenstein's sense of the cityscape was one which was totally rooted in the everyday lives of a wide cross-section of its citizens. This was a teeming urban world related to what is seen in Ruttmann's *Berlin, Symphony of a Great City* (1927) and Vertov's *The Man with the Movie Camera* (1929). Unlike in these films, his own urban scenes from *The Strike*, *The Battleship Potemkin*, and *October* show social turmoil, but Eisenstein's citizens also strongly interact with the landscapes of the city, the factory and port, from which they seamlessly emerge.

Before Chicago, Eisenstein's first experience of a large American city had been his point of arrival, New York. He had expected to be more impressed by the height of the city's famed skyscrapers.[5] However, he hadn't anticipated the shock of nocturnal Manhattan on a rainy night:

> At night, perspective and the perception of real distance are destroyed by a sea of coloured, illuminated advertisements. Far and near, small (in the *foreground*) and big (in the *background*), flashing on and off, moving and revolving, popping up and disappearing, they ultimately nullify all perception of real space, and at certain moments they seem like a drawing made up of coloured dotted lines or strips flickering over a single flat surface, the black velvet of the night sky…the headlights of speeding cars and buses, the light reflected from railway tracks and from patches of wet asphalt, together with the upside-down reflections in puddles which destroy our perception of which way is 'up' and which 'down': all these contribute to forming a similar mirage of light under our feet; and as we make our way through this double world of neon advertisements, they seem not to be on a single plane but a system of stage 'flats' hanging in the air, past which rush the lighted streams of traffic.[6]

Eisenstein's first conscious impression of Manhattan at night is that of a space where normal perspective is reversed: the patterns of neon lights in the foreground appear small, whereas the electric advertising in the background appears large. This impression is extended by the sense of a double mirage of lights, where it's not certain which is above or below. This experience reminds Eisenstein of René Guilleré's article about the jazz age, in which he explains that at this time single-point perspective was replaced by a complex synthesis of several perspectives, viewpoints which are shown simultaneously from above and below. Guilleré points out that art, literature and music from this period make use of multiple perspectives. Jazz, based on multiple parts played at the same volume, has superceded the perspectival planes of classical Western music: Guilleré mentions how in jazz everything is carried forward into the foreground. He explains the result of this method on the audience in cinematographic terms: a camera angle is widened, pulling the image right up to us and into us, so that we are forced to participate in the world of the image. This, he tells us, is the reason for close-ups in cinema, to show someone out of proportion as she or he would look when they are only half a metre away from us. This approach to perspective abolishes illusory depth; and creates a different relationship between people and their environment, bringing them much closer together. As a result, Guilleré states that we enter our environment, and it is perceived through us – the environment and us co-exist: we function through one another.[7]

This use of multiple perspectives was later termed an 'all-over' space, the spatially ambiguous yet dynamic planes of painters like Stuart Davis, De Kooning and Pollock, from the late 1930s to the 1950s. And Davis, inspired by Cubism, was also influenced by jazz in his work, especially in his landscapes, for example *Swing Landscape*. Eisenstein clearly sees the connection between Cubist painting and jazz. He points out that one only has to glance at Cubist painting to realise that what happens there has already happened in jazz. He also understands that classical architecture, based on Renaissance perspectival conventions has the same relationship to the Classical period in music, as the landscape of the modern city relates to jazz.[8]

The 'all-over' space of a rainy Manhattan at night was a type of space Eisenstein would encounter in various forms on his travels in Mexico, in his attempt to make an audiovisual film portrait of that country. It was in his filming of *Que Viva Mexico!* that he would realise how closely people and their landscape environment interact, and it was in Mexico that his concept of 'nonindifferent nature' was born, as well as its relationship to his developing ideas about audiovisual cinema.

Que Viva Mexico!

Eisenstein's arrival in America was for him a momentous event. He had even chosen his hotel in Paris, the Hôtel des Etats-Unis, in anticipation of his sojourn in the United States.[9] It was not easy for artists to travel outside the Soviet Union, let alone to the largest capitalist country, as there was always a concern that they might not return.[10] The memory of his arrival in New York, apart from its vivid qualities, was particularly expressive of what he was expecting to encounter in America. The first thing he saw from the liner were 'rosy four-faceted columns' gradually rising from the greenish surface of the Atlantic, so tall that their bases were for a long time invisible beneath the line of the horizon. He described these Manhattan skyscrapers as being Babylonian in scale, making him aware of the curvature of the earth. They represent enormous energy, explosions of rockets 'frozen in flight', and he mentions their superimpositions of tower upon tower in the most dynamic terms: the slender second set of thirty stories escapes from the wider shoulders of the first thirty, and the third set of even more slender thirty stories bursts from the arms of the second set, to rush to throw itself even higher, to at last become still, at an unreachable height.[11]

This ecstatic vision is complemented by his subsequent experience of the people of Manhattan rushing like a whirlpool through its streets, like the millions of wheels of its hyperindustry spinning. The scale and excitement induced in him by this advanced technology-based dynamism makes him feel as if the earth itself is spinning as a result of all this energy.[12] It was not long before he would realise that behind this most technologically advanced culture lay what he believed was a conservatism of traditional values. He noticed that the soaring skyscrapers were actually stacks of dozens to hundreds of provincial buildings, featuring apartments with old-fashioned armchairs and lace doilies masking the latest technological achievements, like refrigerators, washing-machines and radios. He was amazed by the provincial nature of the manners and ideology of the American middle-classes.[13] Ultimately it was this conservatism which led to each of his film projects being rejected by Paramount in Hollywood, because of the ideological unsuitability of his scenarios, and Eisenstein's desire not to use stars or professional actors.[14] It was another form of the same conservatism which was to lead to the dismantling of his film *Que Viva Mexico!* Perhaps this is one of the reasons that in *Nonindifferent Nature* he juxtaposes his initial ecstatic vision of New York with an extended and rhapsodic evocation of his experiences in Mexico.[15]

After his failure to make a film in Hollywood, Eisenstein felt that he should try to make at least one film before returning home to Russia. He approached the successful American socialist novelist Upton Sinclair for financial support for a film he wished to make about Mexico. Eisenstein had long had a fascination with this country. As a young man, the first theatre production he had directed was *The Mexican* (1921), adapted from a story by Jack London. He had also designed the sets and costumes for it, using colours such as bright blue and yellow to evoke what he had imagined would be a Mexican atmosphere.[16] He had met the famous Mexican painter Diego Rivera in Moscow, in 1927. Rivera was a guest of the Soviet government for the tenth anniversary celebrations of the Revolution. The charismatic painter had described to him the wealth and diversity of the cultures of his native land. Shortly after Eisenstein's arrival in Mexico, Rivera took him to see his murals showing the Spanish conquest, in the Cortés Palace, Cuernavaca. He was also struck by the paintings of other Mexican muralists, in particular José Clemente Orozco and David Alfaro Siqueiros.[17] In addition Eisenstein read what he could find about Mexico, including D.H. Lawrence's travel book *Mornings in*

Mexico (1927).[18] He also read his novel *The Plumed Serpent* (1926), which he admitted that he could not finish perhaps partly because of Lawrence's reactionary ideas at that time, which are a key part of this work.[19] He was inspired by Anita Brenner's *Idols Behind Altars*, her book about the hybridisation of Mesoamerican culture and Catholicism. On his arrival, Eisenstein continued his research into Mesoamerican culture at the National Archeological Museum in Mexico City.[20]

Responding positively to Eisenstein's request, Sinclair agreed to fund a film about Mexico. The director, his assistant Alexandrov and cameraman Tisse immediately set off to Mexico to start work, in December 1930. They were accompanied by Sinclair's brother-in-law Hunter Kimbrough, who was to act as business manager for the production. They travelled the length and breadth of the country to research various aspects of Mexican life and culture, and the three-to-four-month schedule for filming which had been agreed with the Sinclairs soon elapsed. However, when Sinclair saw what Eisenstein had filmed, he was delighted and he allowed him an extension to be able to complete his film. This extension also elapsed, whereupon Sinclair asked his brother-in-law to supervise Eisenstein's filming more rigorously, so that he would know what the director and his assistants were doing, as well as to encourage them to complete the work. Kimbrough turned out to know even less about film than Upton Sinclair, and his complete lack of understanding of what was going on led to an irretrievable personality clash with Eisenstein, and ultimately to the director's break with Sinclair. After thirteen months the film had gone considerably over budget and they had just one final episode of the film to shoot. At last Eisenstein had been able to secure the cooperation of the Mexican government, who were going to supply them with the hundreds of soldiers needed for this particular episode. At this point, to Eisenstein's dismay, the novelist put a stop to his funding of the film. He kept everything that had been shot, and in spite of the efforts of Eisenstein and numerous others, over subsequent years Sinclair sold off the film to various individuals and companies who used it to make short features, travelogues and educational films. Eisenstein was never able to obtain a copy of his film to edit it as he had envisaged, and he never really recovered from its loss.[21] In Mexico he had had complete artistic freedom. He had intended to make a new type of sound film, what he called a 'Film-Symphony' about his vision of the diversity and the destiny of a country which fascinated him, a film he called *Que Viva Mexico!*[22]

Upton Sinclair's knowledge of how a film was made was largely circum-scribed by the conventions of the script-based Hollywood approach, so it was not surprising that a new and unscripted type of film which grew and developed as Eisenstein travelled across Mexico, was something which was beyond the novelist's comprehension. This lack of understanding was exacerbated by his brother-in-law, who insisted that Eisenstein and his team were squandering Sinclair's money without adhering to any valid shooting schedule. To make matters worse, Eisenstein had outstayed his leave from the Soviet Union, and Stalin had sent a telegram to Sinclair saying that the director had 'lost his comrades' confidence' in the Soviet Union, that he was thought to be a deserter and that 'the people here would have no interest in him soon.'[23] The technological possibilities to make his first sound film (which had attracted Eisenstein to the United States in the first place) had crashed against the limitations of the underlying conservatism he mentioned that he had also found there. In addition, in Eisenstein's years of absence from 1929 to 1932, the Stalin-led world of Soviet art was moving rapidly away from revolutionary experimentalism to a conservative Socialist Realism which had little patience for a work as personal and innovative as *Que Viva Mexico!*[24]

Eisenstein, Mexico and nonindifferent nature
In writing about Disney's films, Eisenstein found an explanation as to how they blazed with colour: 'grey, grey, grey. From birth to death. Grey squares of city blocks. Grey prison cells of city streets. Grey faces of endless street crowds.' This was a greyness he had experienced in New York, Chicago, Berlin, Paris, Moscow. He associated this greyness with people oppressed by the sameness of daily routines, with their 'regulated moments of rest', playing out their lives in an already lost game of chess where the squares are not black and white 'but are all of a protective grey colour, day after day'. Eisenstein considered Disney's brightly colourful films to be a revolt against such 'spiritual stagnation and greyness'.[25] But he had found in Mexico ample evidence of other kinds of social injustices, including pervasive corruption and a police force which was more or less under control. The problems were different: there was sloth and back-wardness rather than industrial drudgery. Because of the tropical climate, the poverty was more on show, and daily sights like mangy dogs licking dirty cooking pots were commonplace.[26] But the intensity of colours resulting from the quality of light he encountered there dazzled him, and again and again he made reference to this in his memories of Mexico.

These experiences were part of what Eisenstein called 'the Mexican fever', caught by those who had been to that country. It evoked hallucin-atory colours: 'the gold of the Mexican dawns and sunsets … the warm bronze of pensive faces … the dark green, bluish or light grey foliage … majolica on blue cupolas … the razor-edged green sail of the agave leaf …

the flocks of parrots in shades of light green.'[27] He wrote about flying over the Gulf of Mexico: 'the rose-coloured flamingos fly like arrows over the blue surface of the ocean between our airplane and the bronze-green Atlantic coast that lies at our feet.'[28] Eisenstein mentions the sensation of extreme heat, also part of the 'Mexican fever': from 'the perpetually hot, dry heat of the desert' to 'the hot embraces of the tropics' and 'the searing heat' of the bullfight arenas. The heat accentuates the sense of smell; Eisenstein recalled 'the stupefying aroma of fermented maguey juice' from the *pulque* distillery, which permeated his sleeping quarters in the hacienda at Tetlapayac, his headquarters for the making of *Que Viva Mexico!*[29]

The Mexican heat also helps to bring body and landscape together in other ways. He noted that at certain moments during sunrise and sunset the air would take on a transparency so great that it seemed to him as if it had been stolen. Eisenstein describes how the red-tinted slopes of the mountains in the distance appeared to be suspended in the void which divided the ultramarine coloured sky and the violet shade of the foothills. At a moment like this, he realised that his eyesight moved beyond seeing, and it went into the domain of touch – just like the blind 'see' with their hands.[30] In the intensity of Eisenstein's experience of the twilight landscape his sight becomes like touch. He remembers the 'emotional landscapes' painted on silk by Chinese artists of the eighth century, and realises that 'images of a worldview' are not only present in the 'flickering graphics of the brush' of Huang Ch'üan, an artist from this period, but are there, in the actual Mexican landscapes, surrounding him everywhere. He quotes from Engels, where the philosopher refers to the religious beliefs and spiritual qualities of various kinds which he sees as growing directly from the specific character of the local landscape. Eisenstein develops this idea further by explaining how for those who can see and are sufficiently emotionally receptive to nature it is at this point that his concept of 'nonindifferent nature' reaches its triumphant and joyous culmination.[31] It was the intensity of his experiences of Mexican landscapes, intertwined with their human histories, that enabled Eisenstein to develop his idea of 'nonindifferent nature'. These landscapes were to form a vital component of his scenario for *Que Viva Mexico!*

Que Viva Mexico! and landscape

Each section of Eisenstein's scenario is based on a different Mexican landscape. The first part is a *Prologue*, a funeral set in Yucatan, amongst the Mayan ruins, vast and ancient pyramids and temples. Eisenstein filmed an 'immobile procession', a ritual which for him symbolised a farewell to the Mayan civilisation.[32] Some of the Mayan people he involved in the *Prologue* were chosen because of their physiognomic resemblance to the sculptures on the walls of the Mayan ruins.[33] Even their poses and expressions are alike, so they blend and interact with the architecture in the landscape.[34] The living people he shows become like sculptures and statues; Eisenstein planned to show a variety of groups of them as if they had joined the timeless ruins and had been turned to stone. He parallels the almost closed eyes of the living with the mask-like face of the dead man in the open casket. The only visual movement in this part of the film would have been scenes from various symbolic funerals, emerging from the original one, which would have appeared as a 'shifting procession'.[35] This suggests a sequence of dissolves to blur the living with the dead, and various layers of the past with a present which already seems ancient. In this *Prologue* static living figures would have emerged from the ancient human land-scape of the Mayan ruins. However there is a shot which features human movement and which appears in Alexandrov's version of *Que Viva Mexico!* Here, Eisenstein's use of a Rodchenko-style shot, from an extremely low angle, makes the two men who are climbing the pyramid appear to blend with the architecture. This approach is a development of the Soviet Constructivist low angle shot, used to blend man with structures of the machine age.[36]

After the *Prologue* there is a sequence of four stories. The first, titled *Sandunga*, is set in the tropical isthmus of Tehuantepec, and is named after a dance song which is the unofficial national anthem of the area.[37] The story is very simple indeed. It is a portrait of a matriarchal society which features a Zapotec girl, who is saving up for her dowry to marry her lover, and her subsequent early motherhood. Eisenstein uses this slim narrative to show the overwhelming abundance of life in the tropics: from the dense forests, to the flora and fauna who live freely in them. He portrays an idyllic existence, a paradise where the local Tehuana girls (from the village of Tehuantepec) are described in terms of the tropical landscape. Their shining black hair is described as being like a cascade, and they wear wreaths of flowers on their heads. Lying in the shallow water of a river, they are juxtaposed with alligators basking in the sun. The young people seem to grow out of the landscape like flowers; in Eisenstein's imagination their 'beauty blossoms on the screen'. At the market in Tehuantepec he also notes the mixtures of cultures in this part of Mexico, lying at the narrowest point of the country between the Pacific and Atlantic oceans. The fruit, flower and fish stalls suggest India, the earthenware pots suggest Baghdad, and another aspect of the market evokes the South Seas. In the section showing a dance in the local hall, the tropical flowers, leaves and fruits become decorations for the festivities. After the dance the young man makes his proposal of marriage, and her acceptance sets in motion all the elements of a traditional wedding, including a banquet, elaborately decorated gifts, and girls dancing in their regional costumes. As the celebratory fireworks go off, following local traditions the young women turn their headgear inside out. Eisenstein compares them to a flock of bih-birds spreading their wings. The shots from this episode show the Tehuanas as if emerging from tropical vegetation, in a Gauguinesque way. Their clothes and what they carry feature floral and leaf designs, and when the young people's torsos are naked, Eisenstein makes sure that the shadows from the tropical vegetation play on their skin. The Tehuantepec romance began with a sunrise and the waking of the animal and human life inhabiting this lush landscape. It ends with a sunset as the diurnal animals retire, and we see the young mother, her young husband and their son, contented, totally integrated with the tropical landscape.[38] An alternative ending, also based on a nonindifferent integration between people and landscape, features a transition to the next story through the shape and character of the Tehuana's wedding dress: 'the snowy white "weepeel" – the mountain-like head-dress of the triumphant mother and wife. The snowy serenity. Snowy like the grey-haired Popocatepetl.'[39] The head-dress to volcano transition is shown in Eisenstein's sketches for this breakdown of shots. In these drawings he also shows further graphic match ideas using a triangular arrangement. The suggested progression of shots moves from cacti to sombrero, to a symmetrical montage within a single shot, of a man wearing a sombrero, with some cacti on both sides, and a volcano centered in the background. These transitions also imply Eisenstein's concept of nonindifferent nature.

The second story is in complete contrast, 'as the North Pole differs from the Equator'. The landscape is harsh and consequently the people inhabiting it are austere, arrogant and aggressive. All the action takes place on a high desert plain, at the foot of great volcanoes, in and around the ancient hacienda at Tetlapayac, in the midst of 'vast seas' of the maguey cactus.[40] Once again the story begins around dawn, in this case some time before sunrise, and ends with the setting sun. The social structure is feudal, even though the action takes place at the beginning of the twentieth century.

The owner of the hacienda has complete control over the lives of his workers, the *peons*, who go out daily to harvest the juice of the maguey cactus to make the ancient Indian alcoholic drink *pulque*. The feudal lord's power even involves approving the brides of his workers. Adhering to this tradition, the peon Sebastian takes his bride to the landowner, an old man who simply gives a few coins to the young girl, and continues enjoying the annual fiesta of the hacienda which is in full swing. One of his guests drags the girl away and rapes her, while Sebastian is waiting outside for her to return. A servant tells him what has happened, so the peon attempts to rescue his bride, but he is thrown back out. Meanwhile the landowner, realising what has happened, decides to mask the incident by calling for the fiesta fireworks, music and games to begin. Outside Sebastian decides to get his revenge for what has happened, and three other peons agree to support him. They try to set the hacienda on fire, and they steal arms and ammunition from the landowner's armoury. They attempt unsuccessfully to rescue the bride and are beaten back by gunfire from the *charros*, the cowboys from the hacienda. The peons flee and are discovered the next day. After another battle with the *charros*, during which the landowner's daughter is shot dead, they are taken prisoner.[41] The peons are then buried up to their waists in the desert, and the *charros* ride over them, their horses' hooves delivering the inevitable and final death blows.

The massive sharp spikes of the maguey cactus are emblematic of the cruelty and violence of both this story and the harsh desert environment in which it unfolds. The aggressive forms of this cactus punctuate the shots from the episode. At one point, in their battle with the *charros*, the peons take refuge in a giant maguey cactus. In other shots from later in the story, Eisenstein counterpoints the wounded head of the dead hero Sebastian with a nearby scraggy and contorted cactus (Fig.4).[42]

The third story is set during the same historical period as the *Maguey* episode and culturally it concentrates on the Spanish influences in Mexico. Like the previous two stories it ends at sunset, and the action takes place at various locations, which as a whole comprise an imaginary amalgam of the Spanish colonial style, from Mexico City, Merida, Taxco, Puebla, Cholula and other places representative of this architectural genre. Like in the *Sandunga* episode the story is simple: a picador has an assignation with the wife of another man. Eisenstein uses this basic structure to show the various rituals before and during a bullfight, a huge national fiesta, the floating gardens of Xochimilco in Mexico City, and finally the summit of a mountain at sundown. He shows how Christian and pre-Christian beliefs and rituals are interwoven in these events and places. At the centre of this episode is the annual fiesta in honour of Mexico's patron saint, the holy Virgin of Guadalupe, on 12 December; she is also the patron saint of the pre-Christian art of bullfighting.[43] Eisenstein noticed how Catholic shrines were located at the holy sites formerly devoted to the ancient Meso-american divinities, including that of the Virgin of Guadalupe.[44] The bullfighters in the story pray to her before they enter the arena. Eisenstein juxtaposes the Indian dancers getting their elaborate costumes and masks

Fig.4 Sebastian's remains are paralleled with a nearby maguey cactus.

ready for their ritual dances, with the Catholic bishops and archbishops putting on their equally fine robes for their services. Both types of ceremony are in honour of the Virgin of Guadalupe. After the bullfight the lovers take a boat through the floating gardens of Xochimilco, one of the few surviving sites built by the Aztecs in Mexico City. The Spanish Baroque, the *barroco*, blending with equally complex Mesoamerican patterns are the key element here. The decorated Spanish colonial architecture in the background, the elaborate moves of the bullfighters in their highly embroidered costumes, the intricate lace of the mantillas worn by the bullfight 'belles' in the audience, the religious robes of both Indians and Catholics, and the hundreds of festively adorned boats in Xochimilco, all make up what was to have been an elaborately composed episode featuring complex and intricate designs. The story's main characters become lost in the colourful mobile maze of 'temples of love', the boats of Xochimilco, covered with flowers, in this area known as the 'Venice of Mexico'.[45] Thus intricate patterns dominate this episode, expressed in architecture, costumes, the movements of dancers and bullfighters, and the ancient man-made landscape of floating gardens.

The final story, like the *Maguey* episode, involves violence, in this instance during the Mexican Revolution. This part is entitled *Soldadera*, after the name given to the women in the vanguard of the revolutionary armies who prepare food in advance for the soldiers they adopt. Against a violent and confused background of the continuous movements of armies, their trains and their battles, Eisenstein follows the nomadic life of Pancha, a *soldadera* whose adopted soldier dies in a battle, just after she has given birth. She and her baby are adopted by another soldier. Just when the next battle seems imminent, they are told that the civil war is over, and we see them celebrating the triumph of the Revolution with their former enemies, as they all begin a new life. Eisenstein lists the landscapes and towns for this story: the mountains, the deserts, the woods, Cuautla, Morelos, Acapulco on the Pacific Coast. The *soldadera*s trudge on dusty roads, and at one point Pancha is lost from view among the huge mass of humanity on the move, veiled by the dust. They also travel on the roof of a troop train, where they are squatting, crow-like. Eisenstein describes how, during a battle, the *soldadera*s take refuge beneath the cars of a freight train and hang their holy icons from the car wheel, as well as their small votive lamps on the car axle's springs. In this revolutionary context, unlike during the Russian Revolution, there is no attempt to forego religious devotion.[46]

The *Epilogue* is set in modern Mexico, and Eisenstein begins with a parade of modern industries. He shows current leaders, including generals, engineers and aviators, to demonstrate that in Mexico there is an equivalent to the process of industrialisation of the Soviet Union. Here Eisenstein's description of large scale industry brings to mind the world of Vertov's *Enthusiasm* (1930). Agriculture is also being developed. Then he begins to focus on the people's faces. As in an epic mural by Diego Rivera, Eisenstein shows us how these modern faces are identical to the ones we have seen in all the previous episodes, including at the immobile funeral lost in the depthless time of Yucatan, from the *Prologue* at the very start of *Que Viva Mexico!* The film ends as it began, with the theme of death. To conclude, Eisenstein shows us the *calavera*, the emblematic skeletons in the Mexican fiesta for the Day of the Dead. This is when, starting on the eve of All Saints' Day, the dead make their annual visit to the world of the living. Dancing skeletons appear, dressed in a variety of costumes, representing the dead from all levels of Mexican society, from the president, the leaders of the military, the feudal landowners down to their peons, the *soldadera* and others whose lives we have witnessed in the previous episodes. The film ends on the image of a smiling boy's face which fills the screen, after he has removed his skull mask. He personifies 'the new growing Mexico'.[47] Here is shown the triumph of life over death, the idea which lies at the centre of the fiesta of the Day of the Dead.[48]

Music in *Que Viva Mexico!*

When writing scenarios Eisenstein explained that he liked 'to imagine the music as I work.'[49] Together with his skill and imagination in the visualisations of the events in his film projects, Eisenstein simultaneously had an ability to aurally imagine the music and sound in them. In this respect he worked like a composer, who before composing the music for an opera reads the libretto and aurally imagines the types of music which are needed at each point and for each scene. In his most detailed scenario for *Que Viva Mexico!* there are very few examples of speech or dialogue. Most of the text is descriptive, and suggests two main sources of sound: there is music which always comes directly and organically out of the events which occur, and noise, which has a similarly direct relationship to what is happening. Both of these types of sound are closely related to the strongly traditional nature of the various Mexican cultures which form the context of each episode in the film. It is almost as if there are two scores implied throughout the scenario: a score for the music, and an equally important score for noise.

Eisenstein's idea to use a symphonic form for *Que Viva Mexico!* enabled him to structure a series of four highly contrasting narratives, akin to symphonic movements, framed by a *Prologue* and an *Epilogue*. A classical symphonic structure depends on the formal principle of four highly contrasting movements. These differ from one another in a variety of ways: in tempo, in style, in form, in content. Like each narrative in *Que Viva Mexico!* each symphonic movement is largely formally self-contained, though they can be linked by certain recurring elements. For example two of the four movements can have elements in common, in the same way that the *Maguey* and the *Soldadera* episodes are linked by the themes of violence and death, and the *Sandunga* and *Fiesta* episodes are linked by sharing a romantic and lyrical atmosphere. In addition, each of the six parts of the film features a different folk-song. Eisenstein is concerned that together, the folk traditions, the myths and the music from various parts of the country form a symphonic unity. He is aiming to bring together these different parts of the country into a single filmic unity, a 'Film-Symphony' which for him represents the varied entity of Mexico, audiovisually.[50]

For what Eisenstein calls his 'overture', the *Prologue* set in Yucatan, he uses high-pitched Mayan singing, against drums from Yucatan, with their strange ancient rhythm to accompany the funeral procession which has been frozen in time.[51] This music is intended to evoke a sense of primordial timelessness, an elemental combination of high voices and drums, to provoke a state of trance in those attending the funeral.

As mentioned earlier, the first episode is named after the *Sandunga*, the graceful dance song from the Isthmus of Tehuantepec, which reflects the rich mixture of cultures Eisenstein describes in his scenario. It is a blend of the European waltz, as well as Spanish and Zapotecan musical styles.[52] The song is the expression of a Zapotecan woman's grieving over the death of her mother; she moves from an overwhelming sadness to a sense of release afforded by the acceptance of her loss. The girls from Tehuantepec sing the *Sandunga* as they lie in the shallow edge of the river at the start of this episode. The sensual music of this danced song is present almost continuously throughout this story. It embodies the slightly unreal and dreamlike quality characteristic of the *Sandunga* episode.[53]

Music is used to frame the beginning and end of the *Maguey* story. The morning hymn, *El Alabado*, is sung by the peons before they leave the hacienda to begin their day's work harvesting the sap of the maguey cactus. A song to the virginity of a new day, it is at the same time a hymn to the Virgin Mary, another example of the Mexican mix of Mesoamerican and Catholic cultures and beliefs. Eisenstein closes the episode with the peons singing 'their vesper song just as plaintive, as mournful, as their morning *Alabado*.' After the violence of this section, the music has a cathartic effect, and also gives a sense that nothing has changed (or will change) in the static feudal rhythm of the life of the Mexican haciendas, the 'unapproachable fortresses amidst the vast seas of cactus groves'. The only other music Eisenstein mentions in this stark episode is the rattle of the dance music for the hacienda's annual fiesta, ordered by the feudal lord as a distraction after the incident of the rape of the peon's bride.[54]

The *Fiesta* section features a more complex and varied selection of different pieces of music, to match the complex visual patterns in the episode. As pilgrims from all over Mexico gather for the national fiesta in honour of the Virgin of Guadalupe, the matadors prepare for the bullfights to the accompaniment of 'the tinkling of guitars and the sound of militant songs of the ring'. An orchestra at the bullring accompanies the opening parade with a joyful march as the audience take their seats. Overlapping with the end of the *corrida* there is a complex mix of rhythms as the drums of the Indian ceremonial dances, the pealing of the ancient Spanish church bells and the 'thunder of exploding sky rockets' combine in the plaza, punctuated by the roar and ovations of the crowd from the bullring. Here again is an audiovisual expression of the Mexican blend of Mesoamerican and Catholic cultures; in this instance the non-Christian aspects of Spanish culture are also shown in the bullfighting rituals. Then there is another mix: Spanish and African influences merge in the music for guitars and marimbas which accompany the lovers' retreat into the labyrinth of the floating gardens of Xochimilco. Then, following the Picador's narrow escape from the jilted husband, a song from the huge fiesta ends the episode.[55]

The song *Adelita* dominates the story of the *soldaderas*, the women soldiers who fought alongside and supported the troops during the period of the Mexican Revolution, after 1910. Eisenstein calls *Adelita* the leitmotif of the *soldadera* and so he presents it in different arrangements. It first appears scored for guitars, as the soldiers and the *soldaderas* rest in the evening. Then the soldiers sing it in transit, on the troop train. After a battle during which her soldier is killed, the *soldadera*, weary and grief-stricken, follows the army again. Another soldier carries her child for her and he becomes her new partner. This action takes place against the backdrop of another version of *Adelita*, this time played by military bands, out of tune and out of rhythm, evoking the weariness and depression of the soldiers and the *soldaderas*. When they learn that the civil war is now over, at this point Eisenstein has a military brass band play *Adelita* in its final appearance 'stoutly, solemnly and triumphantly'.[56]

Eisenstein's ideas about the use of music for the *Epilogue* to *Que Viva Mexico!* are to be found in his introduction to the scenario for the film, which he wrote in 1947, for inclusion in the planned publication in French of his writings and scenarios. For the Day of the Dead masks and skeletons he had planned a 'final joyous farandole' to which all the characters from the previous episodes would dance, as well as figures from Mexico's past and present.[57] In another text on this subject, Eisenstein points out that the living are also featured in these masked dances of the dead, in this case 'a wild rumba'. Traditionally, one speaks well of the dead, but there is nothing to prevent Mexicans from using the mask of death during these annual festivities, to satirise the living: 'carnival death demands malicious, heartless, venomous epigrams for each quasi-corpse, to tear off the veneer he sports in life.'[58] It is this Day of the Dead tradition which Eisenstein uses in the climax of his film. All appear equal in death – both in the actual All Saints Day fiesta and in Eisenstein's *Epilogue*, people at all levels of society rub shoulders as dancing skeletons. The *Que Viva Mexico!* characters blend in with the masked dancers from an actual fiesta. The living bishops and generals (and the living President of Mexico) were to have appeared in the documentary-style section at the beginning of the *Epilogue*.[59] In the Day of the Dead conclusion, these dignitaries remove their masks to reveal 'the grimace of a real skull', whereas the 'positive heroes' from the film, those peons, soldiers, *soldaderas* and others, whose lives are blighted by violence and slavery, a form of death in life, remove their skeleton masks to reveal 'living, bronzed faces, creased with mirth'.[60]

The shock of the dignitaries' true death-like nature appears in the sudden pause Eisenstein noted in his experience of dances during an evening spent in a Mexican dance hall:

> The 'Danzon' is under way, that amazing dance, in which from time to time, in the midst of the most sharp motion, a couple suddenly, for several beats, freezes completely motionless, facing one another, and stands as if rooted, until they again continue the tormenting sensuality, or the quick tempo of rhythmic body movements. ... At such moments, the dance hall is frightening: it seems like a stiffened corpse, still trembling inside to the beat of the orchestra's screaming rhythm. ... In the semidarkness, the figures come to life and float away.[61]

The pause traditionally found in the danzon or rumba, or any number of such kinds of dances from Mexico, the Spanish-speaking Caribbean and Latin-America, lies for Eisenstein at the meeting point between sensuality and death. This phenomenon enables Eisenstein to weave a seamless pattern from these traditional dances and their personal and political significance to his audiovisual portrait of Mexico. The double death/life, life/death inversion already takes place during the annual Day of the Dead fiesta. All he has to do is select from what he has experienced in the various landscapes of the country, both rural and urban, and place these chosen elements, both visual and auditory, back into their original and 'live' contexts. This is why the Day of the Dead festival provides an ideal conclusion: it enables Eisenstein to refer directly and naturally to all the past events in his scenario, as death and its simulation are necessarily retrospective, even in the case of the popular epigrammatic judgements on the living dead dignitaries. At the same time it enables him to finish on the optimistic image of a young boy's smiling face, emerging from behind a cardboard mask of a skull, preceded by other smiling faces, uncovered in the same way, who represent the rebirth and continued life of Mexico. Presented audiovisually, at one and the same time this rebirth is the underlying theme of this fiesta and of *Que Viva Mexico!* Now it can be seen why the version of the scenario which Eisenstein made available to the Mexican authorities (and sent to his financial backers the Sinclairs), did not include the musical element to be featured in the final part of the *Epilogue*, the Day of the Dead. With the Mexican authorities' promise to lend Eisenstein hundreds of troops for the *Soldadera* episode, it would not

have made sense to have them know in advance that they were effectively
to be represented in the climax of *Que Viva Mexico!* as examples of the
living dead.[62]

✳ Noise in *Que Viva Mexico!*

Together with Eisenstein's indications regarding music in his scenario,
there is also a 'score' which involves the use of noise. The *Prologue* is
characterised by an immobile silence of death, apart from the thin Mayan
music of drums and high voices. The *Sandunga* episode is framed by the
sound of screaming parrots, with the noise of fireworks at the wedding
fiesta. The same noise of fireworks is heard during the hacienda fiesta in
the *Maguey* story, and these explosions are carried forward in the noise of
the burning hay and the subsequent shooting between the peons and the
charros. In the *Fiesta* episode, the noise augments in scale with the sound of
the shouting and hand-clapping of some sixty thousand people assembled
on the plaza, waiting to enter the bullring's auditorium. Their cries,
outbursts and roars of derisive laughter punctuate the *corrida*. Then,
outside the arena, the sound of exploding sky rockets is heard, as well as
the sound of pealing church bells, mingling with another roar of the
crowd and ovations. At this point the noise 'score' combines with the
music, which itself has a strong noise element: the rolling of beating
drums accompanying the Mesoamerican ceremonial dances in the plaza.[63]

The *Soldadera* episode is particularly rich in noise, starting with shouting
and general chaos in a small Mexican village, as it is being pillaged by the
women soldiers. Squealing pigs and screeching fowl can also be imagined
at the beginning of this story: 'women are catching hens, pigs, turkeys;
women are hastily seizing tortillas and chile in the houses.' As the women
set up camp and begin to cook, the domestic clapping sounds of their
palms as they pat tortillas into shape, imply that peace is near. Then, as the
weary army arrives, clarions signal the call to rest. After dinner the soldiers
listen to the playing of *Adelita* on guitars, then fall asleep. The sleeping
soldiers form a 'snoring chorus', recalling a similar chorus of snoring
soldiers at the end of Act 2 in Alban Berg's opera *Wozzeck* (1917–21).[64]

The next day there is a battle, with the sound of machine-guns roaring,
the clattering hooves of the cavalry, shouts, the noise of gunshots and
exploding shells. After the battle there is a lull, then the whistles of the
locomotives are heard sounding the call for the surviving troops to depart.
The soldiers in the cars sing *Adelita*, as the women with their children
settle on the roofs of the train. Then the sound of the clapping of the
women's palms begins again, this time in counterpoint to the rattling
sounds of the train's wheels. The next day there is another, final battle,

before the news of the end of the civil war reaches the troops. The thunderous noise of the army's triumphant shouts are heard over the band slowly but confidently playing *Adelita*.

The first part of the *Epilogue* is full of the noise of modern industrial Mexico, with its hissing aeroplane propellers and its factory whistles, while the second part, the climax of the film, features a rumba, then a funeral march, followed by another rumba, or danzon or farandole, depending on which of the various versions of the scenario for *Que Viva Mexico!* is being read.[66]

Landscape and music in *Que Viva Mexico!*

The film project *Que Viva Mexico!* is dominated by a variety of landscapes. In his scenario, Eisenstein shows their influence on the lives and society of the people inhabiting them. Given the important role of music and noise in *Que Viva Mexico!*, certain questions can be raised about the role of sound in a film of this type, especially as it would have been Eisenstein's first sound film, had he been allowed to complete it. This was also probably the only occasion when he had the sort of freedom enjoyed by a poet, novelist or painter, to create something with a minimum of outside intervention, especially with regard to the way a subject is shown and interpreted. This impression of Eisenstein's new-found freedom, after the endless restrictions imposed on him by Paramount was noticed by Upton Sinclair, at the start of the Mexican project. He told his friends that this was 'the first time in Eisenstein's life that he was entirely free to make a picture according to his own ideas.'[67] Consequently Eisenstein had the freedom to use music and sound in this film project in any way he wished. This situation raises a fundamental question as to the function of music in any film involving landscape: why does landscape in cinema so often require music? Eisenstein provides an answer to this question in his essay on Walt Disney:

Let the libretto suggest to you that this is an ocean surf, and that – the sounds of a forest; this is a storm, and that – the play of sunlight in branches. How many varied storms and forests, suns in branches and surfs appear here to each individual imagination, how many different ones – to the same person on different days, at different hours, at different moments of his own emotional life. Music has preserved this emotional plurality of meaning in its speech, the plurality of meaning which has been displaced from language that seeks precision, distinctness, and logical exhaustion.[68]

Pathetic fallacy and the emotional plurality of meaning

In this text Eisenstein makes a correlation between the 'emotional plurality of meaning' which music has kept 'in its speech' with the emotional plurality of human responses to landscapes. These responses are dependent on the individual's state of mind at the time, interacting with the plurality of states in which the landscape appears, in calm or stormy weather, or at different times of the day or night. In making this type of correlation, Eisenstein evokes the direct link the Romantic imagination provided between landscape and emotion, for example the so-called 'pathetic fallacy', where an external storm is paralleled with an individual's interior emotional storm.[69] However his focus is on a *plurality* of meaning dependent on the variable states of mind of the individuals experiencing the landscape, and the *plurality* of the states of the landscape itself. The interactions which result from the mixing of these variables create a range of emotional responses which are much greater, more ambiguous and subtle than that provided by the one-to-one nature/emotion equivalence found in the Romantic approach to landscape. Yet it is still possible to retain the idea of 'nonindifferent nature' as there is no discernible separation between the state of the landscape and the state of the person experiencing it. This lack of separation is a direct consequence of the absence of 'precision, distinctness and logical exhaustion' which Eisenstein explains is characteristic of music, as it has retained its emotional plurality of meaning. This plurality of meaning is also present in the emotional response of the individual to the landscape. It is for this reason that landscape and music are so closely connected: they share an 'emotional plurality of meaning.' This kind of plurality is very much in evidence in Eisenstein's approach to Mexico. Instead of being content to explore just one aspect of the country, like the landscape and mixtures of cultures in the Yucatan peninsula for example, he wants to explore the wide range of landscapes and cultures of the whole of Mexico.[70] Shortly after his arrival, he even filmed the immediate aftermath of an earthquake in Oaxaca, an experience which deepened his feel for the country's landscape and its periodically devastating effect on the inhabitants.[71] However, because of the lack of clear separation between nature and the individual in his concept of nonindifferent nature, subsequently he saw the varied landscapes and cultures of Mexico as being a vast extension of his own personality:

> I think that it was not that my consciousness and emotions absorbed the blood and sand of the gory *corrida*, the heady sensuality of the tropics, the asceticism of the flagellant monks,

the purple and gold of Catholicism, or even the cosmic time-lessness of the Aztec pyramids: on the contrary, the whole complex of emotions and traits that characterise me extended infinitely beyond me to become an entire, vast country with mountains, forests, cathedrals, people, fruit, wild animals, breakers, herds, armies, decorated prelates, majolica on blue cupolas, necklaces made of gold coins worn by the girls of Tehuantepec and the play of reflections in the canals of Xochimilco.[72]

Mexico as Eisenstein's self-portrait

There is a drawing of Eisenstein by Gabriel Fernandez Ledesma (1900–83), a Mexican artist who subsequently married the young woman who played the role of Maria in the *Maguey* episode. He shows Eisenstein as a monkey, which is also an imaginary map of the Tetlapayac Hacienda in Hildalgo province. Eisenstein stayed at this hacienda, using it as a base for his travels round the country, as well as for the location of the *Maguey* episode. The drawing, dated 1931, and therefore contemporary with Eisenstein's stay at Tetlapayac, captures the idea of the 'emotional plurality of meaning', as there is no evidence of a dominant emotion in it. The artist has also used Eisenstein's style of drawing, so that at first glance the picture looks like one of the filmmaker's own drawings. The artist has reflected Eisenstein's personality, which in turn is the landscape of Tetlapayac, both inside and outside the hacienda. Eisenstein's idea of the filmmaker *as* the landscape he was filming is also shown in this amusing portrait. Like some of Eisenstein's Mexican drawings, it combines the characteristic sensual complexity and elaboration found in Baroque art, with the ascetic precision of single lines.[73]

Eisenstein described his initial first-hand experience of Mexico, as if he were meeting a female alter-ego: 'when I met Mexico she showed herself in all her contradictions, as though she were a projection of all the various traits and features which I carried and still carry around with me – a knot of complexes.' He reduced this Freud-influenced approach to two divergent Mexican traits: 'the simplicity of the monumental, and the extravagance of the baroque – in both its Spanish and Aztec aspects.' He found that these traits resonated within him: he was using 'the lenses of Eduard Tisse's incomparable film camera' on himself, and by realising a portrait of Mexico he was simultaneously making a self-portrait.[74] At a first glance, the graphic style of Ledesma's drawing incorporates the Mesoamerican influences, the dynamic lines, as well as Eisenstein's caricatural sense of humour which briefly could be mistaken for a self-

portrait.[75] The nearest pictures which approximate a self-portrait of
Eisenstein are not to be found in his Mexican drawings, but in the
photographs taken on his travels through Mexico. Here he is shown in
comical juxtaposition with various Mesoamerican gods, a giant suggestive
cactus, a sugar skull and a dressed-up skeleton from the fiesta of the Day
of the Dead. In other photographs he is seen wearing a nineteenth-century
style colonial explorer's outfit, including a pith helmet.[76] Eisenstein saw
himself as being the latest in a long line of explorers and travellers 'such as
Von den Steinen and Major Powell – all those doctors, missionaries,
adventurers, customs officers, enthusiasts, and colonizers..'. He merged
his personal travel experiences in Mexico with the accounts of their
travels, what Eisenstein called 'the sources of human culture'. Another of
these sources was the German scientist and explorer, Alexander von
Humboldt. Eisenstein describes how in Taxco he was shown the ruins of
a stone house where 'the untiring "great inquisitive", old Humboldt' had
stayed on his exploratory travels through Mexico. Continuing his
description, he blends a local flower with the designs on the great
naturalist's uniform, merging human with landscape and animal. Along the
ruined walls of this large stone house once occupied by Humboldt, he
found dry leafless stalks growing, with 'blood-red, five-pointed, velvety,
fantastic flowers', which reminded him of the great explorer's uniform,
'decorated with stars'. These flowers, named '*sangre de toro* (bull's blood)',
resembled for him spots of blood on the 'gray-yellow dust of that part of
Mexico'.[77]

Mexico: geography and time

Eisenstein's overwhelming hunger for knowledge about Mexico and its
cultures led him to fly above it, sail beside it, travel overland across it, and
even to travel into it, as when on a flight in a small aeroplane, passing by
the volcano Popocatepetl he tells how 'curiosity drove us to peer into the
extinct crater'. Eisenstein realised that the extreme geographical variety he
encountered in the country was accompanied by a huge vertical voyage in
time: 'the culture of Mexico of any one epoch from the vertical column of
history seems to be like a fan spread across the surface of the land'. Each
type of landscape he encountered held its own historical epoch; multiple
eras existing simultaneously across the country:

> when you travel from Yucatan to tropical Tehuantepec, from the
> tropics to the central plateau, to the civil war battlefields in the north
> or to the completely modern Mexico City, you seem not to be
> travelling in space but in time. The structure, the look, the culture

and customs of these various parts of the federation seem to belong to pre-historic times, to the pre-Columbian era, to the age of Cortés, to the period of Spanish feudal rule, to the years of the struggle for independence.

Eisenstein conceived of his film as a path across the centuries which had emerged directly from landscapes. He had intended it to be 'in the form of a sequence of small episodes which would traverse these gradations of history, episodes which themselves grew naturally out of the visual features and the mores of different parts of the country'.[78]

Nonindifferent nature and the cineplastic symphony

These landscapes were so different to what he had known before that when he detected some familiar element, he superimposed this previously lived experience directly on to the Mexican view before him: 'the broad avenues of Chapultepec which join the Bois de Boulogne to tropical plants; and the twisting iron architecture from the days of Napoleon III and Maximilian merges with the bronze faces and blue overalls of the contemporary inhabitants of Mexico City.'[79] This finding of the familiar in the unfamiliar extends to Mexican designs, woodblock prints, and finally to the people, in particular certain characteristic types, as Eisenstein continued to use his 'typage' method, not stars, in filming *Que Viva Mexico!*: 'Mexican lacquerwork is like our Mstyora and Palekh. Toys on the Mexican alamedas, like the toys of Sergiev Posad. José Guadalupe Posada – and our lubok. The *charro* could be a Circassian. And the thickset *mestizo* could be Ukrainian, the hero of one of Gogol's poems or stories.'[80]

And there is another example of the merging of the human with landscape, in this instance through colour:

In Mexico, every house painter is a wonderful designer, even when he is just daubing a wall. Is there an agreement between everyone on the town council, or is their spontaneous harmony – as in an amateur choir – born from their instinct alone? ... In some towns you will come across streets and entire neighbourhoods with walls painted in ochre and yellow, brick red or pale blue, in turquoise or orange, which form an immense canvas whose harmony seems planned. ... From the top of its cathedral, Puebla looks like the dress of an Infanta in a painting by Velasquez.[81]

Elie Faure, the French art historian and author of this description, had met Diego Rivera in Paris, and, like Eisenstein, had been enormously impressed by the painter's extraordinary stories about his country. Eventually accepting Rivera's repeated invitations to visit his country, he was taken round Mexico by the painter and other friends, and he met Eisenstein at the Tetlapayac Hacienda.[82]

Faure showed an early interest in cinema and a sensitivity to its potential as an art form. Already in 1922 he published *De la cinéplastique*, in which he outlined his ideas about cinema as an audiovisual medium. In defining his term *cinéplastique* he explains what he means by 'plastique'. It is 'the art of expressing form at rest or in movement, by every means humanly possible'.[83] In the Soviet Union during this period the term 'plastique' was being used with reference to movement in dance and in exercise patterns, as well as painting and sculpture.[84] Faure, in his list of the plastic arts, includes dance, gymnastics, processions of various kinds, and all techniques of painting, drawing, and engraving, including fresco painting. However he excludes academic sculpture, as he feels that it is too static for the plastic form, in which movement is a vital ingredient. He then argues that cinema goes beyond painting in that it shares with music and dance the possibility of movement which is repeated. The hybridisation of the dynamic characteristics which music, dance and cinema share mean that 'even the most mediocre films' give Faure the impression of 'unfolding in a musical space'. Additionally Faure explains that what *cinema* as a plastic art can provide, is a combination of architecture and movement: 'cinema is above all a plastic medium: it consists of a type of architecture in movement, which has to be in continuous harmony and dynamic equilibrium with the context and the landscapes, against which it rises and falls.'[85] Eisenstein realised that these ideas were describing what he was aiming to achieve in audiovisual cinema. After having successfully completed his first sound film, *Alexander Nevsky*, he wrote that it 'became the first masterpiece of a new art form – audiovisual art. The epic is built on the double development of the visual and musical movements. It is opera become cinematographic. It is the cineplastic symphony prophesied by Elie Faure.'[86]

Eisenstein's statement could have been applied to *Que Viva Mexico!*, had his Mexican audiovisual film been realised in the form he had envisioned. The scenario for it was clearly built 'on the double development of the visual and musical movements', its 'vast and multicoloured Film-Symphony' was epic in scale, and the approach to his use of music was operatic, as has been noted earlier.[87] Eisenstein's mention of symphony and opera in his statement is not as incompatible as at first it might seem, as Wagner, whose music drama *Die Walküre* Eisenstein was soon to direct, structured his operas using symphonic forms and techniques. The question of colour and music is also particularly relevant to both Faure and Eisenstein. With Faure it is clear in the musical analogy of a harmonious amateur choir which he uses in association with the harmonies of colour he noticed in Mexican towns. He also compares the cineplastic film to 'a kind of visual symphony as rich, as complex ... as the symphonies in sound by the greatest composers.'[88] With Eisenstein the colour/music analogy emerges out of his general image of the form of *Que Viva Mexico!* as being like a serape:

> the striped blanket that the Mexican *indio*, the Mexican *charro* – every Mexican wears. And the Serape could be the symbol of Mexico. So striped and violently contrasting are the cultures in Mexico running next to each other and at the same time being centuries away ... we took the contrasting independence of its violent colours as the motif for construction of our film; six episodes following each other – different in character, different in people, different in animals, trees and flowers. And still held together by the unity of the weave – a rhythmic and musical construction and an unrolling of the Mexican spirit and character.[89]

Colour, line and music in *Que Viva Mexico!*
The weave of the serape becomes like the lines of music in a score; its unfolding becomes like Faure's idea of a film 'unfolding in a musical space'. At this point it becomes difficult to imagine *Que Viva Mexico!* as anything other than a film in colour. Eisenstein admitted that he had the same problem:

> in my mind's eye I invariably see it as a colour film, as a series of images in colour ... its shots have remained in my memory not as photographic pictures but as the very objects themselves as they were caught by the lens and as they actually appeared in front of the camera.[90]

Just as Eisenstein was inspired by the saturated colours in 'the heady sensuality of the tropics', he was equally intoxicated by the 'dry asceticism' and brutality of what he called 'the tormenting severity of a line ripped bloodily from nature's multicoloured body'. For him the line, 'the clarity of the drawing' represented a different, sadistic sensuality of order, opposed to a lazy and sensual submission to vibrant colour. He saw the function of line as cutting 'through colour, so the orderliness of a system dissects the varied chaos of forms'.[91]

An awareness of the importance of line in the Mexican landscape led him to notice the harsh geometrical relationships between the natural and the man-made forms: 'the tetrahedron of the pyramid of the Moon and Sun in San-Juan-Teotihuacan rose up before me like an implacable razor. The white faces of Popocatepetl's spurs bisected the blue sky.' He also makes a closer and more dynamic comparison between pyramids and volcanoes, almost as if they were derived from the same creative impulse: 'pyramids you might expect to explode like volcanoes'.[9]

Triangular shapes are another important geometrical feature in *Que Viva Mexico!* [93] They first appear in the *Prologue*, set amongst the pyramids of Yucatan.[94] Then they reappear in the shape of the hammock and the Tehuana woman's head-dress. The latter motif provides the graphic transition to the volcanoes which are in the backdrop of the *Maguey* episode, mentioned earlier. Eisenstein places the three peons who are about to be killed in a triangular composition, with the hero dominating in the middle, which suggests the triangular arrangement of the crucifixion of Christ, flanked by the two robbers, as they are traditionally shown in Christian paintings. This idea is echoed in the subsequent *Fiesta* episode when there is a shot of a simulated crucifixion featuring the trunk of a cactus which has a complex interweaving of triangular motifs.[95] This use of triangular compositions is not only a means to provide a graphic unity to the variety of images in the film, but it also links the natural landscape to the human presence within it: the volcanoes are echoed in the man-made pyramids and later in the arrangement of the three buried peons. The acute triangles of the shapes of the peons wearing the serape, as they sing their hymn to the dawn, are echoed in the even more elongated shapes of the leaves of the maguey. In the shot of the dead peon and Maria, there is a complex of interlocking triangles which link her to her lover, and both in turn to the maguey cactus.[96] The varieties of these triangular compositions become leitmotifs expressing the concept of nonindifferent nature: the interaction of people and their emotions with the landscape that they inhabit.

In addition, the triangular compositions indicate the unbroken continuity of religious development, from Mesoamerican to Christian beliefs, and their current co-existence. Eisenstein mentions an example of this type of syncretism, when he explains that the Catholic cathedrals at the top of some of the Mexican pyramids were there 'in order not to sidetrack the pilgrims, who for thousands of years had come from all the corners of the land to the foot of these very pyramids'.[97] Apart from his use of the triangular geometry of the crucifixion, Eisenstein links these mergings of pagan and Christian beliefs with other triangular arrangements, for example the kneeling line of pilgrims ascending the pyramid in the *Fiesta* episode. Triangular-based images where the pagan element dominates are of the *torito* (the firecracker bull image) from the *Maguey* episode, a shot of a bullfight 'queen' from the same episode, and finally some shots of skeletons from the *Epilogue* featuring the syncretic fiesta of the Day of the Dead.[98] Eisenstein's preparatory drawings for the film also feature strongly triangle-based compositions usually associated with climactic and extreme sensations, including a diagrammatic representation of ecstasy.[99]

Another recurring motif is the ellipse, which relates faces (both alive and in masked form, in particular the Day of the Dead skull masks) to the sombrero, to ritual bowls, to jars, to Mesoamerican motifs.[100] Like the leitmotif of the triangle, this graphic echoing is analogous to a musical technique. Imitation and variation of a diverse range of short and recognisable motifs are used to provide unity and effective expression in music (as for example in a fugue), and Eisenstein uses an analogous technique in visual terms. This was partly a legacy of the influence of Malevich's Suprematism, which Eisenstein acknowledged with regard to his first treatment of a Mexican theme: his production of *The Mexican* (1920), a staging of a story by Jack London. This production, like *Que Viva Mexico!*, had a *Prologue* and an *Epilogue*; they were intended to evoke Mexico, and for Eisenstein what saved the production 'was the fact that the set was more Suprematist than Cubist'.[101] The origins of the triangular and elliptical shapes that he was to use as visual leitmotifs in *Que Viva Mexico!* can already be seen here.[102]

Eisenstein's Mexico: drawings and dance

Eisenstein's experiences in Mexico prompted his return to drawing after a seven year break, which had begun with his work on *The Strike*. As a youngster he had drawn with great facility, a talent which became very useful in designing costumes and sets for his theatre productions.[103] In Mexico he began to make preparatory sketches for shots and shot sequences, a practice he was to continue when making subsequent films, like *Alexander Nevsky* and *Ivan the Terrible*. However he also used drawing to improvise visualisations of certain ideas and sensations which were preoccupying him, in particular the combination of religious ecstasy, sensuality and brutality which he found again and again in Mexican culture, both in its pasts and in the present. In these drawings he tried out thematic superimpositions: counterpointing Christian iconography with Mesoamerican images, blended with the pagan elements in Spanish culture.[104] Eisenstein later realised that his style of drawing changed in Mexico, it 'underwent an internal catharsis, striving for mathematical abstraction and purity of line.' He related this clarity of means to his fascination with 'the mathematically pure course of montage thought.' He affirmed that this passionate concern was already there in his work on his early films. However, in Mexico, this 'abstract, "intellectualised" line' became useful to express the chaos of sensuality with a paradoxically great economy and precision; Eisenstein used it 'for drawing especially sensual relationships between human figures, usually in especially complicated and random situations!' These drawings were the result of a sensual exploration of a synthesis 'of all the varieties of Mexican primitivism: from Chichen-Itzá bas reliefs, via primitive toys and painted implements, to the incomparable pages of illustrations by José Guadalupe Posada for street songs.'[105] This statement recalls the Russian Futurists' enthusiasm for vigorous peasant art like the *lubok* prints, toys, and village houses and farm implements, expressed in paintings by Chagall, Larionov, the Burliuk brothers, and in the graphic work of the artist poet Mayakovsky during the early days of the Russian Revolution.

The dynamic quality of the lines in Eisenstein's Mexican drawings and their sensual and sinuous characteristics bring to mind the clarity and dynamism of dance. He remembered, as a child, being amazed at the outlines of animals which a family friend would draw for him. These lines were indelibly associated in his mind with motion:

> Here, before the eyes of the delighted beholder, this outline took form and started moving. As it moved, the unseen outline of the object traced a magical path ... the line was the track left by the movement. ... I still remember this acute sense of line as dynamic movement; a process; a path. Many years later it made me record in my heart the wise saying of Wang Pi from the third century BC: 'What is a line? A line speaks of movement.'[106]

He describes his fourteen-month sensual exploration of the mostly anonymous Mexican art from the past in almost dance-like terms, as 'greedily palpating (it) with my hands, eyes and the soles of my feet'. In this context it is not surprising when he points out that 'drawing and dancing are branches of the same tree, of course; they are just two varieties of the same impulse'. The dances he is hinting at here are not in the style of European ballet with its star performers, but the African-Hispanic hybrid forms of anonymously performed social dances, like the rumba, or the danzon, found all over Mexico and the Caribbean. Eisenstein had a fondness for these popular dance forms. He admitted that he could not dance the genteel waltz, but that he 'was able to pull

Fig.5 Two of Mayakovsky's drawings of Mexico, from his notebooks, 1925.

off a foxtrot with great panache, albeit a jerky, black version in Harlem.'[107]

The 'mathematical abstraction and purity of line' used by Eisenstein in his Mexican drawings was also ideal for exploring the contours of the harsh landscapes and the geometrical outlines of the peons outlined against them.[108] He believed that perhaps the strongest impulse which had driven him back to drawing was 'the actual, astonishing, linear structure of the stunning purity of the Mexican landscape'.[109] He saw the peon in this landscape in an almost Suprematist manner, albeit in strongly emotional terms: 'the figure of the peon – this combination of a white triangular shirt, an emaciated blackened face and the round outline of a straw hat – is at once a tragic symbol and an almost graphic formula.'[110] The clear harsh light of Tetlapayac heightened the blackness of the shadows, and encouraged the use of back-lit silhouettes in the black and white film.[111] The immense sky created by the low horizon line emphasized the insignificance of the human presence in this landscape. When Mayakovsky visited Mexico in 1925, some of the landscape drawings he sketched at

Fig.6 An example of visual three-part counterpoint: a shot from the
Maguey episode from *Que viva Mexico!*

this time have the same dominance of the horizontal in their composition,
the use of the silhouette, and sharply outlined geometrical shapes
(Fig.5).[112] Eisenstein noted the presence of solid black shapes and their
importance in this brutal and unforgiving landscape:

> the black wing of a vulture – the *zapilota* – that lives off carrion.
> The black silhouette of a Franciscan in Pueblo [Puebla]. The black
> cross of a gravestone, and the black tunic of the *licenciado* [bailiff]
> who had come to check the fields of an enraged *hacendado*
> [landowner]. The long black shadows of the *tlagiceros* [farmworkers]
> wandering home at sunset with their mules, knowing that no
> matter who inherits the haciendas, their lot will be the same: to
> extract the oily juice from the heart of the cruel cactus.[113]

Mexico and montage within the shot

These elemental black shapes encourage two-dimensional images, as is
shown in a shot from the *Maguey* episode, where a long lens has been used
to flatten the space between the ground, the figures and the sky. As a
result of this composition, the line of the clouds, the line made by the
heads of the figures, and the line of the ground form a three-part

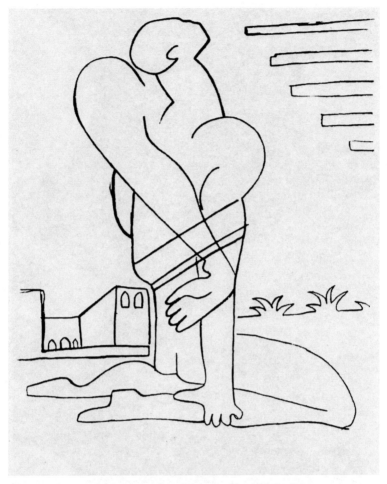

Fig.7 Pencil drawing by Eisenstein of an execution by firing squad.

counterpoint, which embeds the people in the landscape, above and below (Fig.6). A similar process is used by Eisenstein in his drawing of an execution, where each element of the picture is made two dimensional, unifying the maguey cactus, the peon and the hacienda, which all suggest theatre flats. The implied perspectives in the outlines of the hacienda and the rifles of the 'off-stage' firing squad suggest a low angle shot, making the peon into a vast iconic shape, growing out of the desert landscape (Fig.7). This great expansion of foreground space is what Eisenstein called 'foreground composition'.[114]

He used the same technique, combined with a low angle shot to make

Fig.8 A montage within the shot from the Fiesta episode from *Que viva Mexico!*

Fig.9 Montage within the shot: masked figures against a
whirling Day of the Dead funfair.

the maguey cactus a vast and iconic presence in the landscape, dwarfing
the human figures dotted on the line of the horizon.[115] Already in *The Old
and The New* he produced a similar type of composition by having a huge
distorted typewriter in the foreground, using a 28mm lens to achieve this
spatial distortion.[116] He developed this compositional technique in
Mexico: 'only a camera lens can do this, and only a 28mm lens at that; it
also has an amazing capacity for distorting the close-up, artificially
exaggerating its size and shape.' The use of this wide-angle lens enabled
him to explore the possibilities of dialectical montage, not from one shot
to the next, but *within* the same shot: 'these (foreground compositions) are
the skulls and monks, masks and carousels of the Day of the Dead in the
Mexican film.'[117] An example of this kind of montage within the shot can
be seen in the low angle shot with the white skull motif in the foreground,
which is simultaneously contrasted with the towering presence of monks
in their black cassocks in the middle-ground, and the altar boys in the
centre background (Fig.8).[118]

To Eisenstein this image signified 'the Jesuits' Catholic asceticism, ruling,
with a rod of iron, the sensual magnificence of Mexico's tropical beauty.' In
the *Epilogue*, he added irony to 'this deeply tragic theme'. Here the skulls

Fig.10 'The profile of the Mayan girl with the entire pyramid of Chichen-Itzá.'

were cardboard masks, and 'life-sized carousels and Ferris wheels spun behind them, flashing through the empty sockets of masks.' Shots from this section of the *Epilogue* gives a sense of what Eisenstein is describing (Fig.9). In a similarly composed low angle shot, bordered below by a line of heads wearing skull masks, one of the towering figures only needs to remove his mask for the effect of the spinning carousel or Ferris wheel to flash 'through the empty sockets'. For Eisenstein this combination of images near and far was not just a visual conceit. The moving image montage within the shot produced a complex meaning, it 'seemed to say with a wink that death is no more than an empty cardboard box that, come what may, the whirlwind of life will punch holes in without thinking twice'. He also mentions another instance of montage within the shot, this time from the *Prologue*: 'another good example is combining the profile of the Mayan girl with the entire pyramid of Chichen-Itzá'(Fig.10).[119]

An additional example of Eisenstein's use of montage juxtaposition within the shot is found in the *Maguey* episode, where the head of a landowner is unflatteringly compared to the head of a Pekinese dog (Fig.11). He had already used this technique in *The Strike*, where he had experimented with a variety of similar human/animal juxtapositions, comparing spies with a monkey, a fox, an owl and a dog, using dissolves of their heads. However, there is an instance at the beginning of this

Fig.11 The landowner and the Pekinese dog: montage within the shot.

sequence of juxtapositions where *within a single shot* he compares the head of a spy with the head of a monkey.

Mexico's sensual contrasts: the ascetic and the baroque

The maguey cactus, which for Eisenstein was emblematic of the extreme cruelty of the feudal life of the haciendas, was transformed by him into a complex and baroque image, made unstable by the lack of a horizon line, and the confusing intertwining planes of the cactus leaves. This transformation can be seen in a shot of a peon, who is framed by the baroque curves of the maguey cactus (Fig.12). He also operated a similar transformation in words, again using the maguey (also called the agave) cactus leaf as the means of transition:

> The razor-edged green sail of the agave leaf with its relentlessly sharp tip (formed as the end of the leaf dries) splits up into the green curls of lianas. ... The green, curling lianas loop for miles. There is nothing to breathe. ... The hot embraces of the tropics are moist. Here the whole world is immersed in a hot marshy hollow, its surface coated by a boiling yellow-green mire.[120]

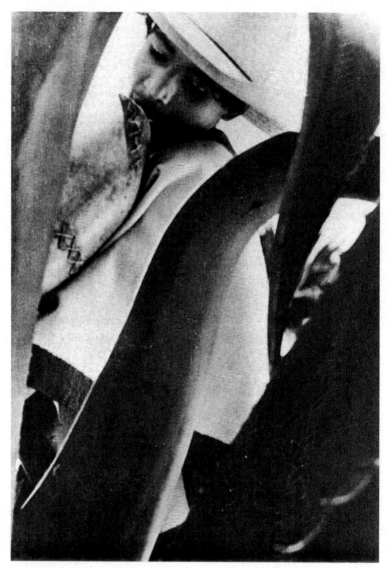

Fig.12 A peon framed by a baroque Maguey cactus.

Here, using images from different aspects of the Mexican landscape,
Eisenstein articulated the contrasts he noted in Mexican culture: on the
one hand 'the simplicity of the monumental, and the extravagance of the
baroque – in both its Spanish and Aztec aspects'.[121] The ascetic sensuality

Fig.13 A merging of peon with landscape.

of the *Maguey* episode, visually expressed in hard-edged triangular forms
epitomised by the maguey cactus leaf, gives way, through a close-up of the
same plant, to the sensuality of the curved line, producing intertwined
forms, as noted above.

These curved interweaving shapes are found in the greatest abundance
in the fertile tropical landscapes of Mexico, where 'the green, curling lianas

Fig.14 The maguey cactus is extended into the sky by a cloud.

loop for miles'. Eisenstein directly relates these vegetal curves in the landscape to the curves of the human body. At times he blends the figures of the peons with the maguey cactus (Fig.13). And he blends the cactus with the sky, by showing an arm of the maguey which looks as if it is extended by a mass of white cloud (Fig.14).

He also intended to interweave living human bodies. He describes how, from a small fortress in Acapulco, he saw a landscape of intertwining bodies, a moonlit scene he had planned to use in the *Soldadera* episode:

'the latent wanderings of sensuality seemed incarnate in the interweaving of bronzed bodies.'[122] These were 'the *soldaderas* and their husbands – soldiers – held in close embraces'. He compares them to 'the saturated, overgrown rapacity of the lianas.'

The mutual embrace of these bodies suggests to him a mutual comparison involving the lianas 'which interwove like bodies and (the) bodies which interwove like lianas'. This vegetal/human landscape suddenly loses any sense of objectivity and distance when Eisenstein says that 'the close embraces' that he sees 'seemed embodied in me'.

He also notices that these bodies evoke the aftermath of a battle, 'a field of death cast in silver'. However he knows that it is actually a scene involving the mass creation of new life, which he compares to 'a great cornfield where more and yet more generations of bronze children were being conceived'.

These opposite views of the same subject reflect his own nature, which like Mexico itself 'is tender and lyrical, but brutal too'.[123] This disappearance of any emotional distance between the self and the landscape is what characterises Eisenstein's concept of nonindifferent nature. At one point in the *Maguey* episode, he makes the peons disappear

Fig.15 Shot of an 'all-over' composition as the peons enter a cactus grove.

in a cactus grove: their bodies become dematerialised in the complex dappled shadows (Fig.15). Briefly the images on the screen anticipate the delirious all-over textures of Abstract Expressionism, where human and vegetal forms inextricably merge.

In this scenario there are no star actors to disrupt the direct impulse from screen to audience. It was what Faure had envisioned in 1922, three years before Eisenstein had directed *The Strike*: a type of cinema which would function as an audiovisual art, where the role of stars would have become redundant. Cinema would consequently move away from a theatrical model and become a medium closer to dance and music.[124]

All-over spaces, trance and delirium

Faure remembers seeing the 1906 eruption of Vesuvius, with its vast cloud of ash and debris, 'a great mobile structure continuingly renewing itself before our eyes through its internal forces, and which the immense variety of human, animal, vegetal and inert forms participates in building'. This is Faure's image of the cinema of the future, a medium which makes use of a kind of optical illusion to blend landscape, human and animal and other living forms, what he calls a 'cineplastic' medium.[125] The image of the huge and continuously mobile cloud of ash which suggests to Faure a wide variety of illusory forms is an example of an 'all-over' structure, one which in turn evokes the fertile and teeming surfaces found in various Mexican churches. Eisenstein mentions 'the columns of carved figures crowding out the altar decorations in a frozen multitude', a description which suits the extreme 'all-over' proliferation of detail, as in the representations of human, animal and vegetal forms covering the vault of the small church of Santa Maria Tonantzintla in Puebla. He lists this church as one of several which exhibit a Mesoamerican/Catholic syncretism: 'de Guadalupe, Los Remedios, Santa Maria Tonantzintla – Catholic Madonnas who in the days of Cortés, usurped the positions and places held by pagan goddesses and divinities.'[126] The interior of Santa Maria Tonantzintla is a combination of Spanish Baroque ornamentation pushed to a delirious extreme by the influence of the antecedent sacred presence of the Aztec earth mother goddess Tonantzin.

This sacred duality is also present in another Spanish institution: the bullfight. Eisenstein noticed the contrast between 'the severity of the peon's white costume – a costume which, in both colour and angularity of silhouette, is like a *tabula rasa* of costume altogether' and the 'sculptural quality of gold and silver bas-reliefs, with their excessive use of gold embroidery, which burn above deep blue, or green, or orange and cherry coloured satin beneath the black hats of the protagonists in the *corrida*.'

The extravagance of these rich embroideries relate to the effusively decorated Baroque interiors of the Mexican Catholic churches. Eisenstein saw the further relationship between the *corrida* and the church, in 'the blood of bull or man, which after mass each week douses the sands of countless Sunday corridas in a sensual communion.'

This simultaneity of pagan and Christian elements appears in a series of curvilinear drawings titled *Crucifixion of the Matador*. These involve single shot montages of a matador, a crucifix and a bull, in superimposition, expressed in a baroque intertwining of lines. In one drawing Eisenstein pushes the variation on this syncretic theme further by producing a surreal image of a matador crucified on the horns of a bull (Fig.16). This drawing, combining the brutal and the delirious, seems extreme, but not when one reads Eisenstein's analyses of what he calls 'the striking ornamental displays of natural forms in Aztec, Toltec and Mayan architecture'. He explains that these decorations according to one school of thought were 'either executed in a marijuana-induced trance, or in a flashback of one'.[127] This leads him to analyse their monstrous and horrific effect as being related to the decomposition and recomposition of animal-based forms. He describes almost Cubistic distortions, which result in a kind of vertigo. He deciphers the stretched out and decomposed forms he finds in the ancient Mexican architecture and sculpture at Las Monjas Palace in Uxmal, and the pyramid at Teotihuacan. In his analysis these monstrous stylisations become a dynamic and disturbing film montage, derived from the perceptual games the architecture and the sculptures encourage in the viewer. He evokes the dizzying effect he experienced when faced with sculptural details like a broken up human face, which encourages in the viewer a collapse, then a reconstruction of the process of perception. Images of the heads of serpents perceptually break down and are dynamically re-assembled (as in a film montage) into the representation of a bear, with its eyes, face and claws. All of a sudden a hook at the corner of a building assumes the appearance of a nose, leading the viewer to seek its corresponding grotesque eyes on either side of it. Lower down in the building, teeth reveal a monstrous transformation of jaws.[128]

The oscillation of perception forwards and backwards between the basic elements of a human face and the grotesque stylisation which enables details to be stretched out, so that its human characteristics disappear, creates a mental imbalance, a dizziness in the viewer. This state of mind provokes the participation of the spectator in the actual creation of these ecstatic images of the stylised and pulled apart features of the human head. It is as if the viewer enters a trance state, a state of

Fig.16 Eisenstein's drawing from his *Crucifixion of the Matador* series.

possession through these images which are themselves the result of possession in the artists who made them.[129]

Mind, landscape and the human body

The densely packed yet dynamic sculptures covering the walls of these Mesoamerican structures are examples of all-over textures which much later were combined with the Spanish Baroque style to produce the Mexican Catholic church interiors mentioned above. The underlying principle remains Eisenstein's concept of nonindifferent nature. This principle comprises what could be termed a 'total' experience, one which involves a unity of mind, landscape and the body. Examples of such 'total' experiences Eisenstein mentions include the trance-inducing dances of the *danzantes* groups, and the imitation crucifixions involving branches of cactus.[130] Another instance of an experience involving a complete unity of mind, landscape and body is to be found in the lines of pilgrims ascending ancient pyramids on their knees to reach the Catholic churches which were built on their summits.[131] Such an example is the pilgrimage to the church of Los Remedios:

the steady flow of human figures, bathed in sweat, crawling on their knees from the base of the pyramids to their consecrated summits. Their knees were bound with rags. Some had tied cushions to them and these were torn to shreds. Often outlandish headwear fashioned from feathers (the brotherhood of the *danzantes*). Cloth over the eyes. Streams of sweat. Old ladies among the pilgrims carried someone in pain in their arms; they wore cheap blue shawls. Panting, they reached the last step. The binding was ceremoniously removed. After the darkness and torment, the suffering man saw before him the wide-open doors bathed in the ruddy candlelight of the temple of the Madonna de Guadalupe, de Los Remedios, the Cathedral of Amecameca.[132]

The scene inside the church at the top of the pyramid, already accentuated by the removal of the blindfold, becomes for the pilgrim a total sensory experience: 'there were the cries of the pilgrims' children. ... The tones of the organ. The fumes from the candles. Heat and frenzy.'[133]

Eisenstein had had an interest in the phenomenon of frenzy, particularly in crowds, ever since as a child he had read Zola's novel *Lourdes*. When he was travelling around France, before coming to the United States, he visited Catholic cathedrals in Rheims, Chartres and Amiens. He also went to holy places associated with miracles, like Domrémy (where Joan of Arc first heard her 'voices'), and Lisieux (the home of Sainte Thérèse de Lisieux). At this time he was reading the texts of various saints, including John of the Cross, Ignatius Loyola, Theresa d'Avila and Thérèse de Lisieux.[134] In her autobiographical writings, Thérèse de Lisieux (1873–97) mentions how her mood was strongly affected by bad weather:

nature seemed to participate in my bitter sadness, now for three days the sun has not allowed even one of its rays to shine, and the rain has been falling in torrents. (I have noticed that during all the difficult times in my life, nature was the reflection of my soul.)[135]

This is a vividly personal account of nonindifferent nature, another example of the link Eisenstein's idea has with nineteenth-century Romantic thought. However Eisenstein also noted that this late nineteenth-century mystic was capable of 'earthy, Rabelaisian, red-blooded humour' in her letters of instruction to the nuns in her care.[136]

The nearest Eisenstein got to Lourdes (his stay in France did not coincide with its dates of pilgrimage) was the imitation Lourdes grotto in Marseilles: he noticed its proximity to a small side-street where there was nothing but brothels. He was fascinated by this kind of involuntary association of religious ecstasy with sexual ecstasy, sometimes with amusing results. Researching Catholicism in the south of France, as well as other forms of local culture, he found that attractive girls were featured in depictions of saints like Thérèse de Lisieux, in the votive photographs which were for sale near churches and cathedrals. When he looked closely at the postcards of scantily-clad girls available in Toulon's tobacconist shops (for the benefit of sailors) he noticed that they featured the same girls, as these pictures and the holy ones were printed by the same company: 'since that firm was economically-minded, it employed the same models in both lines simultaneously.'[137]

Another mystic Eisenstein read in his research on religious ecstasy was St John of the Cross (1542–94), a member of a reformed Carmelite order, who knew and was influenced by St Theresa d'Avila. A victim of internal Catholic politics, he was tortured over a period of eight months by unreformed Carmelite monks. During this time of extreme suffering, one evening he heard a popular love song being sung in the street below his prison cell. This inspired him to compose a set of mystical poems which were strongly influenced in their form by the popular music of his time, for which he had a passion. In these poems he expressed the love of God in terms of the human love between lovers, following the tradition of the *Song of Songs* from the Old Testament. Landscapes, and their flora and fauna are lovingly described in his song-like poems, as in these stanzas from *The Spiritual Canticle*:

My beloved mountains,
Solitary luxuriant valleys,
Mysterious islands,
Sonorous rivers,
Soft sounds of the airs' caress.

Calm night
At break of dawn,
Soundless music,
Sonorous solitude,
The supper that refreshes and excites.[138]

In this poem, the love between a bride and bridegroom is expressed in the features of the surrounding landscape, including the music of the sounds emanating from it. St John referred to nature and landscape as 'the knowledge of the evening', a form of the knowledge of God which differed from 'the daylight knowledge of God in Himself'.[139] His concept of 'the knowledge of the evening' implies a sensual and ecstatic connection between the self and landscape which Eisenstein experienced in Mexican dawns and sunsets.[140]

In the poem *Deep Rapture*, subtitled *Rimes after an ecstasy of profound contemplation*, St John uses the repetitive patterns of the *villancico*, a popular dance song of the time. In each verse there is a close juxtaposition of opposites, intended to express ideas beyond the limitations of language:

> The more we rise to great heights,
> The less we understand.
> A cloud is dark as the night is bright:
> The wise will never know
> That which transcends all science.[141]

The oppositional juxtaposition of images in the third line of this verse is analogous to Eisenstein's concept of dialectical montage, used to express ideas beyond the one-to-one object to idea relationship in photographic reproduction.

Mexico and Eisenstein's concept of ecstasy

Eisenstein understood that repetition was a key constituent in both the portrayal of the ecstatic state as well as one of the methods of achieving it. He explained how his fascination with 'the onset of mass ecstasy as crowd psychosis' was more than satisfied in Mexico, where he observed the behaviour of crowds at bullfights and the sacred dances of the Mexican *danzantes*, whose use of repetitive melody he found stupefying.[142]

The use of repetition can be used to create an all-over texture, one which implies that the repetition continues beyond the frame, beyond what we perceive as being the beginning and end of an experience. This is the technique which was used in the decoration of the interior of Santa Maria Tonantzintla. The delirious extent of the repetitions of the motifs of the relief sculptures blend wall and ceiling in a continuous all-over texture, which has been deliberately made so that it cannot be seen in a single glance, or shot of film. These repetitive Baroque surfaces have their musical counterparts in the obsessive repetitions found in Mexican popular dance forms, like those Eisenstein planned to use in *Que Viva Mexico!*, like the *Sandunga* (which he had planned to repeat throughout the *Sandunga* episode) and the rumba which he had intended to use in the Day of the Dead *Epilogue*. The repetition characterising these musical forms is accentuated by their lack of variety of dynamics, they are performed at a more or less consistent level of volume. This consistency results in the lack of foreground and background in the music: as Guilleré observed in jazz music, all planes are in the foreground. This technique is also used in the more extreme examples of obsessive repetition in Baroque music, for example in J. S. Bach's *Preludes II* and *VI* from the first volume of *The Well-Tempered Clavier*. Again the consistency of repetition results in a consistent level of volume, producing an hypnotic all-over texture which implies that these pieces are but a fragment from much greater entities. This idea lies at the root of nonindifferent nature: the use of delirious detail in repetition and the resulting all-over texture brings individuals out of the limits of their body; their consciousness opens out and blends them with the surrounding landscape.

Eisenstein, in his study of ecstasy, explores the meaning of the Greek roots of the word: a combination of *ex* (out of) and *stasis* (a state). For him ecstasy involves a transformation where someone goes into a state which is beyond the norm, involving a *qualitative* change into something new. He explains that he can encourage this kind of ecstatic transformation in the viewer just by showing a shot or shots of someone in an ecstatic state. However he realises that the provoking of this altered state in the viewer can be realised compositionally in a more complex and effective manner when the ecstatic state is shown to go beyond its individual human limits. Then this altered state will spread to the surroundings of the character, the landscapes being presented with the same characteristics of frenzy.[143] An early example of this nonindifferent externalisation of frenzy in Eisenstein's work is to be found in the water jet sequence in *The Strike*. In *Que Viva Mexico!* this externalisation of an inner frenzied state is found in the curving sprays of fireworks bursting out from the *torito*, the exploding bull's head used to celebrate Mexican fiestas and which the peons use as a weapon in wreaking revenge against their feudal master in the *Maguey* episode.[144] In his scenario, Eisenstein features the non-perspectival spaces of fireworks again and again.[145] These all-over spaces bring to mind Eisenstein's evocation of Manhattan on a rainy night. His description also suggests a firework display:

> At night, perspective and the perception of real distance are destroyed by a sea of coloured, illuminated advertisements. Far and near, small (in the *foreground*) and big (in the *background*), flashing on and off, moving and revolving, popping up and disappearing, they ultimately nullify all perception of real space, and at certain moments they seem like a drawing made up of coloured dotted lines or strips flickering over a single flat surface, the black velvet of the night sky.[146]

Eisenstein's research into states of ecstasy led him to the *Spiritual Exercises* of St Ignatius Loyola, a series of instructions for contemplative prayer.[147] These exercises involve an elaborate programme for the modification of all aspects of human behaviour. This transformation of key aspects of the everyday life of an individual leads to a mental state necessarily beyond the norm, a state of exaltation or ecstasy.[148] A similar process of behaviour modification, not in a private but in a public context, takes place in the fiesta for the Day of the Dead: here there is a transformation of every aspect of everyday existence. Eisenstein shows us a variety of dignitaries, both civil and military, as well as those whom we have already seen taking part in the film.[149] All are represented in a form of a Mexican image of death or *calavera*, either as a skeleton, or wearing a skull mask. The ubiquitous representation of death sets this festival apart from the other Mexican fiestas. And Eisenstein has already shown us several examples of these festivities: the *Sandunga* episode's marriage fiesta, the annual fiesta of the hacienda at Tetlapayac, the fiesta in honour of the Virgin of Guadalupe.

What distinguishes this Day of the Dead fiesta from the others is its highlighting of the presence of death in the everyday. Eisenstein incorporates the spinning Ferris wheels and carousels in the Day of the Dead imagery and the dance music forms a key part of the *mise-en-scène* in this episode, as does the dancing.[150] The three dancing men who energetically gyrate their hips in Grigory Alexandrov's version of *Que Viva Mexico!* recall the erotic pelvic 'winding' motions of the Guédé dances, during which the dancers are possessed by the Lord of the Graveyard, Baron Samedi, in traditional Haitian religious ceremonies. For both the spectator and the participant, the activities of the Day of the Dead fiesta are a total sensual experience, involving music, dance, costumes and masks. Eisenstein presents scenes in which everything and everyone, the living and the dead, participate frenetically in Day of the Dead sounds and images, thereby intending to provoke a similarly ecstatic state in the audience who are watching the *Epilogue*.

The *corrida*

Eisenstein shows another aspect of Mexican life involving ecstatic behaviour and death in the 'total' spectacle of the bullfight, from the *Fiesta* episode. Here he avoids showing the sordid details D.H. Lawrence chose to depict in his evocation of a Mexican *corrida*, like the disembowelling of horses by a bull.[151] Instead Eisenstein concentrates on the delicate and deadly pirouettes of the famed matador Liceaga, as he avoids the bull's ferocious horns by death-defying timing.[152] The

Fig.17 Eisenstein's drawing and collage of a Mexican *corrida*.

ecstatic dance-like motions of the matador are rapturously received by the crowd, and they provoke audience reactions like jumping out of the seat, spontaneous clapping and crying out. These are the effects Eisenstein describes as being the result of what he calls 'pathos', which he explains has the effect of bringing the viewer to the point of ecstasy.[153] Bullfighting had a similar effect on Eisenstein himself: 'the barbaric splendour of this sport of blood, gilt and sand attracts me madly.'[154] He expressed this ecstatic reaction in a collage dominated by an elliptical sun, with Baroque-style angels intertwined in its rays. Below is a bullring where a matador is delivering a death-blow to the bull; over the whole floating space a syncretic Mexican/Christian god presides (Fig.17). The ecstatic 'all-over' composition of this collage is strikingly reminiscent of the collage-style sketch for the design of 'The Promised Land' scene from the finale of Vladimir Mayakovsky's play *Mystery-Bouffe*[155] (Fig.18). Mayakovsky describes the ecstatic cityscape for this scene in his stage directions:

> The doors fly open and the city is disclosed. But what a city! The wide-open frames of transparent factories and apartment houses tower up to the sky. Trains of railway cars, tram cars and automobiles stand wrapped in rainbows...In the midst of the city

Fig.18 A design for 'The Promised Land' scene from Mayakovsky's
play, *Mystery-Bouffe*, 1919.

is a garden of stars and moons, surmounted by the shining crown
of the sun.[156]

It was after the final rehearsal of Meyerhold's second production of
Mystery-Bouffe in 1921, that Eisenstein first met both Mayakovsky and the
famous director: four months later he was accepted at Meyerhold's new
directing workshop.[157]

Que Viva Mexico!, Blok and Mayakovsky

Mayakovsky's *Mystery-Bouffe* was based on the form of the medieval
mystery play, an early form of 'total' theatre, comprising a unity of music,
theatre and dance, based on stories from the Bible mixed with pre-
Christian tales.[158] The mystery play was a form of street theatre, often
involving processionals and making use of the popular songs and dances

of the time. In his updated version of the mystery play, Mayakovsky incorporated the Communist anthem *The Internationale*, and subverted the biblical story of the Flood, including a visit to hell and to a Revolutionary paradise ('The Promised Land'), followed by a return to earth.[159] In *Mystery-Bouffe*, Mayakovsky drew from the hybrid carnivalesque forms of street theatre, based on mixtures of various sacred and secular traditions.[160] Eisenstein found similarly potent mixtures of theatrical and religious traditions in the Mexican fiestas like the Day of the Dead, and the fiesta in honour of the Virgin of Guadalupe, with its masked figures.[161] These performances involving hybrids of Christian and Mesoamerican religious traditions fuelled Eisenstein's ideas for *Que Viva Mexico!* in the same way that popular theatre traditions had inspired Futurist theatre like Mayakovsky's *Mystery-Bouffe*.

Before Mayakovsky, the poet Alexander Blok had been inspired by the Russian fairground puppet theatre traditions in his *Balaganchik* (*The Fairground Booth*, 1906). Béatrice Picon-Vallin points out that Meyerhold's first production of Mayakovsky's *Mystery-Bouffe* in 1918 was the equivalent in importance of what Blok's *Balaganchik* had been for the eminent director twelve years earlier.[162] Eisenstein's games with the cardboard skull masks in the Day of the Dead section at the end of *Que Viva Mexico!* recall Meyerhold's use of cardboard cut-outs of the figures of the Mystics, who preside over the first scene of *The Fairground Booth*.[163] Remembering his student days, Eisenstein tells of how he had heard stories of Meyerhold's marvellous production of Blok's play, and he also mentions the scene designer Nikolai N. Sapunov's sketches of the Mystics.[164] In his book *On Theatre* (1912), Meyerhold describes how the Mystics are transformed during his production:

> Frightened by some rejoinder, they duck their heads, and suddenly all that remains at the table is a row of torsos minus heads and hands. It transpires that the figures are cut out of cardboard with frock coats, shirt-fronts, collars and cuffs drawn on with soot and chalk. The actors' hands are thrust through openings in the cardboard torsos, and their heads simply rest on the cardboard collars.[165]

Eisenstein clothes his skeletons and produces a similarly macabre shock when these skeletal figures reveal that behind their cardboard skull masks lies the emptiness of a real skull.[166] In his production of Blok's play, Meyerhold played the key role of Pierrot. At the end, the drama over, he plays the flute, and then he finally appears as himself, as the actor

Meyerhold who casts a penetrating stare into the audience.[167] Eisenstein's variation on this transformation is a positive one: at the end of *Que Viva Mexico!* the boy removes his skull mask and he beams at the cinema audience as himself.

At the conclusion of a masquerade which takes place at the end of *The Fairground Booth*, Blok features another deathlike transformation in his stage directions. He describes the masked dancers who 'having flattened up as if crucified against the walls ... seem like dolls from an ethnographic museum'.[168] Eisenstein had a picture of himself taken in the ethnographic museum at Chichen Itzá, during a power blackout. Taking advantage of the appearance in the darkness of a mysteriously looming sculpture, he used a torch to uplight his face, transforming it into a mask, and heightening the resultant parallel with the gigantic figure behind him by sitting in a similarly crouched position.[169] In his article *Museums at Night*, Eisenstein evokes the startling experience of the huge stone figures of the ancient Mayan gods appearing to come to life in the flickering light of the matches:

> The whimsicality, absurdity, disproportion and...size of the statues increased as they suddenly leapt out at you from the darkness when the match flame flickered here and there ... the unexpected flashes as matches are struck in different parts of the room made these still, dark monsters come alive. ... Because the angle at which the light burst in altered as the matches burned down, it was as though the stone monsters had had time to change position during the intervals of darkness. They had exchanged places in order to look at the violators of their eternal rest from a new viewpoint – through wide-open, gaping but dead granite eyes.[170]

This experience evokes the nocturnal world of Blok's *The Fairground Booth*, with its mysterious apparitions, living ghosts in the darkness, where Columbine, a commedia dell'arte figure is mistaken for the figure of Death: 'oh, she is as white as the snow-caps on the summits! Her orbs reflect a mirror-like emptiness. Do you really not see the scythe behind her shoulders? Do you not recognise Death?'[171] This description inhabits the same world as Eisenstein's dressed up female figures of death in his *Epilogue*.[172] Familiar with Meyerhold's production of Blok's play, he recalls Blok's fairground booths when he sees the tarpaulin booths in Mexico City's red light district.[173]

When Eisenstein used live ammunition in his filming of the battle between the peons and their masters in the *Maguey* episode, he indirectly but vividly brings the resultant bloodletting to the screen. He shows the effect of a bullet shot into a cactus, which then 'bleeds' its juice: 'the bullets thudded into the fleshy body of the maguey, which opened its oily lamina like the arms of a crucifix, torn and shot through, and flowed with blood.'[174] This symbolic technique had been used to similar effect by Blok in *The Fairground Booth* when the clown is struck by another character with a wooden sword, and a stream of cranberry juice spurts from the clown's head.[175]

Eisenstein's approach to his filming of the Day of the Dead is related to the influence of the masked dance, the interest in puppetry and fairground theatre booths which appeared again and again in the paintings, theatre and music of the early twentieth century in Europe. Picasso's paintings of commedia dell'arte figures, Satie's *Parade* (with designs by Picasso), Stravinsky's ballet *Petrushka*, Meyerhold's production of Lermontov's *Masquerade*, and Blok's *The Fairground Booth* were amongst a few examples of this fascination. Dance and music were vital elements in the theatre of this period, and composers had a significant role: Meyerhold commissioned Glazunov to provide the music for *Masquerade*, and the composer-poet Kuzmin composed music for Meyerhold's production of *The Fairground Booth*.[176]

Pathos, ecstasy, and audiovisual cinema

The energy and force of expression which Meyerhold, Blok and Mayakovsky found in various forms of popular theatre was not only due to its seamless synthesis of drama, dance, poetry and music, but they were also inspired by its use of archetypal images and narratives. Blok used the static and numinous presence of his Mystics at the beginning of *The Fairground Booth* to mock the static actors in productions of Maeterlinck's dramas.[177] Mayakovsky's 'The Promised Land' scene in his *Mystery-Bouffe* was an ironic borrowing from the Biblical promised land featured in Christian medieval mystery plays. Eisenstein's concept of nonindifferent nature emerges directly from the crucible of ideas that Meyerhold, Blok and Mayakovsky derived from various forms of vernacular performance. His statement that 'our feelings, our consciousness and our frames of reference reflect the real world about us' is directly related to the use of archetypal images and forms in popular and often anonymous art. In reference to his statement he lists the popular Catholic sculptures of madonnas, as well as the 'columns of carved figures crowding out the altar decorations' in Mexican churches. He also mentions the anonymous and secular baroque designs: 'the inlay work on rifles and embroidery on the sombreros of the *charros* and *dorados*, the stitching on the matadors' capes.' The 'feelings', 'consciousness' and 'frames of reference' of nonindifferent nature also include the Mexican landscape and its people. In this regard he mentions the 'gold of the Mexican dawns and sunsets and the warm bronze of pensive faces, succulent fruit with unheard-of names hanging down beneath the dark green, bluish or light grey foliage.' The interaction between his emotions, consciousness, frames of reference and the exterior world is explained by Eisenstein as being a 'displacement of reflections between Mexico and me'. This oscillation between the outside and the inner state he found in the phenomenon of the Mexican *danzantes*, where in the practice of their repetitive dances there is an 'equality between the mechanism of psychic meditation and the basic physical system.'[178] The oscillation between the material and the spiritual produces the shaking of the body, which Eisenstein explains is the physical manifestation of a state of ecstasy. He had seen this phenomenon in Harlem which he describes in the form of a montage of contrasting, oscillating film shots:

> Lexington Avenue was the blacks' Fifth Avenue.
> The central road through Harlem.
> On the right stood a dance-hall.
> On the left, a Methodist chapel.
> There, a brothel.
> Here, a house of salvation.
> There lustfulness was externalised, in the inimitable rhythm of
>   dancing.
> And here divine illumination flowed in the same shuddering of
>   one's limbs.
> Ecstasy knows only one way of taking hold of someone.
> Whether the intoxication of being possessed comes from God or
>   the Devil, the rhythmic quaking is the same.
> The pathos is identical.
> And the pathos is, in essence, ultra-black.
> By its nature, because of the theme and content.[179]

Eisenstein defines pathos in terms of its effect on the audience: 'the effect of pathos in a work is to bring the viewer to ecstasy'.[180] He explains that he does not wish to define it in terms of theme and content, as the pathos which causes ecstasy is a result of social conditioning, both for what Eisenstein calls the author and the viewer.[181] In this instance the viewer would be someone experiencing an audiovisual film. In the case of Harlem, the pathos is 'ultra-black'; in the case of the *danzantes*, a combination of Mesoamerican influences. In these cases the ecstatic state results from physically taking part in the audiovisual experience of dance and music, both of which also contain a strong element of repetition and oscillation.

Creativity and the archaeology of thought

The parallel between the repeated oscillations between the inner and outer worlds of the dancers and musicians, and the material repetitions in the dance and music they are performing recalls a formal characteristic Eisenstein noticed in Edgar Allan Poe's influential detective story *The Purloined Letter*. In it, Dupin, a masterly detective, finds an important missing letter which has all the time been invisible to everybody (including the reader) except himself. Poe spends much of his story outlining the details of the police's fruitless search for this purloined letter, when Dupin finds it in an overly obvious place, too obvious for anyone to notice. The process of finding the letter is identical to the form of the story itself; only at the end does the reader find out the secret, which has also been a secret for all but one of the characters in the story. Eisenstein points out that Poe 'supplies both the principle and its direct subject-related (situational) realisation, *at one and the same time*.'[182] Or as Poe has Dupin explain: 'the material world abounds with very strict analogies to the immaterial'.[183] The material facts of the story are directly analogous to the abstraction of its form.

Eisenstein's *serape* was an example of an everyday object from the Mexican material world which for him represented a distillation of his vision of Mexico. The violently contrasting colours of its stripes were emblematic of the various Mexican cultures 'running next to each other and at the same time being centuries away.'[184] In his travels through the country he had discovered this valuable motif for the construction of *Que Viva Mexico!* However, Eisenstein was aware of the limitations of using an abstracted model like the *serape* for the purposes of '"expanding" it into a construction', if the abstraction had not resulted from lived experience. He calls the process of identifying the abstraction '"naming" the formula.' He then affirms that 'naming' the formula correctly is only possible 'when you have sensed it *precisely*, experienced it *precisely*'. He explains that 'this method later becomes applicable to all questions of form. Finally, the form itself begins to be read as a "literal" reading of the formula of content.' This is a method whereby content and form are unified by means of an abstract principle born from first-hand experience. An example of the method was vividly brought to life years later, when he was working on *Ivan the Terrible* in Alma-Ata, from 1941 to 1944. Eisenstein described an overwhelming, almost ecstatic moment during which he 'experienced in the rarified, mountain air of Alma-Ata, my entire field of vision suddenly shattering before my exhausted eyes (or brain?) and part of it (the lower left hand side) dissolving into bright zig-zags, like a fan of clearly defined stripes of white, dark blue and dense brown.' The surprise for Eisenstein was not just the appearance of this visual impression, but that 'its pattern and range of colour were in precisely the style of Peruvian ceramic painting, and I had found that so overwhelming precisely because its graphic and tonal stylisation made it quite impossible to guess the nature of the external impressions that had given rise to them...' His only explanation was that 'such random, ornamental forms could only have been realised in multiple visual shifts, in dreams in twilight states.'[185] He described these visual shifts as a dual process, involving a 'conjoined unity of seeing and perception – a reflection of reality, refracted through consciousness, and a reflection of reality refracted through the prism of sensual thought'.[186] This double action of consciousness and sensual thought, the 'organic dyad of perception' results 'in increasingly complex problems of form, until eventually separate chance manifestations of formal solutions and 'discoveries' are synthesised.' Here Eisenstein is describing how creative work takes place as a result of an imbalance in the processing of sense impressions, and how 'chance manifestations of formal solutions' and so-called 'discoveries' (what could be termed intuition) contribute to a synthesis which becomes the overall balanced vision of the work. He then goes further to explain that the individual approach adopted by artists in their creative process reflects both their manner of analysing this process as the work is formed, as well as their actual use of this process in the development of the work itself: 'individual stylistic mannerisms are even found both to be elements of studying a method of art as it comes together and as elements of the actual method of the arts.'[187] In this way Eisenstein's discovery of the 'formal solution' embedded in the visual structure of the Mexican *serape* became the basis for the construction of the whole of *Que Viva Mexico!*

Eisenstein returns to the linking of the ecstatic experience with perception when he describes the creative process in terms of an earthquake involving seams of different types of thought:

> seams of sensual thought which only inspiration can dislodge, inducing an active trembling of the whole body from head to toe; from the topmost layers of consciousness down to the deepest bases of primary, past, sensual and pre-sensual thought, where the actual terms 'thought', 'memory' and even ... 'feeling' have almost no place.[188]

Here, in this archaeology of thought, Eisenstein is dealing with a consciousness in an ecstatic state. This consciousness operates on an instinctual level, and exists beyond imagination, emotion, even thought itself.

All-over space and sensuous thought

It was from his experience of the Mexican landscape, together with its inhabitants, that Eisenstein actually understood what he called 'prelogical, sensuous' thinking. This was a phenomenon he had only previously read about in anthropological studies like James Frazer's *The Golden Bough* and the research of Lucien Lévy-Bruhl:

> It is here in *terra caliente* (burning earth) that I come to know the fantastic structure of prelogical, sensuous thinking – not only from the pages of anthropological investigations, but from daily communion with those descendents of the Aztecs and Toltecs, Mayas, or Huichole who have managed to carry unharmed through the ages that meandering thought.[189]

When Eisenstein visited a collection of Diego Rivera's murals (including some featuring Mesoamerican themes) at the Ministry of Education in Mexico City, he was reminded of the prelogical, sensuous and meandering thought he had also previously encountered in the unpunctuated Molly Bloom soliloquy. This long text forms the last chapter of James Joyce's novel *Ulysses*, and it is an evocation of a state of mind existing between the conscious world of the daytime and the subconscious world of sleep. This impression of sensuous thought again arises from Eisenstein's cumulative experience involving the repetition of Rivera's motifs, which leads to an ecstatic moment, a flash of vision not unlike his later experience on the mountain in Alma-Ata:

> Suddenly Diego's frescoes melt together, growing identical, incessantly flowing – no commas, no stops – resembling that last chapter of Ulysses, the inner monologue of Mrs Leopold Bloom.
>   Diego flows across these walls in one gorgeous multicoloured stream, not destroying like lava, but like mysterious Nature in periods of springtime and fertilization, vitality overflowing from one shape to another, ever reemerging in an infinite diversity of forms and creations.[190]

Nature and the human presence in it become dynamically united in one 'all-over' texture which cannot be caught in a single glance, and which is ecstatically fertile, not destructive.

Eisenstein and Mexican artists

Eisenstein was inspired by Rivera's diversity of forms throughout *Que Viva Mexico!* Some examples of this transference from paint to screen can be found in the elliptical shapes of heads and faces, the echoing ellipses of the tops of open jars, the intertwining baroque line, and the comparative profiles of characteristically Mexican faces of various origins.[191] Eisenstein describes the repetition of curves which he noticed in Rivera's murals for the Ministry of Education in Mexico City, the 'repeated curves of the backs of peasant, soldier, corn and sack, and soldier, corn and sack again'. He notices that what he calls the 'optical precedent' for his perception is to be found in the 'abundant treelike nopal cactus – the fleshy pancakes of which project themselves in an infinite variety of curves, from circles to straight lines, depending on the angle where they are caught by the spectator's eye, gathered in masses or ranged along ... walls.'[192]

In his description Eisenstein has caught Rivera's use of the curve to link the human presence in the landscape with both objects and plants. The subjective nonindifferent aspect of this link is heightened by Eisenstein when he notes how the 'fleshy pancakes' of the nopal cactus change in a multiplicity of ways according to the spectator's angle of view. This experience is for him the 'optical precedent' for the echoing motifs of Rivera's repeated curves in his murals. This multi-point perspective is related to the use of multiple camera set-ups, and is also characteristic of the Chinese landscape scroll, with its analogous repetition of shapes and motifs. Eisenstein's mention of walls is not accidental, as the nopal cacti are arranged along the walls, like murals. Later in his text he points out that his medium of cinema also depends on the wall for its effect. He describes his work as 'moving frescoes'.[193] In addition there is a musical element here, as mural and scroll share the temporal progression and the repetition of motifs which exist in both music and cinema.

Eisenstein associated the *Soldadera* episode with another Mexican muralist and contemporary of Rivera, José Clemente Orozco, who had painted some dramatic and evocative images of the *soldaderas*. Eisenstein characterised Orozco's paintings, in contrast to Rivera's expansive and epic murals, as concentrated bursts of explosive energy: 'Squeezed. Narrowed. Pressed. Concentrated in an outburst of one tremendous, unnatural, clenched, crashing fist. ... The surface explodes. The bodies and columns plunge headlong. An agglomeration of surfaces. Revolutionary force. Cyclone.'[194]

However, the projecting angles of a coffin in the *Prologue* recall the dramatic foreshortenings often used by another Mexican muralist of the time, David Alfaro Siqueiros. Eisenstein was fascinated by his representation of a 'coffin of intense aquamarine', part of Siqueiros' unfinished mural painting, entitled *Burial of a Worker*, and he traced such representations of coffins to the influence of José Guadalupe Posada, the popular illustrator of song sheets. Eisenstein was aware that Posada was the spiritual father of the Mexican muralists, and he especially admired his depictions of characters for the Day of the Dead fiesta. He featured his *Calavera Catrina*, a haughtily dressed skeleton of a *bourgeoise*, in the *Epilogue*, and other dignitaries as clothed skeletons, evoking Posada's images.[196] These Mexican artists worked directly from scenes of Mexican life and history, and Eisenstein worked in a similar manner. One of his assistants in Mexico, Aragon Leiva, later wrote in the newspaper *El Nacional* that in Eisenstein's film 'there were no professional actors, no scenes or artificial and candied sets, no artificial lights; the scene was nature, and the actors humble peasants, soldiers and men of the people.'[197]

Landscape painting and nonindifferent nature

The relationship of Eisenstein's film to Mexican landscapes was like the relationship between the Persian miniaturists and the Uzbekistan landscapes, which he filmed when he began working on *The Great Fergana Canal* film project in 1939:

> Everyone is familiar with Persian miniatures and the large number of features characteristic of them. A figure, sitting on a rug, stretches forwards so that the entire length of his body lies, flat, within its borders. I always thought that if you could begin filming like that, then it would be in the style of the Persian artists.
> But when I reached Uzbekistan, it turned out that there was no distortion of reality at all. That is merely the way the various things and objects are arranged there. And if you look directly at what you can see, there really does turn out to be a colossal quantity of things there, which you can see set out like that.[198]

Eisenstein gives specific examples of environments and landscapes in Uzbekistan which have been devised or modified by human action, so that the distance between landscape and the human depiction of it has been greatly diminished:

> If you go to an old, good teashop, and drink tea on the fourth

platform up, then you will be able to see all the figures arranged like that sharply defined miniature.

If you ride out to the paddy fields, which are also arranged in terraces, you will get the same impression.

We are all used to the stylised forms of trees in miniatures – circular, oval and so on. But if you go past mulberry trees of a certain period, you will see that they have been pruned in just that way.[199]

In the region of Alma-Ata, about eighty miles from the Chinese border, in the mornings he wondered at the appearance of slim trees outlined against the pale blue sky. And yet he knew that the previous evening he had seen mountains there. Suddenly he notices, above the trees at an extraordinary altitude, a chain of mountains. Their foothills look just like those he has seen so often in Chinese landscape paintings, where they appear as a pictorial stylisation brought to life by brushstrokes.[200]

Here Eisenstein found that Chinese landscape painting, far from being a stylised interpretation of actual landscape, was a direct and ecstatic rendering of a lived-in landscape, an expression of nonindifferent nature. Eisenstein goes on to compare directly the actions of the Chinese artist to his own actions as a maker of audiovisual cinema. What a Chinese landscape artist has captured with paper and brush, be it an action, an event, an object, a landscape or a sense of space, is realised exactly in the manner that a filmmaker builds these things when confronting the complex method of using a film camera audiovisually.[201]

Musical landscape and nonindifferent nature

Fascinated by the Chinese landscape scroll, Eisenstein knew that it was one of the oldest traditions of the visual representation of landscape. We saw in the first chapter how he realised that these horizontal scrolls functioned very like a film of a landscape flowing past. As well as having an analogy with film, the Chinese landscape scroll used echoing motifs, suggesting musical repetitions. At the same time he noted that a direct comparison could be made between the horizontal and vertical divisions of a Chinese landscape scroll and the structure of a polyphonic music score. Eisenstein also brings together Chinese landscape painting, music and film in one indivisible whole by comparing the landscape scrolls, painted in a series, to the symphony. The scrolls are formed from a sequence of a series of landscape shots, as a symphony is formed from a series of movements derived from a set of motifs.[202]

This idea of a musical progression in terms of landscape recalls

Eisenstein's dynamic and visionary description of Mexico: '...wherever you look, the whole country seems to have just risen from the two oceans that wash her shores – everywhere she seems to be in a state of "coming into being."'[203] This image of the birth of a country is simultaneously for Eisenstein the birth of audiovisual cinema; the montage of epochs he sees in the Mexican landscape becomes Mexico *itself* as a form of audiovisual montage. His film would be a 'rhythmic and musical construction and an unrolling of the Mexican spirit and character.' It would be 'held together by the unity of the weave' of the vividly coloured striped serape, a symbol of Mexico, with its violently contrasting cultures and epochs.[204] He also describes *Que Viva Mexico!* as 'unwound completely' on Mexico's landscapes, evoking both the Chinese landscape scroll and the unwinding of a reel of film. For Eisenstein the role of landscape is primarily and 'invariably musical and emotional': it is nonindifferent nature.[205]

The subjective experience, landscape and audiovisual cinema

For Eisenstein objectivity is impossible.[206] As human beings we are part of the landscape; our existence and the existence of landscape are manifestations of matter. Both are subject to the laws of being, and so both take part in 'a continuous process of becoming'. For this reason we cannot put enough objective distance between us and these laws of being, so we can only be subjective about them. However the poet (and consequently the artist, the writer, the filmmaker) can convey their subjective experience through description, by using structure, images, and the recreative process of analogy. The feeling of oneness with nature is inevitably a subjective state – it can only be known in the form of experience. In order to create a sense of distance from this subjective experience a change in habits or moods is needed. This change will either raise or lower the threshold of our sensory perception, which has the effect of making us notice things which we would normally not notice in our daily experience of life.[207]

Eisenstein's experience of the United States was to have provided this jolt out of the everyday. But apart from the initial ecstatic descriptions of his first view of Manhattan's skyscrapers soaring from the ocean, his subsequent experiences proved ultimately disappointing. It was only with his arrival in Mexico that he really found himself pushed into another state, experiencing a sufficiently substantial change of mood and habits to enable a mental and physical transformation to take place, essential for the transition to a state of ecstasy. In Mexico he saw ecstatic states in others (during religious ceremonies, bullfights, as well as recorded in the sacred forms of the ruins of Mesoamerican architecture) and he experienced them himself: during the *corrida*, through his contact with the *danzantes*, his experiences of the African Mexican danzon, and the Day of the Dead festivities. His interactions with the Mexican landscapes also provoked in him what he described as a 'primeval, purely sensual state' of ecstasy, where one becomes transported beyond understanding, beyond conceptualisation, beyond imagery, beyond consciousness, into '"pure" effect, feeling, sensation, "state".'[208] It was this state which enabled Eisenstein to become aware of Mexico itself as a process of becoming, a country 'coming into being'.[209] Because of the intense subjectivity of his experience of Mexico, he came to see the country as an evolving self-portrait, its landscapes as consequently being nonindifferent.

Eisenstein sees the phenomenon of what he calls 'nonindifferent nature' as being the means by which the passage of visual representation into music takes place. He calls landscape in silent films 'inner plastic music', a form of visual music.[210] According to Eisenstein, this 'inner plastic music' in silent film, in order to be heard, had to go beyond itself into another dimension. It had to make this transition to produce sound: the landscapes in silent film had to become nonindifferent in order to produce audiovisual cinema. This process was directly analogous to Eisenstein's transformative experiences in Mexico, in his attempt to produce his first audiovisual film. For him the representation of landscape is the part of the film which is the least burdened by narrative tasks, the part which is the most flexible to express moods, emotional states and spiritual experiences.[211] These characteristics are shared with music, which can express what is otherwise inexpressible by other means.[212]

Eisenstein believes that nonindifferent nature is subjective. Like music it is within ourselves. Nature is not particularly nonindifferent, but *our* nature is nonindifferent, as we approach the world to recreate it, not with indifference but with 'passion, actively and creatively'.[213] For these reasons nonindifferent nature and music are inseparable and therefore are vital in audiovisual expression.

4
Synaesthesia

only colour, colour and again colour is really capable of solving the problem of commensurability, of finding a common denominator for sound and vision.[1]

An audiovisual problem

In describing his collaboration with the composer Sergei Prokofiev on his first completed audiovisual film, *Alexander Nevsky*, Eisenstein tells of a situation he was unable to resolve using words: he could not express the effect he had in mind for the scene in which pipes and drums were to be played in celebration of the Russian victory. Eisenstein had already decided that in this audiovisual film he would not attempt a recreation of the past as in a 'waxworks exhibition or unskilled stylisation'.[2] In turn Prokofiev had decided that his music for this thirteenth-century historical film would not attempt to recreate what was imagined to be the music of that era, but that he would use a twentieth-century idiom to make these events from the past contemporary.[3] Consequently, Eisenstein had no musical reference to which he could point the composer in order to realise what he, as a non-musician film director, vividly imagined. He was unable to communicate to Prokofiev the exact effect he wanted the audience to 'see' in the music he needed for this moment of joyous celebration.[4]

Eisenstein's impression of this scene was simultaneously aural and visual, hence his use of the word 'seen' in a metaphorical sense, to express at the same instant sound and image. Perhaps it could be said that he 'audiovisualised' these pipe and drum musicians. However, he resolved this dilemma visually by ordering some 'prop' instruments to be made, and having them filmed being played without sound. When he projected this film for Prokofiev, the composer quickly produced a score which for him corresponded to what he saw being played. The sounds of the tambourine-like drums were easy to replicate, and Prokofiev used a combination of woodwind instruments in their high registers to create a shrill reedy sound with rapid notes, which was suggested to him when he saw these silent players of the archaic aulos-like pipes, and flutes; in ancient Greece the aulos or double pipes were played in Dionysiac ceremonies.[5] Eisenstein probably found them appropriate to the mood of archaic and frantic celebration which they evoke at the two points in the film in which they appear.[6]

Using the visual to evoke music and sound

In his earlier films *The Strike* (1924) and *October* (1928), Eisenstein had already experimented with the use of visual material to imply sound. He describes a short sequence in *The Strike* featuring a meeting of the strikers. This meeting is concealed from the authorities by appearing to be a casual stroll accompanied by a worker playing an accordion. In order to evoke the continuous sound of the accordion Eisenstein had it filmed in close-up and combined it in double exposure with the images of the workers strolling in the countryside. Here his aim was to stimulate in the audience the hearing of this music by using only a visual technique. He noted that his double exposure involving the accordion also had the effect of drawing together the images in the montage of this sequence, a technique which was later developed in the use of music or montage sequences in sound films.[7] The visual superimposition of workers with the accordion would, with the coming of sound, be replaced by the counterpoint of *sound* with the image, as put forward in the *Statement on Sound*, in 1928.[8] Another implication of the double exposure Eisenstein used in this sequence is the duplicitous nature of the action which is being depicted. In the Eureka version of *The Strike*, an accordion is played to accompany this section, so any implication of the sound of this instrument is lost.

However, for Eisenstein the technique of double exposure is not just the superimposition of two sets of images, but a continuation of the effect of persistence of vision, the phenomenon which at the time was thought by many to make film possible.[9] The impression derived from a simple sequence of film strips is due to how in the mind a strip is superimposed over the strip which comes after it. Eisenstein extends this concept of double exposure into his examination of what he believes is montage development in its highest form: audiovisual montage. The film experience at its most basic level consists of a stream of still images, then there is the montage of film sequences which consist of a stream of shots, and finally the audiovisual montage, which combines a kind of 'double exposure' comprising a stream of shots with a stream of music and sound.[10] Eisenstein's analysis of how he suggested the presence of accordion music purely visually in a pre-sound era film quickly becomes a structural analysis of how cinema, and audiovisual cinema works. He takes the microcosmic level of the concept of persistence of vision and extrapolates it via the technique of double exposure to the macrocosmic level of film sequences, as well as audiovisual montage. To achieve this extrapolation in his structural analysis he treats the aural part of the audiovisual film in visual terms.

In *October*, Eisenstein analyses his examples of implied sound in a simpler and more direct manner. He mentions several examples where he attempted to suggest noises of various kinds to his audience. He tried to evoke the rumbling of the wheels of machine guns by showing the effect of their sound on people nearby, who look around their doors to see what is causing this noise. He also had the wheels of the gun carriages made to seem bigger than they were by filming them from a low angle. In another example from the film he used 'a system of alternating and slow-motion iris diaphragms opening and shutting the palace doors' to give an impression of the sound of the Aurora battleship's guns echoing through the Winter Palace. He filmed some of the palace's crystal chandeliers twinkling in the light to evoke their shaking due to the gunfire. In these examples he is suggesting various noises using visual means, noises which would not be effectively recreated using musical equivalents in the score for *October*.[11] In these instances the audience would not only be watching the film and hearing its music, but would also experience a third layer, of noise, suggested visually, almost synaesthetically.

In the Eureka version of *October* the sequence of the evoked rumbling of machine guns appears to be absent. However there is a sequence in which a machine gun being fired is rapidly intercut with the gunner's face. This strongly evokes the sound of a machine gun, as well as its power. For me, the synaesthetic effect of this rapid intercutting is stronger when the orchestral music is cut out. In this version of *October* there is only a single iris closing a shot of the Mensheviks' meeting to evoke the echo of the salvo from the Aurora. The rhythmic alternation Eisenstein describes ('a system of "iris" diaphragms, in a correctly gauged rhythm – an opening and shutting out of views of rooms ... to capture the echo's breathing rhythm as it resounded through the galleries',) is lost, especially as this sound version of *October* has an extensive presence of sound effects, including a very blurry echo of the salvo, and even the tinkling of the chandeliers.[12]

Eisenstein on synaesthesia: thoughts and experiences

Eisenstein defined what he understood as synaesthesia on at least two occasions. In his simplest definition he describes it as being 'the production from one sense-impression of one kind of an associated mental image of a sense-impression of another kind.'[13] This description of synaesthesia would match the above instances from *October*, of the visual to aural transfer of associated sense-impressions. There is also a more complex definition of synaesthesia in which Eisenstein states that this process of association of sense-impressions involves emotion. Here synaesthesia is the ability to unite in one whole a variety of feelings gathered from different sources through different sense organs.[14] This definition is more appropriate with regard to an example of implied music in *October*, when Eisenstein used close-up shots of musicians playing harps to suggest the 'harping on' of counter-revolutionaries at a meeting.[15] The implied music of the harps (which audiences would hear in their imagination) is there because it reflects the *emotional* response of the director to the meeting he shows on the screen. Here he unifies the very separate images of a meeting and the harps being played with an emotional metaphor which operates synaesthetically, satirising those participating in the counter-Revolutionary conference.

Eisenstein acknowledges the role of synaesthesia as a psychological phenomenon. It provides the means to bring together on equal terms the audiovisual elements of audiovisual polyphony. However he is also wary of its effects.[16] He describes an unusual form of synaesthesia to exemplify its problematical nature:

Cases are certainly known to medical pathology in which a regressive type of patient is possessed of synaesthetic perceptions to such a degree that he cannot walk across a multicoloured carpet without stumbling. He perceives the polychrome patterns of the carpet as though they were actually at different depths or heights, and as he gauges the need to lift his foot in accordance with them he is inevitably caused to stumble by the disparity between the different heights to which he raises his feet and the absolutely smooth surface of the floor.[17]

By giving this extreme example of synaesthesia in such detail, Eisenstein is demonstrating that there exist various levels of intensity of this perceptual phenomenon. He mentions that he himself has on one occasion briefly experienced the type of synaesthesia suffered by the patient stumbling over the carpet:

I, for instance, have a vivid personal recollection of an instance when, in bright sunny weather, on the smooth asphalt outside the Telegraph Office in Myasnitskaya Street, I stumbled over the sharp, dark shadow cast by a street-lamp just as if the thing lying in front of me had been a log of wood or a steel rail. It happened in a moment of extreme mental absorption in some abstract problem.[18]

Eisenstein explains that it is at such times of extreme concentration that the normal controls exerted by our conscious mental functions give way to what he terms 'immediate impressions.'[19] In these instances the mind ceases to work in an everyday manner and briefly stops the normal mediation of sensory experience. Extreme examples of synaesthesia are pathological, but Eisenstein points out that in poets and artists it is strongly present, however not usually beyond normal limits. He explains how these normal limits paradoxically provide a richer and more diverse subtlety of thought than is possible in extreme cases of synaesthesia.[20]

Eisenstein describes his encounter with the 'memory man' S., whose phenomenal powers of recall were being scientifically investigated by Lev Semenovich Vygotsky and Alexander Romanovich Luria. Vygotsky (1896–1934) was an influential Soviet psychologist, especially interested in thought and language. He was one of the pioneers of psycholinguistics. Alexander Romanovich Luria (1902–77), was a psychologist and disciple of Vygotsky. One of the founders of neuropsychology, he wrote a monograph on 'S': S.V. Shereshevsky. A former student of Luria, Michael Cole states that Luria and Vygotsky regularly met with Eisenstein to discuss how the abstract ideas at the basis of historical materialism could be successfully communicated through cinema.[21]

S. was able to remember seemingly limitless amounts of information, unrelated to any process of discrimination or sense of value. He was able to achieve this through an elaborate and totally involuntary synaesthesia. Eisenstein recounts how S. had kept until his adulthood all the processes of primary sensual thought, which we normally lose as our ability to think logically develops. His overwhelming capacity for synaesthetic response would normally have become atrophied, with the development of an ability to generalise. However his involuntary synaesthetic associations had been retained, which impeded his ability to make conscious connections between things, a characteristic of intelligent thought. Eisenstein learnt that S. also had the ability to make automatic and exact reproductions of complex drawings, a skill which is normally lost as we begin to understand the relationships between the parts of a drawing or picture, and to relate consciously to the things depicted in them.[22] This unmediated and involuntary nature of synaesthesia made Eisenstein wary of artists who put forward systems of direct and absolute correspondences between the different senses, and even corresponding emotional states.[23]

A case in point was the Russian composer Alexander N. Scriabin (1871–1915). Influenced by Wagner's concept of the *Gesamtkunstwerk*, Scriabin aimed to achieve a complete synthesis between the senses in his work. In his orchestral score for *Prometheus*, subtitled *Poem of Fire*, he wrote a score for a keyboard which projected coloured lights in parallel with the music's changing harmonic structures. In order to be able to do this, he created a set of equivalences between keys and colours, to stimulate emotional states and spiritual qualities: C, red; G, orange-pink; D, yellow; A, green; E, whitish-blue; B, similar to E; F#, blue, intense; Db, purple; Ab, red-purple; Eb, steely; Bb, with a metallic shine; F, red, dark.[24]

Eisenstein would have noticed these equivalences, which he would have seen in the *Blaue Reiter Almanac*, a publication with which he was familiar.[25] Scriabin desired to achieve a complete and mystical unity between all the senses, and therefore all the media in his work. In *Mystery*, his last uncompleted piece, he planned to incorporate an olfactory score.[26] In such a proposed mystical union of the senses Eisenstein detected the limitations of a Wagnerian megalomania; he noted that the tendency to be egocentric and solipsistic is very well known in those who work synaesthetically. He cites an anecdote in which the philosopher G.V. Plekhanov (an acquaintance of the composer) met him on a sunny day, and asked him if the good weather was due to the composer's direct influence.[27] So it was the absolute and therefore superhuman characteristics of these direct synaesthetic relationships that Eisenstein found problematical. While he admired Scriabin's desire to 'demolish the contradictions between picture and sound, between the visible world and the audible world', he realised that in practice 'no two seekers of such absolutes are ever able to agree with each other.' What Eisenstein wished to avoid in his conception of audiovisual cinema was Scriabin's path 'into the cosmos, into super-sensuality and super-consciousness' inevitably leading to a generalised mysticism, paradoxically brought on by solipsistic thought. He felt that cinema should operate within the scope of the human experience, 'within a human module, within the limits of the human mind and emotions'.[28]

Eisenstein on his audiovisual collaboration with Prokofiev

Eisenstein saw cinema as a collaborative means of expression, and it was his practice of collaboration, involving a certain amount of 'give and take', which proved to be so fruitful in his work with Prokofiev on his first completed audiovisual films *Alexander Nevsky* and *Ivan the Terrible*.[29] When Prokofiev later wrote about his collaboration with Eisenstein, he mentioned his great respect for music, to the extent that the director would be prepared to make necessary adjustments to his montage to 'preserve the integrity of the musical fragment'.[30]

According to Eisenstein, he and Prokofiev would always 'bargain' for a long time before it was decided who should be first to make the next decisive audiovisual step. This would be a choice between the composer having to write the music having seen the relevant section of unedited film, or to compose it once Eisenstein had already edited it. With respect to the first choice, it would be up to the film director to develop the montage from Prokofiev's existing score; with the second option, the principal artistic choices, in the form of his film montage, would already have been made by Eisenstein. With the latter choice it was then up to the composer to create an appropriate construction using the available techniques of musical composition, based on the director's 'architectural' plan. On the other hand, the first choice implied for Prokofiev what Eisenstein thought of as a fundamental creative problem, the responsibility for determining the developing rhythmic structure of the section. This option involved the *composer* drawing up the 'architectural' plan itself, which would then determine how the film director's audiovisual montage would operate. Eisenstein describes in detail the complexities of what he refers to as the internal mechanisms of this procedure.[31] When he is confronted with a recording of Prokofiev's score, and he has to create a film montage to match it, these are the steps he outlines:

1. You must have in your memory a mental record of all the unedited film, the 'plastic' material which can at any point be manipulated and transformed.
2. Listen again and again to the recorded music, until the moment arises when you can imagine a series of images which could correspond with the music, or a section of the music which could correspond with an imagined filmed sequence.[32]

These correspondences can be of various types:

- a texture of an object or a landscape which can be matched with a timbre in the music;
- the possibility of synchronising a series of close-ups with a certain rhythmic pattern in the music;
- the matching of the music with a corresponding section of visual representation, producing an internal harmony, inexpressible in rational terms.[33]

This list of audiovisual correspondences is necessarily limited, as the combinations depend on a vast range of variables, both in terms of the content of the music and of the film, and many other factors relating to the overall creative intention. For Eisenstein there are other difficulties at this point in the process of combination:

- the visual part of the combination is as yet chaotically unrealised;
- what Eisenstein describes as a 'spirit of combination' which hovers above a 'primeval chaos of representation' is nevertheless dependent on the laws of musical development which are evident in the recording of the score;
- the mind of the film director has to leap from any part of his unedited film to any other part of it, in order to mentally rehearse what film montage would correspond with each section of the music;
- the montage of the film also has to follow its own laws, otherwise it will not work visually.[34]

Eisenstein notes at this point how this *audiovisual* process was very like the method he used to create the montage for his pre-sound films. The basic difference was that instead of selecting pieces of montage to a pre-existing recording of music, he had in his mind what he describes as a 'musical score' or 'inner melody' to which he edited his shots. He explains that this melody is frequently so powerful that at times the entire rhythm of his actions is determined in advance during the days when he is editing scenes to correspond to these sounds. He goes on to give examples of the type of distracted behaviour he experienced when he was editing very different sections of *The Battleship Potemkin*. When editing the 'Mist' and 'Mourning for Vakulinchuk' sections, he would carry out everyday activities in what he describes as a '"wilting" rhythm', in marked contrast to the abrupt and aggressive behaviour he exhibited in daily activities when he was editing the sequence of the massacre on the Odessa Steps.[35] This is very similar to the synaesthetic behaviour Eisenstein described when he was absorbed in 'some abstract problem.'[36] Here there is an analogous transfer and superimposition of one set of perceptions and emotions to another unrelated set, in a seemingly arbitrary manner. Eisenstein gives an example of the actor Michael Chekhov, who was acting the part of a distracted man in the theatre in the evenings: from the morning and throughout the day at home he would fall over chairs, upset cups and break dishes.[37]

Eisenstein confesses that he does not really know how a composer's inner compositional processes work, but he does attempt to elucidate some of what he thinks took place in Prokofiev's mind during their audiovisual collaborations. What particularly impressed him about Prokofiev was his ability to capture, after watching a scene from the film only two or three times, its emotional effect, rhythm and structure. As a result of this gift, the composer could provide the very next day a fully-scored *'musical equivalent of the visual representation'*. As an example of Prokofiev's audiovisual talent, Eisenstein describes how the composer had achieved a complex *'interweaving* of accents of action and music' in his score for the episode from *Ivan the Terrible* where Ivan implores the boyars for their support. He also noticed that Prokofiev had only rarely synchronised the visual accents with the musical accents, and that these joint accents were solely conditioned by the montage and by the development of the action during this particular scene.[38]

How did Prokofiev achieve so rapidly such a remarkably flawless audiovisual combination, which needed no amendments, either to the film or to the music? Eisenstein found the answer to this question in a surprisingly mundane manner, when he remembered how the composer had articulated his new telephone number when he had called it out to him. He had subsequently realised that Prokofiev's voice had closely followed the pattern of the figures in his new number, in terms of dynamics (soft to loud), and the rhythm of the combined names of the numbers announced in an emotionally charged way. Eisenstein demonstrates Prokofiev's 'performance' of his new number, k 5–10–20, extension 35, by notating it in the typographical manner of the poets Velimir Khlebnikov or Tristan Tzara: 'K5! 10!! 20!!! Extension 30!!! 5.'[39]

The composer had evidently recognised the pattern of the increasing size of the first four numbers, reaching a musical climax on the figure 30, before the final number which repeats the first one, at the same volume level. This was a musician's way of remembering his new telephone number. For Eisenstein this mnemonic technique is the key to Prokofiev's ability to translate his perception of visual representation directly into a musical form.[40] He also refers to it as his talent for 'creating images in music.'[41] Eisenstein breaks down what he believes to be the composer's audiovisual compositional technique in this manner:

1. the finding of a pattern in what first appears to be a 'primeval chaos of representation';
2. the addition of an emotional interpretation to this found pattern.[42]

The second part of this audiovisual process then leads to the third action, what Eisenstein describes as the way in which the audiovisual formula is 'mastered sensually'. This is the way in which Prokofiev translates the telephone number into an intonational pattern, which Eisenstein calls the melody of the 'tune' of speech, which is also the foundation of music. Therefore, in the third and final part of this audiovisual compositional process, the 'formula', which is the emotional interpretation of the found pattern, becomes translated by the craft of the composer into a piece of music – it is 'mastered sensually'. For Eisenstein the mnemonic process is what is common to both Prokofiev's memorisation of his new number, and his ability to translate images into music: a person's mnemonic method is largely the key to that individual's thought processes. He acknowledges that mnemonic techniques can be very varied, from a straightforward process of association, to something more compositional and complex. As an example, Eisenstein mentions how a series of words to be memorised is linked through action and content to create a *'concrete picture'* in one's memory.[43] This statement could be understood as a process which is analogous to Prokofiev's audiovisual compositional technique. The series of words corresponds to the series of images in an edited or unedited film. This series is then connected by a found pattern, which Prokofiev translates into a piece of music, the aural equivalent of Eisenstein's 'concrete picture'. Whether the associational process features images, words or music, the compositional technique, involving a combination of memory, emotion and transferral from one medium to another, is the same.

Eisenstein gives a specific example of how Prokofiev demonstrated to him an aspect of his audiovisual composition technique. The composer showed him the audiovisual relationships he had featured in a song about the sea, which was being performed for a recording which was to have been included in *Ivan the Terrible*. Prokofiev pointed out to him the parts in the music which he had connected to various characteristics of the sea: waves, a splash, the sea's depth, the feeling of a tempest. As these elements were not all featured in the score at the same time, Eisenstein compared this form of depiction with various camera set-ups, used to film, say, a fortress. If this building were only to be filmed 'head-on', it would not appear in a fully three-dimensional way. In addition this single image of the fortress would lack the emotion which would be expressed by the choice of the various camera angles used to depict it.[44] Eisenstein describes Prokofiev's audiovisual composition method in terms of 'tonal camera angles': 'having grasped the structural secret of a phenomenon, he clothes it in the tonal camera angles of instrumentation, making it sparkle with shifts of timbre, and forces the whole inflexible structure to blossom forth in the emotional fullness of orchestration.'[45]

Eisenstein also describes his observation of Prokofiev when the composer was working on the first step of his audiovisual technique: the finding of a pattern in what first appears to be the 'primeval chaos of representation' mentioned above. In the flickering light from the screen, the director notices the composer's fingers drumming on the elbow rests of his chair, as he is concentrating on watching the edited sequence of images. Eisenstein concludes that Prokofiev, in his state of heightened awareness, is not beating time, but instead is measuring 'the structural canons governing the lengths of time and tempo in the edited pieces, harmonizing these with the actions and intonations of the characters'. At one point the composer exclaims in delight as 'he watches a piece with a cunning contrapuntal construction of three movements which do not coincide in rhythm, tempo and direction: protagonist, group background and poles flashing by in the foreground as the camera passes them.' Here Prokofiev seems to be experiencing Eisenstein's visual counterpoint instantaneously as music: 'the following day he will send me the music which will permeate my montage structure with a similar sound counterpoint.' This facility would suggest that Prokofiev, when he was concentrating in this way, experienced the tempo and visual rhythms he was watching in the edited sequence synaesthetically. Eisenstein realised this when he described this aspect of the composer's audiovisual technique as a 'wonderful synaesthetic synchronization of the sounds with the image on the screen'.[46] This synaesthetic facility would also explain how he was able to check whether the music that he heard instantly in his mind's ear would get in the way of the speech uttered by the protagonists who were featured in the sequence. Eisenstein noticed that it was not wise to interrupt Prokofiev at this point in his creative process – the composer's mind was not working on an everyday level, but one where synaesthesia was possible, a state of mind where emotion and thought revert to become identical.

Prokofiev on his collaboration with Eisenstein

In her description of this audiovisual collaboration, Tatiana Egorova provides a view from Prokofiev's pragmatic stance. She shows the three stages of the composer's audiovisual compositional system:

1. a survey, stop-watch in hand, of roughly assembled episodes and the determination of the exact time [ie duration] of the necessary music fragments;
2. writing a piano version of the scenic music and recording it on tape;
3. coordination of music and representation and, if the result is satisfactory, the beginning of work on the orchestration.[47]

To stimulate Prokofiev's audiovisual imagination, Eisenstein would provide the composer with sketches of the most important scenes.

Prokofiev called these drawings 'squibs'. He would refer to them when he had to compose the music before Eisenstein had found the melodic, rhythmic or dramatic key to the montage of a particular scene. The director also gave Prokofiev a list of descriptions of each musical theme, including his commentary on the scenes for which they were intended. Prokofiev called these descriptions 'themelets'.[48] This collaborative method indicates the extent to which Eisenstein was in some instances working like a composer, but without having the training to use musical notation to write down what he heard in his inner ear. He explains how he did not choose sections of film to correspond to Prokofiev's music, but to correspond with the 'score' of what was being 'sung' within him. For Eisenstein audiovisual montage cannot be constructed without listening to the 'inner melody' which determines its compositional development.[49] However, he also had the ability to 'let go' in his collaboration with Prokofiev, as when, for the scene of the attack which begins the 'The Battle on the Ice' in *Alexander Nevsky*, he edited the film to match the composer's previously composed and recorded orchestral score.[50]

This account of the remarkable collaboration between Eisenstein and Prokofiev is another indication of how close the editing of film is to the process of musical composition. Rhythm, tempo, accents and counterpoint are vital elements common to both music and film. In his approach to audiovisual cinema, Eisenstein also adds musically synaesthetic analogies such as harmony, melody, timbre, score, instrumentation, and orchestration. Both artists had a vision-to-sound synaesthesia, and Eisenstein also experienced its sound-to-vision counterpart. His use of terms such as 'tonal camera angles' indicate a complete audiovisual interchangeability; he was at home in any combination of sound and vision, helped by his reversible sound-to-vision, vision-to-sound synaesthesia. Prokofiev also had some sound-to-vision synaesthesia, which would explain how he was able to compose an effective score for a sequence before Eisenstein had edited it, with the additional help of the director's 'squibs' and 'themelets'. The reason why they had to bargain so hard as to who would be first to make the next audiovisual decision was also the reason why their collaboration was so effective: their synaesthetic and audiovisual abilities were surprisingly similar and yet complementary.

Eisenstein, synaesthesia and Kabuki

Eisenstein's awareness of his own synaesthesia led him to explore various artistic traditions in which this phenomenon played a key part. Already in 1928 he wrote about synaesthesia in an article about Kabuki theatre and the potential its techniques have for use in audiovisual montage. He explains how in this theatre tradition the senses are addressed equally, the Japanese aim to achieve 'the final *sum* of stimulants to the brain, ignoring *which* path that stimulation takes. Instead of accompaniment the Kabuki reveals the method of *transference*: the transference of the basic affective intention from one material to another, from one 'category' of stimulant to another.'[51] This absence of differentiation is characteristic of perception before an ability to think logically is developed, before there is an understanding of relationships between various things that are being perceived. To illustrate this state, Eisenstein mentions the cases of people who are cured of their blindness, but on being able to see don't have the ability to differentiate between objects which are near and those which are further away; to them everything seems to jostle on the same plane.[52] In Kabuki theatre all the senses which are stimulated are treated as if they are on the same plane, so the conditions for transfer between the senses, synaesthesia, is readily made possible:

> Watching the Kabuki, you involuntarily recall the novel by an American writer about a man whose auditory and optical nerves were transposed so that he perceived light vibrations as sounds and air tremors as colours; that is, he began to *hear light and see sounds*. The same thing happens in the Kabuki! We actually 'hear movement' and 'see sound'.[53]

In an epigraph to his chapter 'Synchronization of Senses' (from *The Film Sense*), Eisenstein quotes a passage from a story published in 1926 by the Welsh writer, Richard Hughes. In this extract Hughes describes his protagonist as he gradually dissolves into infinity. His senses become mixed so that he hears the surrounding green café tables as a 'tinkling arpeggio'; the sunlight becomes a blaring bass in a booming sky, and the rattling sound of a passing cart is transformed into a set of bright colour flashes.[54]

As an example of synaesthesia from Kabuki theatre, Eisenstein (in his article from 1928) mentions a scene during which a protagonist leaves a besieged castle. His increasing distance is shown by his moving away from the representation of the castle at the back of the stage, then by a backdrop which appears and shows the castle gate in a smaller size, followed by another backdrop of abstracted landscape colours, which hides the castle from view. Finally, the greatest distance from the castle is expressed synaesthetically: in terms of sound, by the music of the *samisen*, a Japanese instrument resembling the mandolin.[55]

Eisenstein could easily see this process translated into audiovisual cinema terms: first there would be a close-up of the gate behind the hero, then the gate would be seen in long shot, then a landscape shot would appear, and finally perhaps another landscape shot, this time with the *samisen* music appearing. This music would suggest the passage of time, and therefore the great distance travelled by the hero.[56]

Synaesthesia and other types of thought

Eisenstein also noticed a synaesthetic system of correspondences in Chinese philosophy. To illustrate this, in his book *The Film Sense*, he reproduces a diagram from the Sung tradition, showing colour and sound equivalents as well as associated parallels involving the seasons, compass directions, the elements, and examples of human behaviour. However, we have seen how Eisenstein had doubts about the proposed correspondences put forward by Western artists centuries later, especially between colours and sounds. He noticed that the French poet Arthur Rimbaud's correspondences between vowel sounds and colours in his poem *Le Sonnet des voyelles* did not match those of others who had put forward such equivalents. Eisenstein compares the German writer A.W. Schlegel's chart of correspondences between vowel sounds and colours, with Rimbaud's list from the first line of *Le Sonnet des voyelles*:

| A.W. Shlegel: | A red, | | I blue, | U violet, | O purple |
| Arthur Rimbaud: | A black, | E white, | I red, | U green, | O blue.[57] |

Eisenstein doesn't list the German 'E', and the vowel sound 'U' in German doesn't sound like 'U' in French anyway. So these factors would also account for a divergence in correspondence between these sounds and their perceived colour equivalents. Eisenstein prefers and quotes Lafcadio Hearn's more flexible and dynamic approach to synaesthesia, in his case between words and their corresponding colours: 'words are like those little lizards that are able to change their colouring according to their surroundings.'[58] Eisenstein explains that this lack of absolute correspondence, for example between various sounds and colours, is the path to creating '*new chains of association*' in a work of art. Flexibility of association provides 'a perpetual stimulus to seek new forms of that fusion of sounds and colours'. In turn these new fusions can result in the blazing of 'new trails in our awareness of reality', which he sees as being one of the aims of art. As an example of this method, Eisenstein tells how in 1923–24, he formulated 'the aim of creating new conditioned reflexes on the basis of existing unconditioned reflexes'.[59]

These statements involving synaesthesia, association, conditioned and unconditioned reflexes can be clarified by examining how each phenomenon relates to the other. Synaesthesia and the process of association can be considered to lie at opposite ends of a continuum (Fig.19). This continuum represents the variety of a person's response to a sensory stimulus. For example, synaesthesia is an involuntary and automatic response, while association and disassociation are largely voluntary and conscious responses. Both unconditioned and conditioned reflexes are automatic, and so these responses are placed at the synaesthesia end of the continuum. Conditioned reflexes are learned, so association and disassociation play a more important part in creating them. This is why they are to the right of the unconditioned reflexes in the diagram. The more synaesthesia becomes conscious, the more it approaches the process of association and its opposite, disassociation. Metaphorical thinking and

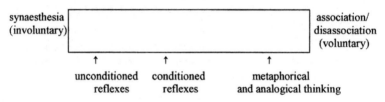

Fig.19 Diagram of a stimulus response continuum.

analogical thinking are strongly voluntary, yet they are a form of association which normally has an initially unconscious and therefore involuntary aspect. The positioning of the responses to a stimulus will vary according to the individual: the diagram reflects an individual's possible set of responses. For example, in the case of someone who is strongly, perhaps even pathologically synaesthetic, the conditioned reflexes would be placed more towards the right in the diagram, pushing the metaphorical and analogical thinking further to the right also. By far the largest part of this type of synaesthete's responses is involuntary. Luria's account of his study of Shereshevsky, *The Mind of a Mnemonist*, shows what can happen to someone's thinking processes, when responses to stimuli are of this pathological type. For example Shereshevsky found Eisenstein difficult to understand, as he kept responding synaesthetically to the varied qualities of his voice:

> there are people who seem to have many voices, whose voices seem to be an entire composition, a bouquet. The late S. M. Eisenstein had just such a voice: listening to him, it was as though a flame with fibres protruding from it was advancing right towards

me. I got so interested in his voice, I couldn't follow what he was
saying.[60]

We have looked at the synaesthesia end of this continuum, so now we can
see how Eisenstein uses association and disassociation in his ideas on
audiovisual cinema.

Association

When Eisenstein was making his earliest films, for example *The Strike* and
October, he was already thinking in terms of the sound film. He explains
that sound was an 'inner urge' which for him sprang from the silent film
medium. He realised that this type of film had 'to go beyond the limits of
plastic expressiveness alone'. The silent moving image (the 'plastic ...
image') inexorably and inevitably implied sound. Eisenstein wanted to use
this phenomenon, which he called 'the sound image', to attain a maximum
degree of effectiveness of expression and communication: 'from its very
first steps our silent film strove by all attainable means to convey not only
the plastic but also the sound image.'[61] As examples of such 'sound
images' he mentions the sequence in *The Strike* featuring a group of
workers led by an accordionist, the tinkling of the chandeliers in the
Winter Palace caused by gunfire nearby, and other examples from *October*
already described above.

These sound images rely to a certain extent on the phenomenon of
synaesthesia, but they are less inconsistent than the colour-sound type of
synaesthesia which tends to vary considerably according to individual
experience. The sound images Eisenstein used are closer to the
phenomenon of the conditioned reflex: when the audience see an
accordion being played, they will instantly imagine the sound it makes as
they are familiar with this instrument, and they normally experience it
audiovisually. The same type of reflex applies to the tinkling chandeliers,
the roar of the machine gun fire in *October*, and the imagined noise of the
factory whistles seen blasting in *The Strike*. Even if they are simultaneously
imitated in a piano and orchestral accompaniment, the audience will still
hear them as noises because of the strength of the automatic conditioned
reflex. The only instance where this kind of reflex is completely
neutralised is when the actual sound the object or person makes appears
on the soundtrack. In a currently available version of *The Strike*, the sound
of an actual accordion is heard during the sequence featuring the workers
led by the worker-accordionist. As a result, the sound image disappears
completely, as everyone in the audience hears the same accordion and the
same music. Any room for an inner individual imagining of the music has

been lost: the whole process of audiovisual perception has become over-defined and less evocative. Consequently the sound film has a tendency to neutralise the expressive possibilities of the sound image.

Colour, and music and sound in film

Eisenstein found the solution to this problem in his use of colour in film. He believed that 'as the silent film cried out for sound, so does the sound film cry out for colour.' He saw the use of colour as being possible in black and white film, as this type of film represents colours in an abstracted form, by a variety of shades on the grey scale. For example, Eisenstein states that grey is the dominant colour in *The Battleship Potemkin*. This colour consists of three types of grey, 'the hard steely gleam of the battleship's boards', the mellow grey of the mists in the film, and a third type of grey, which combined 'the gleam of the first and the mellowness of the second – a variation of the sea surface photographed in the grey gamut'. The only point in *The Battleship Potemkin* which features actual colour is when at the end of the film the red flag is flown from the ship's mast: 'the red of the flag pierced *Potemkin* like a fanfare.' Eisenstein describes this hand-painted effect in musical terms; he synaesthetically associates the sound of the fanfare with the Bolshevik red colour, its bright colour/sound 'piercing' his film. The associations here are with the colour of a bleeding wound, with the fanfare announcing the violence of the future Revolution. This is how Eisenstein associates colour with sound in a film, through *meaning*: 'its effect was due not so much to the colour itself as to its meaning.'[63] The synaesthetic interpretation of the redness of the Bolshevik flag in terms of the sound of a fanfare is Eisenstein's own private connection: nothing in this part of the film indicates this type of association. However it is only necessary for the *appearance* of the red flag, with its emotional associations for the audience, to create an effect for them which could be described as being like a fanfare. The sudden red colour in an otherwise entirely grey film causes a surprise, for which Eisenstein has carefully prepared the audience with a long and suspenseful montage, accompanied by an equally suspenseful score by Edmund Meisel. Here he has developed the colour/sound type of synaesthesia into a *conceptual* synaesthesia, where the involuntary and unconscious phenomenon becomes a deliberate audiovisual technique, used to express a complex combination of emotion and idea.

Eisenstein underpins this audiovisual method with a scientific analysis of colour and sound on a microcosmic scale. He points out that, like sound, the visual element is also based on vibrations, 'admittedly in a different band of physical wavelengths', and is also characterized by tones.

He then states that the visual equivalent of sound is colour, and develops this analogy in musical terms; he makes pitch correspond 'to the play of *light*', and a tonality analogous to 'colour tone'.[64]

The visual line and the melodic line

This musical sound/colour analogy enables Eisenstein to further develop the comparison by associating what he calls 'a "linear" element of plastic art' with the line of a melody. Both the visual and the melodic line comprise a 'higher unity' which has been born of movement: the temporal progression of tones in a melody, combined with the representation in time which the linear element of the montage articulates.[65] This linear element can be present in a sequence of shots, as well as within a single shot, as the passage of time is a factor in the perception of both of these means of filmic depiction. Eisenstein defines the linear element or 'linear contour' as 'the imaginary path that runs through the purposefully, specifically juxtaposed elements of depiction'.[66] For clarification of what this 'imaginary path' consists, it is useful to turn to another and related analogy which Eisenstein uses to deal with the complex question of audiovisual unity: his concept of overtonal montage.

Eisenstein's overtone analogy in audiovisual cinema

Eisenstein also develops this analogy from a scientific phenomenon in acoustics: in this case the harmonic series, in his 1929 article *The Fourth Dimension in Cinema*. The harmonic series are the 'partials' or overtones which form part of the resonance patterns of sound which are heard when a fundamental tone is played or sung. The overtones are not played but originate in the type of voice or instrument which is being listened to – they are the less dominant sounds which determine the sound quality or timbre of the notes. Eisenstein points out that composers like Debussy and Scriabin make a deliberate use of the harmonic or overtone series in their music, and he then makes a direct comparison with optics. He compares the play of overtones and how they change timbre in music and sound with the way different lenses distort space. As an example, he mentions the change in visual effect produced by a 28mm wide angle lens compared to that produced by a 310mm long lens.[67] This almost scientific analogy is then extended to include 'the secondary resonances of the actual filmed material' which Eisenstein specifies as being 'the visual *overtonal* complex of the shot'. He describes these visual 'secondary resonances' or overtones as a 'whole complex of secondary stimulants (which) always accompanies the *central* stimulant'. In terms of his musical analogy, the '*central* stimulant' corresponds to the 'basic dominant tone'.

Eisenstein points out that the musical overtones, deliberately used harmonically and melodically by Debussy and Scriabin in their compositions, and his use of visual overtones are also similar because they can only take place as part of a process involving time, which he calls 'the fourth dimension'.[68]

By this stage in Eisenstein's development of his music/film analogy, he has moved away from the scientific precision of the musical overtone, to his generalised concept of visual overtones as a 'complex of secondary stimulants'. Nine years later, in his article 'Montage 1937', he further extends his definition of the visual 'overtone' by adding the element of emotion, and by referring specifically to the sequence: 'I have defined the "overtone" as the summation, or rather the general emotional "resonance" that derives from the sequence.' He now acknowledges that his definition is not the same as 'the concept of "overtone" in musical terminology'. He lists some of the 'individual component factors' which contribute to the 'overtone': acting style, the 'play of linear elements', movement, light, and what he describes as 'the emotional associations of form and the interplay of the forms themselves'. The concept of the 'linear element' can be recognised in Eisenstein's previously mentioned comparison between this idea and a melodic line in music. However, this type of audiovisual montage is only based on what he calls 'the parameter of "meaning"', whereas the overtonal montage is 'an *emotional generalisation* about all the elements in a sequence'. Though the *musical* overtone part of the analogy has by this point almost disappeared, the concept of overtonal montage as an 'emotional generalisation' of various elements is quite close to a description of how a piece of music works. To clarify what he means, Eisenstein expresses the effect of overtonal montage as follows: 'the overtone begins to sound like an overall image of the sequence.'[69] Though he intends the overtone he mentions here to be of a visual nature, he describes it synaesthetically as 'sounding' like the sum of visual and emotional resonances which make up the 'overall image' of the sequence. In order to unify the very different characteristics of music and cinema, Eisenstein brings each medium together using the idea of the 'overtone', which he applies to both: '*sound* and *visual* perceptions are *not reducible* to a single denominator. They are constants in different dimensions. But the visual overtone and the sound overtone are constants in a *single dimension!*[70]

Some useful metaphors for working with audiovisual cinema

Eisenstein's use of the mathematical term 'constant' refers to the scientific foundation on which he builds his audiovisual comparisons: the concepts of vibration, and of resonance and overtones, which he finds are common to both the musical and the visual elements in a sound film. He extends these parallels to meaning, emotion, and also time, which, as was mentioned above, he calls the fourth dimension. Meaning, emotion and time are far beyond the scientific parallels with which Eisenstein began his analysis of music and the visual. In order to avoid vague over-generalising, he brings music and film once again closer together: 'for both we introduce a new uniform formula: "I feel".'[71] The relation to synaesthesia is through the feeling or emotion which makes this phenomenon possible, but the scientific word 'formula' denotes a conscious creative act.

This precise word reminds the reader that Eisenstein is not just dealing with imprecise abstractions, but he is describing a working method for making effective audiovisual cinema. He does this by using a variety of analogies to bring the elements of music and sound and the visual aspects of cinema together into the same conceptual space in order to be able to work on them to produce an audiovisual unity. He also avoids loss of meaning through abstraction by underlining the effect of the perceptual elements in the audiovisual combination, by stating that '*both visual and sound overtones are totally physiological sensations*'.[72] He begins with the involuntary perceptual phenomenon of synaesthesia which he develops into a conscious conceptual synaesthesia, comprising various useful metaphors for working with audiovisual cinema (Fig.19).

Wagner's leitmotif and its use in audiovisual cinema

Eisenstein believed that it would be possible through the medium of audiovisual cinema to surpass previous artists' visions and attempts to achieve a successful audiovisual unity. In terms of predecessors in this regard he mentions Diderot, Wagner and Scriabin.[73] Eisenstein noted that Diderot believed that the compositional principles of both vocal and instrumental music were derived from the intonations of emotional speech and from the sounds of nature.[74] When applied to a musical genre like opera, this approach, as discussed by Diderot in *Le Neveu de Rameau*, incorporates both vocal and instrumental music, as well as theatre and dance. These compositional principles not only result in an audiovisual unity, but also in an audiovisual continuum with nature.[75]

The Russian composer Scriabin further extended Diderot's ideas of an audiovisual unity as a continuation of nature in his unrealised project entitled *Mystery*. He was inspired by Wagner's idea of the music-drama as a synthesis of the arts, a *Gesamtkunstwerk*. Scriabin intended his *Mystery* to be a gigantic and universal magical act incorporating his music, as well as his texts, and dance, colour, taste, touch and perfume. It was to be performed in a temple of his own design at a spectacular natural site in India, either in the mountainous north, or in the tropical south.[76] Though Eisenstein admired Scriabin's audiovisual vision, as was noted earlier he was sceptical about the composer's messianic solipsism.

More useful to Eisenstein was Wagner's concept of the *Gesamtkunstwerk*. He studied the composer's writings, and before working on *Ivan the Terrible* he directed a production of his music-drama *Die Walküre* at the Bolshoi Theatre in Moscow, in 1940.[77] This direct contact with Wagner's music and stage practice enabled Eisenstein to experience at first hand the composer's use of the leitmotif, a technique he had developed to seamlessly interweave his music with the action taking place on the stage. Though he felt that Wagner had achieved the application of his leitmotif technique magnificently, he did feel that the composer sometimes applied it to absurd lengths. However Eisenstein thought that Wagner's use of the leitmotif could be usefully applied to music for colour film. He noted that Wagner used the melodic patterns and melodies of his leitmotifs to bring out certain themes in the stories being enacted by his characters. His leitmotifs were modified and developed as the themes, characters and action developed. In his production of Wagner's opera, Eisenstein wished to avoid a one-to-one relationship, as for example between a certain colour and a character, so that as the action developed the same character would not always wear the same colour. This implied that the leitmotifs would become associated with developing themes in the action rather than just the characters.[78]

Examples of these over-arching and developing themes, expressed in terms of colour, can also be found in three of Eisenstein's many abandoned film projects. A sketch of a film survives from the mid-1940s about Pushkin's life.[79] Eisenstein's text for *A Poet's Love* involves an intricate use of colour leitmotifs which develop directly from the story, together with indications about the music he had planned for the film, some of it to be composed by Prokofiev. In this sketch is also mentioned another idea for a colour film, this time about the plague, 'in which gradually the blackness spread and overran the joyfully coloured landscapes, the costumes of those dining, the luxuriance of the gardens and the radiant sky itself'.[80] Eisenstein had already used this idea in his scenario for Paramount, *Sutter's Gold*, which showed the destruction of the Californian landscape by the Gold Rush, followed by an invasion of thousands of lawyers dressed in black.[81] Eventually he used a swallowing up of colour by darkness to show the rise to power of Ivan the Terrible's own personal army, the *oprichniki*. Cloaked in black, they invade the screen, at the end of the sequence in colour from Part II of the film.

Consequently, in an audiovisual context, the colour leitmotif would not be limited to an association with just one musical leitmotif, as in synaesthesia, but both colour and musical leitmotifs would be associated with ideas derived from the visual structure of the audiovisual film. Eisenstein points out that the key role here is determined by the '*image structure*' of the whole work. This structure is not derived from stereotypical correlations, but by establishing in the images of the '*specific creative work*' correlations of sound and colour, and sound and image, which are determined by the theme and the idea embodied in the work.[83]

Eisenstein also points out that this principle remains functional whether the composer is writing the music for an edited or an unedited sequence, or conversely the director is editing his sequence to the music: the idea and theme of the work dictate the nature of the audiovisual correlations.[84] With this approach to audiovisual unity the music brings out the invisible elements of the film: all the ideas, moods, thoughts and themes which lie beneath the visual surface of the images.

Disassociation

The process of disassociation provides another technique which can be used to combine colour film and music. Eisenstein is keen to distance himself from using absolute relationships in a work of art. As an example, he quotes from a description of a goldsmith who uses decorative patterns which have been generated by an oscilloscope, in response to tones from various vibrating tuning forks. This artisan regards these patterns as having the effect of the visual equivalent of an octave, or a Debussyan 9th added note chord. Looking at his work it is evident that they do not suggest octaves or chords at all, as there is no absolute relationship between the curves depicting sound waves and the effect of these sounds as they are heard. Consequently Eisenstein points out that in art absolute relationships are *not* decisive, but arbitrary relationships *are* key within a network of images which are determined by a specific work of art.[85] The problem of finding a common denominator between sound and vision, a problem of commensurability, is not solved by making use of colour/sound combinations which are revealed through synaesthetic perceptions, or by other similarly absolute correspondences.[86] Eisenstein believes that this difficulty will never be resolved by a given system of correlations between colours and symbols. To avoid the rigid monovalency of meaning which is associated with absolute correspondences between sound and vision, he proposes the need for a colour scheme to be abstracted from the film in order to create a set of audiovisual relationships which varies and develops in emotional meaning as the sound film progresses.[87] Though colour is mentioned here, Eisenstein reminds the reader that what he is saying applies equally to black and white films, whose varying tones correspond exactly to colours. Even within the limits of black and white, a single tone can not only avoid being allocated a single value, in terms of creating an image which is absolute in its nature, but it can even take on totally contradictory values, which depend only on an overall system of imagery which has been determined for the film in question.[88]

Here the relation of colour to sound becomes something which operates like a metaphor, an equivalence which can have more than one meaning, and which in some cases brings together opposite or paradoxical meanings. This idea is a development of one of the invocations from the *Statement on Sound*: '*the first experiments in sound must aim at a sharp discord with the visual images.*'[89] By avoiding absolute correspondences between colours and sounds, and thereby creating too specific meanings and emotions, Eisenstein becomes free to decide which combinations of vision and sound best suit the purpose of expressing the work's theme and idea. Simplistic colour/sound equivalences which could get in the way of the overall idea behind the work are consequently neutralised.[90]

What Eisenstein wishes to avoid is 'the ordinary colouring of a work;' he wants to work with colours as a composer works with sounds. This approach will enable him to work audiovisually, to work with 'music in colour'.[91] He describes an example of this audiovisual method in composerly terms:

> Suppose that you have black, blue and red – for the colouring of costumes, furniture, and so on. What is important when you start handling colour film is that the themes of black, blue and red should become independent expressive themes. The real black polish of boots could be elevated to the meaning of blackness, which you are then using in this case as a tragic colouring.[92]

In another example he explains that the blue colour of wallpaper should not merely remain the colour of wallpaper but that it should have 'its own emotional value, connected with a precise idea'. For Eisenstein 'there is no difference at all between working with colour and with music. Once you have understood how you should treat the musical resolution, you have laid the groundwork for handling colour too.' He then attacks the approach of synchronising the pairing of sound and image as being uncreative. The process of deliberate disassociation between these two elements should result in 'an arbitrary unity of sound and depiction'.[93]

This is the point at which audiovisual expression begins: 'the art of audiovisual montage begins at the moment when, after a period of simply reflecting obvious connections, the filmmaker starts to establish them himself, selecting such connections as reflect the essence of the content it is his aim to portray and to impress upon the spectator.'[94]

To illustrate this kind of audiovisual montage he mentions the way in which the creaking of a boot is not featured with the depiction of the boot. Instead it appears when a human face is seen, listening anxiously to this sound. Here the passive everyday association with the creaking sound and the image of the boot is severed, and the connection which is made between the anxious face and the creaking sound of the boot is the point at which audiovisual cinema becomes an effective expressive medium.[95]

The abstraction of colour in *Ivan the Terrible*

In the colour section from *Ivan the Terrible*, Eisenstein deliberately disassociates the music from the coloration of the scene. He does this by taking the dance music which is associated with the whirling dance at the beginning, and he repeats it in other sections of the scene where the dancers are not present, like during parts of Ivan the Terrible's conversation with Vladimir Staritsky. Here the music functions as a backdrop; it is not foregrounded as in the more abstract whirlings of the dance section, which Eisenstein describes as 'almost pure abstract spots. Each frame has been made almost black and white. You see the turn of gold brocade on the sleeve. The next turn is the red sleeve, the next is a hop. A splash of colour, a dance of spots.'[96] The fast editing of the close-ups of the dance gives the spectator a sense of being in the middle of the rapidly gyrating dancers. The limited range of colours used and separated from shot to shot (red, gold, blue and black) means that they themselves become abstracted, hence Eisenstein's reference to each frame in this part of the sequence becoming 'almost black and white'. This process of abstraction brings the separate elements of music, dance and colour closer together.

The same technique was used by James Joyce at the beginning of the Sirens episode in his novel *Ulysses*. As the content of this episode is strongly musical, Joyce structured it using the musical form of a fugue. In a 'prelude', before the actual 'fugue' begins, he hints at the main themes to be developed in the chapter by presenting them in an abbreviated form. This has the effect of abstracting these themes from their context, so that the reader notices in particular their colour, the words themselves and their musical attributes:

Bronze by gold heard the hoofirons, steelyringing Imperthnthn-
    thnthnthn ...
A husky fifenote blew.
Blew. Blue bloom is on the
Gold pinnacled hair.[97]

Eisenstein explains how Joyce's truncated phrases, 'these glorious old
lines', inspired his approach to editing the beginning of the colour
sequence in *Ivan the Terrible*: 'I threw spots of colour, the first dancing
colour frames of a dance in the Alexandrov sloboda – abstractly, like a
dance of colours – into the beginning of the episode so that the golden
horde of *oprichniki* could later arise from the gold and change into the
theme of golden majesty and the wisdom of heavenly azure. ...'[98]
Eisenstein points out that what is important is that the colours here 'are
torn away from their original association with an object'.[99] This process
was discovered through chance by one of the pioneers of abstraction in
art, the Russian painter Kandinsky. When he saw one of his paintings, on
its side in a particularly strong evening light, he was struck by its
overwhelming effect. He realised that this impression was due to the fact
that he was unable to make out its subject: his painting's colours had
become separated from the objects with which they had been associated,
and the result was an involuntary abstract painting. In addition Kandinsky
associated this abstraction with music: it was at a performance of the
prelude to Wagner's opera *Lohengrin* that he had a strong emotional and
synaesthetic reaction to the music. He felt that the composer had realised
in music the luminosity of the twilight hour: 'the violins, the deep tones of
the basses, and especially the wind instruments at that time embodied for
me all the power of that pre-nocturnal hour. I saw all my colours in my
mind; they stood before my eyes. Wild, almost crazy lines were sketched in
front of me. ... Wagner had painted 'my hour' musically'.[100] In Eisenstein's colour sequence in *Ivan the Terrible*, something similar happens. In
describing his articulation of colours in this sequence dominated by dance,
he refers to them almost synaesthetically, in musical terms:

At first all the colour themes are tied up in a knot. Then the red
theme is gradually teased out, then the black, then the blue ... the
red theme begins with a red sleeve; it is repeated with the red
background of candles; when Vladimir Andreyevich (Staritsky)
goes to his death, the theme is picked up by the red carpet, which
is cut up by the set and breaks off at the door. You need to
distance yourself from the various red objects, take their overall

redness and combine the objects according to their common feature. The Tsar's red shirt also works there in its hue in a certain section.[101]

Colour leitmotifs in *Ivan the Terrible*

These themes work in a similar way to Wagner's themes or leitmotifs, which are also associated with various symbolic elements in his music dramas. Eisenstein cites an example of how Wagner uses a musical leitmotif which works audiovisually:

> When a sword is mentioned in Wagner's *Die Walküre*, the theme of the sword is played in the music. There is a part in Act One where a sword is struck into a tree, and this sword must be pulled out at the end. And just as the hero approaches the sword, the orchestra starts playing particular elements of the theme of the sword. And at the end, when he pulls this sword out, the theme is played in its entirety.[102]

In Eisenstein's case the themes are associated with colours. In the sequence in colour from *Ivan* they function like colour leitmotifs, which underline meanings which are invisible but present. In response to a question from a student Eisenstein points out that here 'the red supplies an ominous theme and acts as blood.'[103] In Kandinsky's case the process of abstraction produces a dance of colours and shapes whose meanings are unattainable, whereas Eisenstein uses abstraction to create meaning. It was this lack of perceptible meaning which he believed diminished the effectiveness of Kandinsky's work. When commenting on an excerpt from the painter's music and colour theatre composition *The Yellow Sound*, Eisenstein states that 'in such confusion and vagueness' he eventually senses something very hard to define clearly, what he calls 'a core of mysticism'.[104] Nevertheless there *is* ambiguity in Eisenstein's use of colour, as he uses it to simultaneously express meaning and emotion. When he uses a specific progression of colours, it 'acquires an imagist significance and takes upon itself the task of expressing emotional shades'. However, these 'shades' are metaphorical ('imagist') nuances, which share some of the lack of clearly articulated meaning in evidence in Kandinsky's abstractions. The 'emotional shades' of his directed progression of colours invariably bring Eisenstein to their musical equivalent: 'the colour scale, whose laws of development permeate the objective appearance of coloured phenomena, will be an exact replica – in its own sphere – of the musical score emotionally colouring the events.' He explains this statement by providing a detailed account of

the workings of a counterpoint of music, action and colour in an audiovisual film sequence:

> the theme expressed in colour *leitmotifs* can, through its colour
> score and with its own means, unfold an inner drama, weaving its
> own pattern in the contrapuntal whole, crossing and recrossing the
> course of action, which formerly music alone could do with full
> completeness by supplementing what could not be expressed by
> acting or gesture; it was music alone that could sublimate the inner
> melody of a scene into thrilling audiovisual atmosphere of a
> finished audiovisual episode.[105]

Colour in opera and theatre: Eisenstein and Kandinsky

The progress of the abstracted colours in an audiovisual film becomes like
a musical progression, which is determined by the filmmaker in a 'colour
score'. This synaesthetic analogy enables Eisenstein to understand the
sophistication of Prokofiev's talent as a composer of music for film. He
points out that 'any composer can translate the rustle of leaves into his
music'. However he describes Prokofiev's exceptional abilities in terms of
his colour-to-sound synaesthesia: he could 'translate the rhythm of a shot's
yellow tone into the accompanying musical tone'.[106] Eisenstein's continued use of synaesthesia, whether he uses it conceptually or
involuntarily, suggests that artists like Scriabin and Kandinsky did have
some influence on him. Though he is disparaging about Scriabin's
solipsism and egomania, the way in which this composer combines an
orchestral score and a coloured light score in his symphonic tone poem
Prometheus (1910) seems nevertheless to have influenced Eisenstein's
approach to combining music and theatre lighting in his 1940 production
of Wagner's *Die Walküre*, at the Bolshoi Theatre. Though he had to cope
with a greatly reduced register of colours, due to technical problems, he
describes how he managed somehow to achieve a certain level of
audiovisual expression with the limited means at his disposal.[107] In one of
the scenes (*Wotan's Farewell*) he manages to light the stage a metallic
bronze colour, which changes fluidly into silver. Then, 'with the embrace
in the music, it suddenly changes into the deepest, lyrical blue...'
Eisenstein also describes Wagner's score for *Die Walküre* in visual terms, it
'is not too rich in its coloration, but it flares up, burns, bathed in light,
organically and in the spirit of movement within the music'. His
description of one of the character's leitmotifs at one point in the music
drama is totally synaesthetic: 'in the Magic Fire, Loge's theme runs like a
thread of blue through the purple of fire, the underlying element.'[108]

Eisenstein vividly evokes the technical difficulties involved in matching his stage lighting score with Wagner's music. The stage electrician's face is begrimed and perspiring as he does everything he can to match the assistant director's moving finger, which, like an orchestral conductor he moves 'in time to the score, synchronously with the frenzied orchestra, now wailing, now seething, now roaring, now mellifluous as it reaches the finale'.[109] However, as already noted, Eisenstein is disparaging about Kandinsky's theatre and music composition *The Yellow Sound*. He is dismissive of the painter's attempts to use synaesthetic techniques in his work: 'this "Yellow Sound" is a programme for staging the author's vague perceptions of the interplay of colours understood as music, of the interplay of music understood as colours, of the interplay of people ... not understood at all.'[110]

In this 'stage composition' Kandinsky's musical background as an amateur pianist and 'cellist enabled him to be quite specific about the music he imagined for certain sections, without using staff notation. At one point in the work he describes the music as being stormy and harsh, featuring insistently repeated A flats, A's and B's. In another part of the work (also quoted by Eisenstein in his 'Colour and Meaning' chapter from *The Film Sense*), Kandinsky describes an audiovisual counterpoint between the music in his orchestra and the light on the stage, involving a dull yellow illumination which fills the stage. It increases in intensity, until the entire stage is lit in bright yellow. At the same time this increasing intensity of yellow light has been matched by the music which moves down lower and gets progressively darker.[111] Here Kandinsky describes his imagined music in synaesthetic terms, making an equivalence between low notes and darkness, contrasting with the increasing light on the stage. These contrapuntal combinations of sound and colour from 1912 are conceptually not too far from Eisenstein's experiments with Wagner's *Die Walküre*, at the Bolshoi Theatre in 1940, in his 'synthesis of sound and colour', which he called 'chromophonic counterpoint' and a 'chromophonic combination of streams of music and light'.[112]

Line, dance and colour

As well as being concerned with combining music with colour, Kandinsky had a longstanding interest in the synthetic properties of the line. In 1920 he put forward the idea of using what he called 'the movement of line' to establish a link with the movement of the human body. This concept involved inventing a form of notation for dance of various kinds, both traditional and modern, by transferring 'line into the movement of the body and movement of the body into line'. Amidst the profusion of modern dance studios which flourished in Moscow in the early 1920s, Kandinsky believed that dance or the art of movement was to be one of the main sources of a new type of synthetic art.[113] This new form of art would be a further development of Wagner's *Gesamtkunstwerk*, but with dance and movement as a significant component.

Years later, in 1946, in an article about how he learned to draw, Eisenstein states that drawing and dancing 'take their root from the same impulse'. He tells with delight how a reviewer had described his drawings of people 'which had been put on to paper "as if they were dancing."' Echoing Kandinsky's connection between dance and the line, he proudly mentions that the critic had seen the line of his drawing as 'the trace of a dance'.[114] In 1947, in a lecture to his student directors, Eisenstein uses the concept of a line to explain the way he uses colour in the colour sequence from *Ivan the Terrible*. Here he uses line to demonstrate movement in time, a dance of colours related to the dance which is featured in this sequence. In his description the lines of colour become lines of music, which result in a multi-coloured polyphony: 'a golden line is swallowed up by a black one. Parallel to this, a red line expands and a blue one starts somewhere. This is a typical polyphony, with many voices.'[115]

Colour harmonies and colour lines

However, amidst his polyphonic analogy, Eisenstein remembers the importance of the vertical, harmonic factor in this music of colours, when he mentions the colour content of individual frames: 'as regards the colour tonality of individual frames, each time it is connected to the principle of a chord. Take shot 76 (in *Ivan*), for example; the gold has been practically devoured: the black has grown, and the blue has only just started and the frame must be balanced internally.'[116] Here Eisenstein is analysing the succession of film frames as a series of colour compositions, each one comprising a variety of colour harmonies. In the late nineteenth century, the French painter Edouard Vuillard, noted for his striking colour compositions, also thought of his work in a similarly synaesthetic way. In his journal, in August 1890, he wrote of his aim to conceive of a painting as a set of chords, thereby distancing himself from any naturalistic approach to his work.[117] This is an earlier form of Eisenstein's technique of disassociating colour from objects in order to use it to express both meaning and emotion, instead of avoiding the issue of colour in cinema by defaulting to a naturalistic representation: 'what must be "separated" in the present instance are the colouring of an object and its "colour sound," which form an inseparable whole in our notion of colour.' This 'colour sound' then becomes an effective way of expressing emotion and meaning. Echoing Vuillard, Eisenstein states that 'the impact of the expressive means proceeds in chords'. However, so that it can function not just as a vertical colour harmony, but horizontally over time, the 'colour sound' becomes a *line* of development of emotion and meaning. To clarify this process, Eisenstein again makes use of an analogy involving counterpoint, but not in terms of a multi-coloured polyphony. This time he compares the line of colour in an audiovisual film with the line of music: 'the "colour line" is much more difficult to feel and to follow through the "line" of object representations although it permeates the latter as does the "line" of music.' Here two simultaneous but different processes of abstraction of 'object representations' are taking place, one which is musical, and a related one which is to do with colour. Consequently there are three lines of development for the audiovisual filmmaker to consider: the line of object representations, of music and of colour. To these three lines Eisenstein adds two more independent lines of sound, for dialogue, and sound effects. He also explains that the line of music in itself can be subdivided into the different instrumental parts or lines in the orchestral score for the music.[118] So in this analogy there are a *minimum* of five lines of possible independent development in an audiovisual film. If his analogy of colour in film as consisting of multiple 'voices' were to be included, then even more contrapuntal lines would need to be added to this polyphonic analogy. But confusion can be caused by mixing Eisenstein's analogies; he applies each one to a specific case. For example he also uses another synaesthetic analogy to demonstrate the relation of colour to *tempo* in an audiovisual film. Eisenstein explains that an entire film cannot be sustained by using only one colour, as colour in cinema is ambiguous and mobile, like music. A pale blue cannot be sustained for a whole film: 'there is bound to be the same division as there is in music: andante, which you resolve in pale blue, say; and allegro, in red and black.'[119]

Eisenstein on Disney and colour

In analysing Disney's treatment of colour, Eisenstein compares the drawn line not to dance but to melody. He believes that Disney's most valuable contribution to audiovisual cinema 'has been his skill at superimposing the 'drawing' of a melody on top of a graphic drawing', which he feels is unsurpassed by anyone: 'he has an incomparable feel for an intonational gesture in music, and he can weave this gesture into the outline of his figures.' However Eisenstein remarks that when Disney starts working in colour there is no corresponding change in his technique, he just colours in the outlines of his cartoons, everything remains the same, 'except that it is now in colour'. Nevertheless, Eisenstein notices that Disney attempted some correspondences between colour and sound in his film *Bambi*, albeit unsuccessfully. His conclusion is that Disney cannot synchronise colour and music in his work.[120] He also points out that the drawing of his back-ground landscapes in his colour films is poor, unlike the excellent graphic quality of his figures. This discrepancy results in an inorganic separation of figure and ground, which in turn upsets the organic unity between the music and the image.[121]

Eisenstein as an audiovisual composer

As has been shown above, when Eisenstein writes about his audiovisual method and his approach to making sound films, he frequently expresses himself in composerly terms. Perhaps it would be more accurate to state that he works like an *audiovisual* composer. When he describes his audio-visual working method, the phenomenon of synaesthesia is usually present. Even when he writes of his work on pre-sound film montage, he uses a synaesthetic analogy involving music and film, referring (as was mentioned earlier) to the '"score" of what was "being sung" within us'. He believes that no montage can be built unless there is an 'inner melody' according to which the audiovisual correspondence is composed.[122] At the same time, when music and film are both present he underlines the importance of not replicating one means of expression in the other. If film replicates music, or music replicates film, then the effectiveness of both media will be diminished, 'just as the expressiveness of the profile will be lost by encasing it with parallel lines'.[123] This is why Eisenstein feels that the relationship between film and music should involve a degree of complexity, but at the same time there has to be something in common between the two media, otherwise confusion would be the result of the audiovisual combination. In making this statement, Eisenstein is indirectly describing the fundamental principle of musical counterpoint: the combin-ation of separate lines of melody which are held together by common motifs and harmonies. When he analyses the way a sequence from *Ivan the Terrible* (showing Ivan at Anastasia's coffin) is structured audiovisually, he uses a sort of graphic musical score in which the music and sonic elements are shown on the same level of equality as the visual elements (Fig.3). He calls this type of audiovisual notation a 'polyphonic chart'. The various interweaving lines of spoken and sung voices, of visual depictions of the characters and the setting in this scene are collectively labelled 'orchestration'. Eisenstein breaks down the passage of time into the elements which are present in a shot, or in part of a shot. In his notation of this scene he uses hatching to highlight the counterpoint of spoken and sung voices, which he terms 'the *combined* sound of several audial lines'.[124] He uses cross-hatching to show the visual elements of the audiovisual counterpoint, thus making it clear when more than one significant element appears in a shot at the same time. Interestingly, the chart as Eisenstein has notated it does not correspond with the Criterion version of the film. The order of shots is different and his analysis is much simpler than the montage in this version. However the *principle* of these interweaving visual and sonic elements remains the same in this scene, and its expressive audiovisual effect is undeniable.

Eisenstein is also clearly working as an audiovisual composer in a different way, through a composer, in his collaboration with Sergei Prokofiev. When Yevfrosinia Staritskaya, Ivan the Terrible's aunt, is singing a lullaby to Vladimir, her son, Eisenstein adds a double meaning to the innocent traditional words of the song. The simple lyric tells of a beaver washing itself in the Moscow River and climbing up a hill to dry itself. It looks around in case there are hunters around who want to kill it for its fur. Eisenstein wanted Staritskaya to start the lullaby with the folk melody. Then, as she thinks of her ambition that her son Vladimir replace Ivan and become Tsar of all the Russias, she changes the mood of the song, so that it gradually becomes an incitement to murder. The beaver is paralleled with the Tsar. The hunter becomes the Tsar's murderer and metaphorically takes the beaver's pelt to wear it. Eisenstein describes how Prokofiev followed his precise instructions with regard to how the music should reflect the psychological subtext supplied by the evil Staritskaya. The composer produced the desired effect: 'and when Yevfrosinia sings, and the music echoes her with unbelievable force, and when additionally the orchestra plays Ivan's theme, the effect of this piece is instantly horrifying.'[125] This audiovisual collaboration is a good example of music providing '*a sharp discord with the visual images*', one of the techniques proposed in the *Statement on Sound*.[126] It is also another good example of music being used to supply a change in mood, which would otherwise be difficult for the audience to perceive. Serafima Birman's performance of Staritskaya's role at this point is greatly assisted by the introduction of Ivan's theme into the lullaby. The use of music in this way prompted Eisenstein to tell his students that 'music is acting by other means'.[127]

Before the 'The Battle on the Ice'

Probably the best known in-depth analysis of audiovisual technique is Eisenstein's 33-page analysis in his book *The Film Sense*. He deals with twelve shots lasting a total of 85 seconds, representing the tense calm

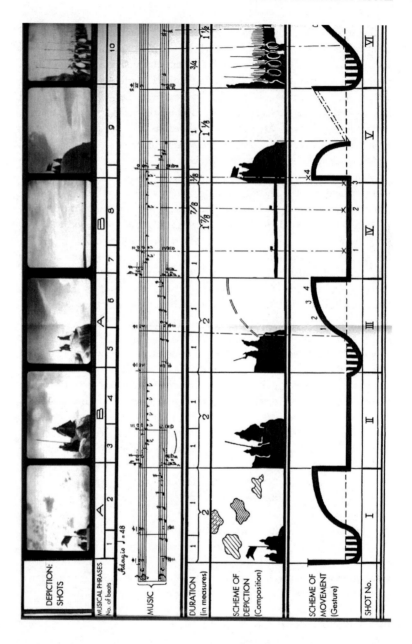

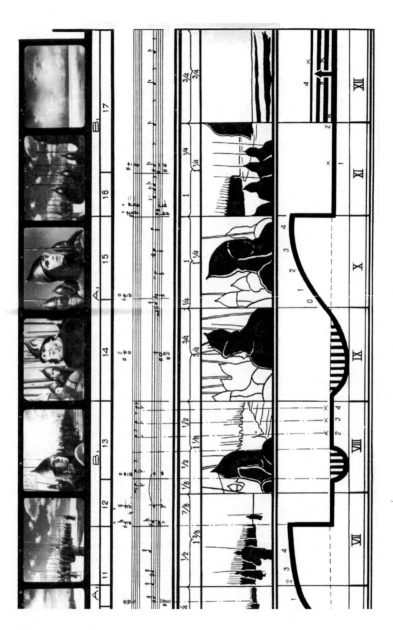

Fig.20 (a and b) Eisenstein's diagram of his audiovisual analysis of the sequence before 'The Battle on the Ice' from *Alexander Newsky* (1938).

before the 'The Battle on the Ice' in *Alexander Nevsky*. This analysis is accompanied by a pull-out page which on one side features the twelve stills and the piano version of the orchestral score by Prokofiev. On the other side is a diagram where Eisenstein shows how they are combined in the film (Fig.20). Parallel to these, he has added the schematised drawings of the contents of each shot, the 'diagram of pictorial composition', together with the lengths of the shots in measures, and a 'diagram of movement', which shows the dynamic audiovisual line developing through this sequence. Above the music notation he has also added a layer showing the structure of Prokofiev's music in relation to the measures, labelled 'music phrases'. Eisenstein explains the advantage of choosing this section from *Alexander Nevsky*: there is little significant motion in each shot – they are almost like stills, and so their effect can be reproduced relatively easily in this type of comparative diagram. The exception to this is the first shot which fades in, an effect which he acknowledges cannot be adequately shown in his diagram. In addition Eisenstein has had to modify the music notation so that the position of the notes in each measure matches the various visual accents in each shot. The notes are arranged in this way so that he can demonstrate the tremendous precision of the audiovisual synthesis in this series of shots, especially in terms of its timing.[128]

Synchronisation and timing

When comparing the diagram with the Criterion DVD edition of the film, some discrepancies appear, notably the accents at the beginning of measures 3, 5 and 7 arrive a beat earlier than is shown in the diagram. Another discrepancy arises as a result of a subjective impression, rather than a factual difference between the audiovisual diagram and the film. For me, the last note of measure 12, the eighth-note, becomes directly linked to the soldier Vasilisa's face, shown in Shot VIII, whereas for Eisenstein it is the chord at the beginning of measure 13 which 'has the "impact" of a full fusion with the close-up'.[129] Another subjective discrepancy occurs in Shot VIII. For Eisenstein the reflections of the sun on the helmets of the receding line of soldiers accompany the four eighth-notes in measure 13, whereas for me this audiovisual link does not happen. Similarly, Eisenstein explains that in Shot IV there are two flags, while the corresponding music for this shot, in measures 7 and 8, features four eighth-notes. He goes on to say that the eye seems to pass the two flags twice. In this way the front line of troops appears to be twice as long as what we really see in the frame. Moving left to right, the eye associates the eighth-notes with the flags. The two remaining eighth-notes lead the eye beyond the right-hand edge of the frame. This enables us to imagine that this line of troops extends there indefinitely.[130]

This description does not match my audiovisual experience of this shot: perhaps Eisenstein's individual synaesthetic response is at work here. However, for me there *is* a direct audiovisual correspondence, as he intended, between the last eighth-note of measure 8 and the flag in shot V.

The roving eye

Eisenstein was very much aware that the experience of his audiovisual montage could vary, especially as in a static image the way the eye's attention is caught may not be the same with everyone. Consequently, an important factor in his analysis is the way the eye's movement is directed by the artist in a still picture, whether this image is a painting, a photograph, or a film shot. He explains to his students that 'a more or less normal person follows the elements as they attract him in a shot'. Taking

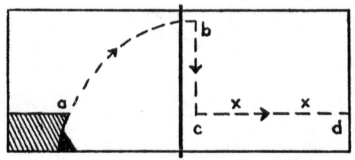

Fig.21 Eisenstein's diagram of the movement of his hand outlining the 'graph of the eye's movement'.

as an example Shot III, he acknowledges that not everyone's eye would be drawn first to the figure of Nevsky standing on the rock at the left of the frame. But he felt that 90 per cent of spectators would see the image in this manner.[131] In his diagram in 'Vertical Montage', he uses arrows and a dotted line to provide a 'graph of the eye's movement' to show the path the spectator's gaze would follow from Shot III to Shot IV, moving inexorably from left to right (Fig.21). In practice I find that this doesn't happen, as in this shot Nevsky turns to look to the soldier next to him, and my eye follows his eye-line leftwards. If this were more of a *still* shot, the eye would probably be directed in a continuous upward curve to the right, as Eisenstein had intended, as it would not be distracted by Nevsky turning to look to the left. Nevertheless the strong *'fall of the eye downwards'* at the beginning of Shot IV is still present, given the considerable contrast in composition between Shots III and IV.[132] Another factor (and perhaps an unfortunate effect of Eisenstein's detailed analysis) is that one finds oneself trying out his way of seeing this sequence after having read his text and explanatory diagrams.

The audiovisual accent

Eisenstein's aim is to direct the movement of the spectator's eye in specific ways across the shot. He also points out how his intentions are paralleled by Prokofiev with his music for this sequence.[133] However it becomes clear that other elements also contribute to the effectiveness of this series of shots. One of these elements is the combined audiovisual rhythm of the musical accents and the straight cuts. It is interesting to

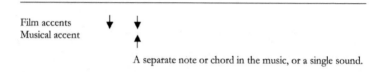

Fig.22 Diagram showing an audiovisual accent after a visible cut.

note how a strong audiovisual accent is caused by a single sound which follows just after a straight cut (Fig.22). An example is the last eighth note in measure 8, which is heard directly after the straight cut between Shots IV and V, and which, as has been already noted, coincides visually with the flag at the left of Shot V. In this type of audiovisual interaction, the sound appears to 'pick up' the visual accent after the straight cut, thereby provoking a simulated synaesthetic response in the spectator.

Missing items

Two items relating to the music for these twelve shots are missing. The first item is missing from the music in the film: the five repeated G sharp eighth-notes in measures 16 and 17 are inaudible.[134] This omission does not have a negative effect on the quality of the music or the film, or the interaction between them. The second item is missing from the *music notation* in Eisenstein's parallel analysis. He has used a piano reduction of Prokofiev's score, so that it can be read more easily for the purpose of comparison with the visual elements in his diagram. In his 'diagram of movement' for Shot V, Eisenstein traces the descending motion of the music which follows the line of descent of the rock at the left of the shot, and he points out that the arc here does not ascend, but goes down. This movement entirely matches the movement of the music, in which a clarinet moves down against the violins playing tremolo.[135] However, when I listen to the music for this part of the film, I hear in the orchestral texture a simultaneously *rising* figure for strings. It is clear that Prokofiev has drawn his 'sound image' not only from the descending line of the rock, but also from the rising line of the cloud above it in Shot V. In his analysis Eisenstein attaches a great deal of importance to the descending line in the music and image in Shot V, especially in terms of the unifying effect of the downward visual aspect which he also finds in Shots II and VIII.[137] But because he has used the probably earlier (or simplified) piano version of Prokofiev's score, he hasn't noticed the simultaneously rising line in the strings, in the final orchestral version of the music for Shot V.[138] However, the presence of this contrary motion in both Shot V and in the music does not detract from the overall effect of this sequence of shots in the actual film. In fact it underlines Prokofiev's skill in making an effective synaesthetically-derived sound image, what Eisenstein described as his 'striking talent for creating images in music'.[139]

The movement line
Eisenstein's audiovisual analysis of the sequence before the 'The Battle on the Ice' provides a useful practical clarification of what he means when he refers to a line of movement. In the text which accompanies his audiovisual diagram he demonstrates how this line follows a variety of contours: graphic, tonal, and in depth, thereby unifying the wide variety of shots in this sequence. Shots III and IV have a graphic contour, a line of movement which Eisenstein explains can be described by moving your hand through the air. Shot I has a tonal contour, as it fades in from a black screen; its line of movement represents a gradually increasing brightness. Shots VI and VII together move perspectively inwards into the picture space. Eisenstein indicates this movement in depth using a dotted line (Fig.23). He relates these three different types of visual movement to each other, and considers them to be part of a continuous line of development.[140] This line of movement is multidimensional in terms of space, and because it moves it also encompasses time, which Eisenstein calls the 'fourth dimension'.[141] The concept of the movement line enables him to demonstrate how he had achieved an audiovisual counterpoint in this sequence which totally corresponds in its pictorial nature with the nature of the movement of the music.[142]

Eisenstein's mention of the pictorial nature of the movement line is derived from art, in this case European art of different periods. He shows

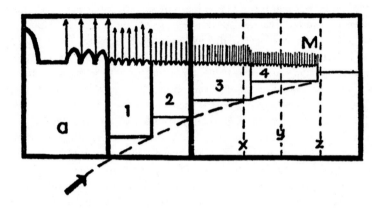

Fig.23 Eisenstein's diagram of the movement into depth from Shots VI to VII.

how the line in depth is found in a variety of paintings, for example Ghirlandaio's *The Adoration of the Shepherds*, where a road moves from the background to the foreground and features two temporally separated events: the voyage of the Magi and the adoration of the shepherds. The tonal line is found in Rembrandt's varying levels of density in his chiaroscuro. The graphic line moves from form to form in the paintings of Delacroix. Eisenstein found these pictorial aspects of composition very useful in analysing his sequence of relatively still shots, as the movement line is a compositional device which is common to painting, music and film. It is therefore ideal as a technique for unifying music with image in the context of an audiovisual film.[143]

Landscape and emotion
Certain elements in this tense pre-battle sequence are derived from the nonindifferent relation between the landscape and its inhabitants, which Eisenstein experienced with such intensity in Mexico. Here his movement line links visually distinct shots, producing a generalised graph of tension which moves from nature to the Russian soldiers, then back to nature again. Prokofiev's music underlines these links with his use of long held-note harmonies. These suggest the epic scale and the flat endless expanse evoked by the frozen lake, whether it appears in the shot or not. The strongly horizontal character of the music is synaesthetically related to the nature of the landscape; it becomes a means of showing what is invisible in most of the shots, but is nevertheless there beyond the frame. In addition, Prokofiev's repeated notes underline this flat expanse, and at the same time suggest intermittent heart beats evoking the tense expectancy of

the soldiers before the battle. Prokofiev's harmonies consist of suspended and unresolved chords which oscillate from one tonal area to another. In the first eight measures he uses a microtonal shift (the enharmonic change from Eb to D#) to heighten the sense of uncertainty. This harmonic ambiguity is framed by string tremolos, which are used to create tension. A technique dating back to the Baroque period in Western classical music, the tremolo was also frequently employed to generate suspense and excitement in music for silent films.

Orchestration

Eisenstein explains that what he had achieved in terms of 'audiovisual solutions' in *Alexander Nevsky*, like the sequence before the 'The Battle on the Ice', had their origin in the 'Odessa Mist' sequence from *The Battleship Potemkin*.[144] He gives an evocative description of a montage progression of misty scenes of Odessa's harbour becoming increasingly clear, until Vakulinchuk's prostrate corpse appears, with a flickering candle in his hands.[145] This candle acts as a symbolic fuse for the uprising, culminating in the seizing of Odessa. In this description Eisenstein makes extensive use of musical audiovisual metaphors to explain how he has assembled this sequence. He describes a buoy as a 'black mass', which for him corresponds audiovisually to a massively solid chord. Here is an example of a synaesthetic association, in this case visual to aural, which takes on a consciously symbolic meaning, thereby producing an audiovisual metaphor.

He then outlines the various motifs which appear in the sequence, which he associates with the elements of earth, air and water: the black hulks of the ships (an extension of the black mass of the buoy), the airy mists, the lead-grey surface of the water and grey sails, and the hard rock of the embankment. He describes these elements as being 'echoed by the mutual play of purely *tonal* and *textural* combinations', he 'sees' them as melodic lines which flow together into a final static chord, Vakulinchuk's corpse. These visual melodic lines interweave as in a counterpoint, moving from background to foreground and vice-versa. They are arranged so that variously they highlight each other, or appear in contrast or opposition to one another. Each melodic visual line also follows its own path of movement: as the mist becomes weaker, shapes become heavier and more concrete. The theme of the water which turns silver provides an audiovisual transition into a white sail. Rhythm is also present in this visual music of forms, in the measured length of each shot, and in the barely perceived '"melodic" rocking' of the buoy and the ships at anchor.[146] Then, almost inaudibly, Eisenstein 'hears' the theme of fire which enters with the flickering candle in the hands of Vakulinchuk. These musical elements are not at all present in Edmund Meisel's orchestral score for this sequence. They are present in Eisenstein's inner ear. They resemble a description of what a composer might hear before setting down this inner music using notation. In Eisenstein's inwardly heard score for this sequence there is counterpoint, modulation, chords, rhythm (of shots, and within the shot), all providing him with a sense of musical progression for this sequence. Finally, he mentions the *orchestration* of these various musical elements, its function being to unify the simultaneity as well as the progressive action in this sequence. He 'hears' the textures of the musical elements described above as being like an orchestration of 'winds and strings, wood and brass!' Eisenstein also uses the idea of orchestration when actors are performing in an audiovisual sequence. To the orchestration of the elements mentioned above (in his analysis of the visual part of the Odessa mists sequence) he adds the soundtrack, and the actors' performance. These elements he describes as comprising 'the range of instruments in my orchestra'. They make up what he calls the 'total performance ... of the synthesising sound film'. As he is delineating an 'orchestration' of audiovisual elements, the music and sound on his soundtrack can themselves become instrumental lines in the counterpoint of the audiovisual whole.[147] Eisenstein uses the musical technique of orchestration in order to highlight at any point the 'content, meaning, theme and idea of the film'. At the same time he uses orchestration to provide a unity of the expressive means he is using in the film. Orchestration balances 'the whole so as to prevent any particular, individual element from undermining the unity of the *ensemble*, the unity of the compositional whole'. He deliberately uses the word 'ensemble', as he aims to extend the technique of ensemble acting to 'orchestrate' the range of the diverse and expressive elements he has at his disposal in audiovisual cinema. He intends to use each one of them in isolation and in combination where appropriate, to their maximum expressive effect within the 'unity of the compositional whole'. Eisenstein also thinks in terms of orchestration as a means to attain a unity between the visual and the auditory in audiovisual cinema. He noticed that in black and white film the most harmonious blending between sound and vision was obtained through various gradations or nuances of light. Just as movement in film corresponds with rhythm, visual texture has its auditory counterpart in the texture of sound or timbre. Consequently he concludes that as light nuances in black and white film are the closest to being like colour in colour film, audiovisual unity would only be fully realised in the colour film. Again he uses the musical technique of orchestration to explain his conclusion: it is only with colour film that 'complete visual orchestration will rise to the level of the wealth of orchestration in music'.[148]

Orchestration: sound long-shots and sound close-ups

As noted above, Eisenstein was very much aware of the role of orchestration in music, involving the use of appropriate instruments to place aspects of the musical material in the foreground, thus placing the other elements into the background. As he was thinking audiovisually, he saw a visual parallel of this aspect of orchestration in the use of camera distances and the resultant framing of shots. When he provides a description of a prisoner in court, he imagines the filming of this scene from the point of view of this person, who experiences the adverse reactions of his neighbours around him, seated in the courtroom. In his montage plan for this scene Eisenstein includes their distant whisperings, in the form of a 'sound long-shot'.[149] Then, taking a short extract from a poem by Pushkin, Eisenstein shows how the poet uses sound and distance in a night scene involving a nocturnal disappearance:

> But no one knew just how or when
> She vanished. A lone fisherman
> In that night heard the clack of horses' hoofs,
> Cossack speech and a woman's whisper.[150]

Eisenstein points out that the dramatic effect of Pushkin's description could be shown in three shots, each having a different camera distance in terms of sound, starting with a 'sound long-shot', and ending with a 'close-up' in sound:

1. The clack of horses' hoofs.
2. Cossack speech.
3. A woman's whisper.[151]

For Eisenstein sound and vision are synaesthetically part of the same 'mental lens', which has the capacity of enlarging or diminishing scale. Sound can be adjusted simply by changing the distance between the microphone and the sound source, just like a film camera can be moved, or a lens adjusted, to change what is needed to be in the frame.[152]

Reverse orchestration

Prokofiev also became interested in the expressive possibilities to be derived from modifying the distance between the microphone and the sound source, in his case the musician or musicians. This interest arose when the orchestral players were placed too close to the microphone for a recording of a section of his score for *Alexander Nevsky*. Though the resulting distortion of the sound was strictly speaking a mistake, Prokofiev decided that this error could be put to good use to evoke intentionally disagreeable sounds, like those made by the German fanfares as heard by the citizens of Pskov.[153]

In 1938, just before he had started work on composing the music for *Alexander Nevsky*, the composer had visited Hollywood and had studied carefully the musical techniques used for American sound films, and especially the new technology for recording sound. Tatiana Egorova points out that this experience would have given him the confidence to experiment further with microphone distances. His experiments led to what could be termed 'reverse orchestration', whereby instruments normally considered loud and dominant in the orchestra could be made weak and soft, and vice-versa. By adjusting microphone distances Prokofiev could make a trombone or other brass instruments sound weak and helpless, and a bassoon sound big and formidable. According to Egorova this innovation led directly to the developing of multi-channel stereo recordings.[154] It was also a sonic parallel to Eisenstein's use of a 28mm wide-angle lens to make an everyday object like a typewriter fill the screen.

Colour, cinema, theatre and opera
Just as Eisenstein puts forward the idea of using the analogy of camera distances to make sound dramatically effective in cinema, he uses a synthesis of colour and music to create a dramatic explosion at the very start of the colour sequence in *Ivan the Terrible, Part 2*. He precedes this sequence with a static image in black and white of the chalice which has been used to poison Ivan's young bride. Then there is a sudden explosion of the colourful dancers leaping on to the screen, at the same time as Prokofiev's loud and energetic dance music.[155] This is a *coup de théâtre*, and Eisenstein's subsequent use of colour in this sequence is very theatrical, if not operatic. Red, blue, silver and gold in turn permeate the screen, like full stage lighting. He also uses black as a colour, the black cloaks of the *oprichniki* gradually turning the film itself back into black and white. Colours are mostly non-naturalistic: highlights on faces are sometimes blue, and we see Vladimir's face turning from pink to dark blue then back to pink. There is no attempt at illusion.

Similarly throughout *Ivan the Terrible* Eisenstein avoids the cinematic illusion of the shot/reverse shot editing patterns normally used for dialogues. Instead, as in a play or an opera, we see one face dramatically approaching another, or both figures in their stage-like setting, in a long-shot. Eisenstein is not interested in invisible editing, the idea that good camera work is unobtrusive. He does not aim to be an invisible director: in a good colour film the spectator should be aware of colour, and the music or sounds used should be consciously audible. He does not believe in 'invisible' colour or 'inaudible' music. He thought that such techniques are just abrogations of artistic responsibility in the practice of making films. They demonstrate a director's inability to be creative in the face of the wide possibilities afforded by the variety of expressive means available in the organic audiovisual film.[156]

In the chapter *Organic Unity*, we saw how Eisenstein was profoundly influenced by Meyerhold's audiovisual approach to theatre. For both directors, music was an integral part of dramaturgy. Eisenstein states that

> music lends to acting or a situation, a scene or a pause in development that irresistible power of emotional impact which, out of all the means of dramaturgic expressiveness, is at that particular time the most effective in giving vent to the dramaturgic moment, the link in the chain of the dramaturgic whole.[157]

In terms of effectiveness of expression, he also regards colour 'as an element of the film's dramaturgy', its application being similar to that of music. In addition, he extends this concept to point out that *all* techniques of cinematic expression should 'participate in the making of a film as elements of dramatic action'.[158]

Before their collaborations on *Alexander Nevsky* and *Ivan the Terrible*, both Eisenstein and Prokofiev had worked audiovisually in the theatre. Eisenstein had started in theatre, and before directing *Ivan the Terrible* we saw earlier how he had directed a production of Wagner's opera *Die Walküre* in 1940. Before collaborating with Eisenstein on *Alexander Nevsky*, Prokofiev had already composed three operas (of which two had been produced) and six ballets. Consequently both artists had considerable experience in audiovisual forms, and in Eisenstein's case he always regarded his films, even as early as *The Strike*, as being audiovisual in conception. Given the close connections both artists had with theatre and opera, it is not surprising that *Ivan the Terrible* is so markedly operatic in nature. The stylised and slow pace of the acting, the staging which often brings to mind the large-scale sets for operas, the paintings on the walls like paintings on theatre sets, and the use of music as part of the *mise-en-scène*, all point to the influence of opera. Prokofiev even re-used the melody from Kutuzov's aria in Scene 10 of his opera *War and Peace*, for the chorus which accompanies the soldiers each placing a coin in the bowl before the storming of Kazan.[159]

Eisenstein's audiovisual terminology and music

With regard to audiovisual terminology, Eisenstein uses various terms like 'tonal' or 'line', which may be applied to both music *and* the visual arts, and which mean specific things in each domain. As has been demonstrated, his meaning when he uses these words changes radically, depending on whether his context is musical or visual. He tends to describe the audiovisual combination in musical terms. For example, when he describes a successful audiovisual scene, he explains that it is music alone that can 'sublimate the inner melody of a scene into thrilling audiovisual atmosphere of a finished audiovisual episode'.[160] He also recommends to a student the use of musical terms in order to clarify elements which involve movement in a film, including the use of colour.[161] The resultant fluidity of meaning in Eisenstein's use of musical terms is due to the innovative nature of his subject: he is writing one of the first texts to explain in great detail how the audiovisual can work in cinema. He is dealing with a subject which is new and has not yet evolved a generally accepted terminology. The advantage of his plurality of meaning is a lack of encrusted taxonomies which can impede dynamic combinations of ideas.

The personal perceptual phenomenon of synaesthesia also has a role in Eisenstein's use of musical terminology in dealing with audiovisual cinema. His type of synaesthesia appears to be primarily aural to visual, and vice-versa. Like some synaesthetes, he assumes that most others experience something similar: for example, when they speak of pieces of music as being 'transparent' or 'dynamic', or having a 'clearly defined pattern', or 'blurry outlines'. He feels that this phenomenon happens as most people, when listening to music, see moving images of various kinds, whether they be clear or undefined, abstract or figurative. These images uniquely correspond in some way to their personal perceptions of the music they have heard.[162]

Eisenstein, colour and texture

However there is another factor which affects Eisenstein's approach to the audiovisual, and this factor is related to his sensitivity to colour and texture, as well as to the nature of colour itself. As he points out, colour in nature has an 'indefinite *status quo*', it only acquires meaning and expression through 'the conscious and volitional impulse in the one who uses it'.[163] For this reason the use of colour in cinema is of primary importance. In a film, colour behaves like music or sound, in that it is an abstraction from nature, which through its powers of association can be mobilised by the artist to create meaning and expression.

Eisenstein's visual-to-aural synaesthesia is in evidence at the end of the first line of one of his texts: 'Colour. Pure. Bright. Vibrant. Ringing'.[164] In this text devoted to colour he then asks himself when and where he came to love it. Searching his memory, he brings to mind an eruption of colours he had experienced amidst the black and white scenery of a Russian winter in a little hamlet, during the Civil War. His text is broken up into a series of shots, as in his film scenarios, and his acute visual memory a quarter of a century later also registers the textures he saw:

> Dazzling snow.
> Women stood on the snow.
> They wore short dun-coloured fur coats with a braid.
> And felt boots.
> Between the fur and the boots, I could see a strip of a sarafan.
> Woollen. Striped.
> Relentlessly bright vertical stripes.
> Lilac, orange, red and green.
> With a strip of white between.
> Another one.
> Deep blue, yellow, violet and crimson.
> Worn through, faded, and moth-eaten.[165]

Eisenstein also recalls, again synaesthetically, a colour memory from a flight in Mexico. He mentions 'the penetrating choir of pink flamingoes, standing out against the pale blue backdrop of the Gulf of Mexico'.[166] Then he describes the everyday objects in his room like a painter: 'I find it dull when there is no yellow pencil next to the blue one to set it off; no red and green striped pillow lying on the blue couch.'[167] He compares the various colours of the spines of his books on his shelves to the striped colours of the remembered sarafans, and their colours become abstracted juxtapositions:

> Dark blue, white, white, orange.
> Red, light blue, orange.
> Red, light blue, green.
> Red, red, white again.
> Black. Gold.[168]

Eisenstein revels in the unexpected cultural juxtapositions of colours and textures made by the artefacts and souvenirs he has on his walls:

> a bright ribbon of Philippine embroidery meanders across an Uzbek wallhanging ... a Mongolian stitchwork design sprawls across the dull crimson background of a wall that so advantageously sets off the whiteness of the cardboard emblems of the Day of the Dead, and the Moorish masks black with bloody wounds.[169]

The proximity on the wall of the Day of the Dead emblems and the Moorish masks stimulate in Eisenstein memories of dances of the Mexican Indians, dances which symbolise 'not the Moorish conquest of Spain, but their own enslavement by the Spanish hordes under Cortés'.[170] The juxtaposition of these colours and textures, together with their associations, has produced expression and meaning.

Another vivid colour memory, from an earlier period in Eisenstein's life is associated with his mother's womb-like bedroom and boudoir, in her apartment where they both lived. As a student he was laid up with measles, and he was lying in his mother's bed, delirious with fever. The room was decorated in pink, and the closed curtains acted like a rose-coloured filter as the sun shone through them into the room, bathing the clutter of its nineteenth-century style drapes and curtains in a bright pink light.[171] The textures of patterns of roses on the portières and brocades, together with the sunlight shining through the curtains, recall Vuillard's paintings of similar effects of light in highly patterned nineteenth-century style interiors.

Another portrayal of this period's enthusiasm for textile textures and nuances of colour, is cited elsewhere by Eisenstein. He is demonstrating the range of possible shades in black and white film, whereby a cinematographer like Tisse is able to achieve an almost palpable illusion of colour with it. Eisenstein quotes from a description by Zola (from his novel *Women's Happiness*) of a 'white sale' in a department store:

> Beneath the chaotic collapse of all these varieties of white, in this apparent mess of textiles, tumbling out of torn open boxes, there was an implied harmonic phrase: whiteness. This whiteness was followed and developed in all its tones, which appeared, grew, and blossomed in the complex orchestration of a master of fugue. Its continuous development swept up souls into an ever-expanding flight. Nothing but whiteness, but never the same white, all the

white tones vying with each other, contrasting, complementing one another, even achieving the brightness of light itself. It began with the matt whites of calico and linen, the muted whites of flannel and cotton sheets; then came the velvets, the silks, the satins in a rising scale, the white tones slowly lighting up, ending in tiny flames at the edges of the folds; and the whiteness took off with the transparency of the curtains, with the muslins it took on a lucent clarity, the guipure, lace, especially tulle, so light that they were like a note vanishing in the highest register; while in the depths of the massive alcove, loudest sang the silver tones of the pieces of oriental silk.[172]

It is a synaesthetic description like this one which prompts Eisenstein to propose a toast to Emile Zola for his masterful lessons in 'visual music'. In Zola's description he detects the influence of Chinese and Japanese painting methods and traditions, especially their musical aspects, as well as the more recent impressionist painters, whose landscapes were also influenced by the artists of the Far East. Eisenstein confirms that Zola's musical visions of actual phenomena were an important influence on his methods of producing visual music in his 'silent' films.[173]

The influence of French Symbolist theatre

The synaesthetic experiments of French Symbolist theatre in Paris were another strong audiovisual influence on Eisenstein. He specifically mentions the staging of a play by Pierre Quillard, *La Fille aux mains coupées*, performed in 1891 at the Théâtre d'Art, founded by the Symbolist poet Paul Fort, in 1890. In the form of a 'dialogue poem', this play involved a narrator, placed at the side of the stage, and actors who, veiled by a gauze curtain, moved and declaimed verses against a background of a golden panel of icon-like figures of angels, painted by Paul Séruzier.[174] In 1894, at another Symbolist theatre, the Théâtre de l'Oeuvre, in a production by Aurelien Lugné-Poe of Henri de Régnier's *La Gardienne*, the painter Vuillard used a curtain of tulle as a screen for the stage. Here the idea was that the tulle screen would 'dematerialise' the performers, whose texts were spoken by other actors in the pit.[175] In these productions it is possible to detect foreshadowings of audiovisual cinematic techniques, like voiceover narrations and dubbing.[176] However, what also interested Eisenstein was the idea that such theatre productions aimed to bring to actuality the theory of correspondences between the senses, a conceptual synaesthesia which fascinated the Symbolist artists. He mentions an extreme example of such an attempt at unifying music, stage setting, perfumes and declaimed poetry, in a production by Paul Fort of *Le Cantique des Cantiques* by J.-Napoléon Roinard, at the Théâtre des Arts, in 1910. In this work, the playwright had apparently been inspired by Rimbaud's poem *Le Sonnet des voyelles*, and studies of correspondences between the senses, like René Ghil's theory of the orchestration of words, and *The Orchestration of Perfumes* by Chardin Hardancourt.[177]

Eisenstein also mentions another Symbolist theatre production (which he does not name) from the early twentieth century, in which was attempted the composition of a 'symphony of colours supplementing the symphony of sounds'. Eisenstein finds these attempts at a synthesis of senses absurd, as he believes that such experiments go against and beyond the 'life-like and realistic qualities' of the theatre. However he affirms that what becomes anti-realist and ridiculous in the theatre becomes a powerful force of expression in cinema. He states that in theatre 'all such attempts at synthesis inevitably wreck themselves and lead only to anti-realism. Yet when these same aims are set for cinema, they not only do not lead away from realism, but actually increase the power of its realistic affect.'[178]

We have already seen an example of the effect of synaesthesia in relation to Eisenstein's editing of the 'mists sequence' in *The Battleship Potemkin*. In addition, he acknowledges the influence of what he calls Whistler's 'misty symphonies', as well as Chinese landscape painting involving mist, in his filming of the mists in Odessa harbour. He points out that Whistler, like many artists from the late nineteenth century, was inspired by Japanese art.[179] The American painter was also influenced by current Symbolist concerns with correspondences between the senses. He used musical terms for the titles he chose for several of his paintings of studies of light, some of which were misty dawn or dusk scenes set near the sea or a river.[180] Eisenstein describes how when they were filming in Odessa harbour, his cameraman Tisse heightened 'the natural tulle of real mist (with) tulle and muslin filters placed in front of the lens for washing away depth' as well as a soft focus lens, to wash away 'the edges of visual depiction'. The gauze and tulle screens of French Symbolist theatre became even more effective when they were used in cinema. For Eisenstein, 'the suite of the mist' type of filmmaking occupied a space between painting and music: '"postpainting" passing into a distinctive type of "premusic (protomusic)."' His fourth dimension, of time, pushed the painterly domain of the filming of landscape towards music: 'the suite of the mist is still painting, but a distinct type of painting that through montage already perceives the rhythm of the change of *real spans of time* and the tangible sequence of repetitions in time, that is, the elements of what in pure form is only accessible to music.' Eisenstein considers that the 'suite of the mist' sequence is in itself a stage between painting and 'the *music of audiovisual combinations* of the new cinematography'.[181] He thus describes the future of the sound or audiovisual cinema in terms of a musical analogy, one which recalls his concept of audiovisual counter-point.

Schopenhauer and music

Eisenstein's unexplained reference to 'the elements of what in pure form is only accessible to music' suggests the influence of Schopenhauer's ideas about the relationship of music to the other arts. As a young man during the Civil War he had spent much time reading Schopenhauer's philos-ophy.[182] Central to this philosopher's world view is what he calls the Will, a life force which 'is the innermost, the kernel of every particular and also of the whole. It appears in every blindly acting natural force; it also appears in the deliberate conduct of the human being.' Schopenhauer believes that the world in its multiplicity and incompleteness consists of Ideas which are material projections (or what he calls 'objectivity') of the Will. He sees the arts (except for music) as being a copy of the Ideas. But he thinks that 'Music is ... by no means like the other arts, the copy of the Ideas, but the *copy of the Will itself*, whose objectivity the Ideas are.' Schopenhauer then explains why he believes that music is above the other arts: 'the effect of music is so much more powerful and penetrating than that of the other arts, for they speak only of shadows, but it speaks of the thing itself,' in other words, the Will.[183] Therefore, music, like Ideas, is a direct objectification of the Will.

If what Eisenstein calls 'pure form' is Schopenhauer's Will, then the elements of the 'pure form' are the Ideas. In this case these Ideas are 'the rhythm of the change of *real spans of time* and the tangible sequence of repetitions in time'. These Ideas are only directly accessible to music as 'it is the same Will which objectifies itself both in the Ideas and in music.'[184]

Schopenhauer's belief in the prime importance of music in his philosophical system had a profound influence on Richard Wagner, and Eisenstein's use of musical structures, like fugue, to order both his visual and audiovisual montage, to some extent can be attributed to Schopen-hauer.[185] We have already seen how musical analogies in the form of orchestration, chords, tonality, counterpoint, fugue and so on, point to the importance of music in all of Eisenstein's work in film.

Schopenhauer's concept that all Ideas have a common source in the life-force of the Will enables the possibility of making analogies between the material world of Ideas and the spiritual world of the Will, as well as between the Ideas themselves. With regard to the phenomenon of analogy and music, Schopenhauer stated that 'since, however, it is the same Will which objectifies itself in both the Ideas and in music, though in quite different ways, there must be, not indeed a direct likeness, but yet a parallel, an analogy, between music and the Ideas whose manifestation ... is the visible world.'[186] The use of analogies and the related phenomenon of synaesthesia are central to Eisenstein's method of audiovisual composition.

Synaesthesia, symbolism and the occult traditions

The evidence of Eisenstein's interest in synaesthesia and the interaction of the senses is also present in his library. According to Hakan Lovgren, in the 1930s he began to acquire books by the Russian Symbolist poets and writers, including Viacheslav Ivanov, Andrei Bely, Valery Briusov, and Sergei Durylin.[187] A marked interest in alchemy and other occult and hermetic traditions was characteristic of artists in the Symbolist movement. However, Eisenstein gives a sardonic account of his early encounter with one of these traditions, Rosicrucianism. When he was billeted in Minsk in 1920, during the Civil War, he attended classes in the disclosures of mysterious rites, explained and presided over by Professor Zubakin, a Rosicrucian bishop practising under the name of Bogori the Second. Eisenstein tells how he was so bored that he fell asleep during the study of the occult traditions of the Cabbala, and the Arcana of the Tarot. Nevertheless he maintains that he kept awake during what he believed was the most important part of the study, the very end: 'it became clear that the initiate was being told that "there is no God for God is he". Now that was something I liked.'[188] Eisenstein also liked the textbook on the occult that was used in the classes, and which he later bought in one of the second-hand book markets in Moscow. In his library he placed it next to Eliphas Levi's *The History of Magic*, on the shelves he reserved for what he called '"the imprecise sciences", (magic, cheiromancy, and graphology, of which more elsewhere)'.[189] Eisenstein was dismissive of contemporary proponents of the occult tradition, for example the Rosicrucian movement, Rudolf Steiner, and the founder of the Theosophists, Madame Blavatsky, who had both been a passing influence on Kandinsky.[190] But to demonstrate the existence of previous attempts to unite the auditory and the visual, specifically in the form of the combination of music with colour, he quotes from Eckartshausen's book, published in 1791, the *Disclosures of Magic from Tested Experiences of Occult Philosophic Sciences and Veiled Secrets of Nature*: 'I have long been engaged in research into the harmony of all sensory impressions,' to make this phenomenon 'clearer and more perceptible'.[191] Eckartshausen explains that he built a clavichord which had glass tubes filled with varicoloured liquids, illuminated from behind by glass candles. The keys of this instrument when pressed would lift to disclose the colours, which would then be covered up again when the notes had died away. He wrote enthusiastically that his clavichord could produce 'chords composed of colours' just like 'chords are made up from musical notes'.[192] Eisenstein then quotes from Eckartshausen's *Theory of Ocular Music*, from a little poem he has written with descriptions of various notes and timbres, as well as the colours he imagines synaesthetically:

> Words: 'A homeless little orphan child'.
> Music: a doleful melody on the flute.
> Colours: Olive-green, mingled with pink and white.[193]

This description resembles an extract from a montage sequence. Here the colours could represent the child dressed in white, seen against the greenery of the countryside, which is mentioned in the next line: 'a meadow filled with flowers'. The colours are now predictably 'green, mingled with violet and pale yellow'. In the third stanza, the poem features the child singing 'plaintively, like a robin redbreast,' and the colours Eckartshausen has chosen here are more unpredictable and personal, typically synaesthetic: 'Dark blue with scarlet and yellowish green'.[194] The dark blue can be imagined as belonging to the sky, but the colours suggested by the singing are totally subjective.

Rimbaud, Baudelaire and synaesthesia

This surprising example of synaesthesia from 1791, long before such a phenomenon was acknowledged, brings Eisenstein to the much better known and more recent example of synaesthesia in Arthur Rimbaud's poem, *Le Sonnet des voyelles*, which he quotes in full. This influential sonnet is also reproduced in his essay *On Colour*, in which he points out that many forget to read beyond the first line of the poem: 'A black, E white, I red, U green, O blue.' As a result, these readers fail to understand that Rimbaud's correspondences between vowels and colours are 'conditioned by very individual forms of imagery'.[195] For example:

> A, a black corset hairy with flies
> Which buzz around the wafts of cruel stench,
> Dark gulfs; E, guileless mists and canopies,
> Spears of proud glaciers, kings white, quivering blooms;[196]

This highly personal but nevertheless extremely direct technique of synaesthetic correspondences is also used in another influential poem, entitled *Correspondances*, by Charles Baudelaire, who was the greatest literary influence on the young Rimbaud.[197] This poem became a kind of manifesto for the Symbolist movement.[198] In it Baudelaire describes the human experience of nature as crossing 'forests of symbols':

> Nature is a temple whose living pillars
> Emit intermittently a confusion of utterances;
> Man goes through it, crossing forests of symbols
> Which observe him knowingly.

Nature exists in the form of a dark and profound unity, which is paradoxically also light, and in it the senses echo one another:

> Like long echoes which from afar blend
> In a dark and deep unity, as vast as darkness,
> Vast like the night and vast like brilliant light,
> Scents, colours and sounds echo each other.[199]

Baudelaire uses synaesthesia to demonstrate this echoing:

> There are scents fresh as children's flesh,
> Sweet as oboes, green as meadows;
> – And others corrupt, rich, and triumphal,
>
> Having the expanse of things infinite,
> Like amber, musk, benjamin and incense,
> Which sing the ecstasy of the spirit and the senses.[200]

Baudelaire's examples of synaesthesia are linked to extreme emotion in the form of an 'ecstasy of the spirit and the senses'. This idea is similar to Scriabin's ambition to unite all the senses to induce a state of ecstasy in his final uncompleted composition, *Mystery*.[201] It is also like Eisenstein's analysis of the relationship of '"creative associations" born of vivid impressions' to emotion and ecstasy, leading to a transcendent state of mind where '"thought," "memory" and even … "feeling" have almost no place'.[202]

Baudelaire derived the idea of correspondences from the Swedish philosopher and mystic Emmanuel Swedenborg (1688–1772).[203] He believed that all material things were in direct correspondence to ideas in the spiritual world: 'The whole natural world corresponds to the spiritual world, not only the natural world in general but also in every particular.'

Swedenborg believed that in the human form coexisted a spiritual and a natural world: 'Consequently, whatever in his natural world, that is, in his body and its senses and actions, comes into existence from his spiritual world, that is, from his mind and its understanding and will, is said to be a correspondence thereof.'[204] It was in describing one of the states of mind that he experienced when he was under the influence of hashish that Baudelaire mentions Swedenborg and his idea of 'correspondences':

> The first object which attracts your attention becomes a symbol with meaning. Fourier and Swedenborg, one with his *analogies*, the other with his *correspondences*, become embodied in both the vegetal and the animal which you are perceiving, and, instead of teaching you by means of their voices, they indoctrinate you by form and by colour.[205]

In this fragment of text by Baudelaire, from *Les Paradis artificiels*, there are several similarities to Eisenstein's approach to cinema. The 'first object' which attracts the attention and becomes symbolic can be compared to the director's description of a close-up, a 'conjoined unity of seeing and perception – a reflection of reality, refracted through consciousness, and a reflection of reality refracted through the prism of sensual thought'.[206] Baudelaire's description of indoctrination 'by form and by colour' through the use of analogies and correspondences is similar to both Eisenstein's aims for audiovisual cinema, and the way he explains his audiovisual methods. One of these methods is directly related to his concept of 'sensual thought'. It involves reflections of reality refracted through an irrational, superstitious consciousness.

The black cat method

Eisenstein stated that he always set up his shots according to the principle of 'a black cat crossing my path'.[207] Aware that he was deeply superstitious, he complained that this predisposition greatly interfered with his life. He admitted that Friday the thirteenth, walking under a ladder, starting something on a Monday, black cats crossing his path – all these things were a problem for him. This superstition was even extended to everyday actions. The mundane act of switching off a light would suggest to him 'Departure into Darkness,' a delayed payment, 'shades of Beggardom'. He realised that this anxiety was caused by his ability to generalise instantly from the most trivial detail. This weakness became a strength in his work on a film, as he was able, from a mass of details, to select the one item which most closely realised the general idea of the whole work.[208] He points out that

> In subject and composition, I try never to limit the frame solely by the way things appear on the screen. The subject must be chosen thus, turned this way, and placed in the field of the frame so that, besides mere representation, a knot of associations results that mirrors the mood and sense of the piece. That is how the dramatic style of the frame is created. That is how the drama interweaves with the canvas of the work.[209]

Here the frame of the shot, far from being static and limiting, becomes a dynamic centre of associations and correspondences. All the technical means in cinema: light, camera angle, the process of montage, is put to work to go beyond representation to reveal 'that conceptual and emotional aspect' of what is before the lens at that particular moment, whether what is in the frame are 'passions (people, models, actors); buildings and landscapes; or skyscapes'.[210]

Eisenstein's 'black cat' method is based on the workings of his own subconscious mind, drawing on a system of direct correspondences between the daily material world and the immaterial world of thought.

Schopenhauer, correspondences and Joyce

We have seen how Eisenstein had already encountered, as a young man, a system of correspondences in the philosophy of Schopenhauer. He was also influenced by his ideas in relation to 'typage', his method of choosing actors for his films.[211] He echoes the German philosopher's belief that the world of Ideas consists of direct copies of the Will itself, when he is describing what he calls his photogenic approach to using actors. Eisenstein selected them according to the ideas their appearance suggested to audiences. Mentioning Schopenhauer, he explains that 'an idea expressed in its completeness is photogenic; that is, an object is photogenic when it corresponds most closely to the idea that it embodies.'[212] By substituting the word 'filmic' for 'photogenic', it is possible to see how Eisenstein's use of Schopenhauer's idea of correspondences was at the core of his ambition to realise an 'intellectual cinema'.[213]

The idea of correspondences between the material and the spiritual worlds, and between matter and thought is one which exists at the meeting point between philosophy and religion. It is present in the ancient Chinese Taoist tradition, which influenced the Chinese artists who painted the landscapes Eisenstein admired and was influenced by in his approach to audiovisual cinema. The Taoist tradition is also at the basis of the system of synaesthetic correspondences in the above-mentioned ancient Chinese chart, reproduced by Eisenstein in his chapter on the synchronisation of the senses in *The Film Sense*.

Eisenstein came across a twentieth-century version of such a chart of correspondences in James Joyce's master plan for *Ulysses*, which he found in Stuart Gilbert's guide to the novel.[214] Eisenstein notes that the colours, substances and art-forms are not only interrelated in this scheme but that the structural laws pertaining to each art were used by Joyce in the form of each chapter:

> there is a spectrum which is broken down by chapters into the primary colours, each one of which dominates a chapter. There are metals and minerals, each one assigned to a particular chapter. The same is done in terms of human labour and the arts: a chapter for painting, a chapter for language, a chapter for music and so on, each one embodying in its structure the laws of that form of art to which it is devoted.[215]

This immensely detailed and intricate scheme appears to be in complete contrast to Rimbaud's chaotic creative principle of the 'dérèglement de tous les sens,' a deliberate disorientation of the senses.[216] Nevertheless Eisenstein was aware of the chaotic element in Joyce's synaesthetic scheme for *Ulysses*. To make his point he quotes the Austrian writer Stefan Zweig, from his article about Joyce's great novel: 'so it is a chaos, but not one muzzily dreamed up by Rimbaud's drunken brain, smothered in the fumes of alcohol and wrapped in demonic gloom, but conceived by a bitingly witty, ironically cynical intellectual and boldly and purposefully orchestrated.'[217]

Rimbaud, Joyce, Eisenstein and the occult traditions
However, the contrast between Joyce's conceptual synaesthesia in his master plan of correspondences for *Ulysses*, and Rimbaud's supposed involuntary synaesthesia in his poem becomes reduced when Eisenstein starts to examine its 'very individual forms of imagery' more closely. He finds that the poet's ordered correspondences of vowels with colours could be traced to his unconscious memory of an alphabet with coloured letters, in general use during the period of his childhood, a sort of conditioned reflex.[218] Enid Starkie, in her study of Rimbaud published in 1938 (which is the possible source for Eisenstein's reference here), believes that a more likely explanation for these sound/colour corres-

pondences lies in Rimbaud's study of alchemy at the time he was writing *Le Sonnet des voyelles*.[219] She points out that the sequence of colours in the first line of the poem: black, white, red, green, blue, are the order of colours which appear during the process that the alchemist uses in the attempt to produce the philosopher's gold. Starkie also demonstrates that the symbolism of the alchemical colours are related to Rimbaud's seemingly unrelated poetic images.[220]

Both Joyce and Eisenstein shared a scepticism of their contemporaries who were exponents of the hermetic and alchemical traditions, figures like Rudolf Steiner and Madame Blavatsky. In *Ulysses*, Joyce described in his fashion the characteristics of the spirit world as they would have been evoked by an adept during a Blavatskyan séance:

> Questioned by his earthname as to his whereabouts in the heavenworld he stated that he was now on the path of prālāyā or return ... he had heard from more favoured beings now in the spirit that their abodes were equipped with every modern home comfort such as tālāfānā, ālāvātār, hātākāldā, wātāklāsāt and that the highest adepts were steeped in waves of volupcy of the very purest nature.[221]

The effect on the young Eisenstein of his attendance at classes in Rosicrucianism has already been mentioned. In 1920, during the same year as his classes with Bogori the Second in Minsk, he found himself amongst theatre people in Moscow, engaged in deep discussions about theosophical matters. In particular Eisenstein remembers a conversation about "'the invisible lotus" which flowered, unseen, in the devotee's breast.' He also noticed that the attitude the actor Mikhail Chekhov had with regard to theosophy alternated between 'fanatical proselytising and blasphemy'. On this occasion, he and Chekhov went out on to the street, where '...dogs frisked playfully around the street lamps. "I have to believe there is something in the invisible lotus," said Chekhov. "Take these dogs. We cannot see anything and yet they can scent something under each other's little tails".' Eisenstein felt that this type of cynicism often goes 'hand in hand with belief'.[222] However, in spite of the cynicism Joyce and Eisenstein shared with regard to the influential mystical beliefs of this time, they were both inspired by the ideas generated by the extensive use of correspondences, analogies and synaesthesia, characteristic of these ancient occult traditions.

One of Eisenstein's unrealised colour films was to be about Giordano Bruno (1548–1600), the Italian hermetic philosopher from the Renaissance, who had been a major influence on Joyce.[223] One important aspect of Bruno's philosophy consisted of his analysis of our thought processes, by an examination of memory and our ability to combine and associate objects and ideas. To undertake this analysis he proposed a new language, an extension of the language of words by means of images. Through time, these images were to be combined and associated into various patterns, to provide new ways of perceiving order in the apparent chaos of the external world provided by our senses. This new language not only combined images, letters, numbers, signs and symbols (any of which could dissolve into another), but it also comprised intentions, words, diagrams, even the sounds of voices. By using complex tables, Bruno stimulated the generation of new aggregates of images and words, in an attempt to show how this process of combination and association is at the centre of the interaction (through time and memory) between the senses and the mind, at the core of the act of thought.[224] It is clear that such ideas, involving the combining and associating of images in time (and occasionally audiovisual images) would have been of interest to Eisenstein, both as a filmmaker, and as someone who wrote his texts very much in a Joycean stream of consciousness mode.

The influence of Bruno on Joyce involved the philosopher's dialectical theory, which posited an ultimate unity with a 'terrestial division into contraries'.[225] Joyce believed that his art was a way of reconciling these opposites in his own mind. This dialectical concept would have caught Eisenstein's attention too, but as he was being offered the chance of working with colour, it was this latter aspect he specifically mentioned in 1940, in his proposal to the Committee on Cinema Affairs:

> the proposal stipulated a natural 'wide spectrum of colours'. The best subject, in that it had the widest range of colours, and was, at the same time, interesting and acceptable ideologically for the leadership, was the highly-colourful (!) Giordano Bruno.
>
> Italy of course...
> Renaissance dress...
> A fire...[226]

This was the fire in which Bruno was burnt for heresy by the Catholic Church; perhaps Eisenstein believed that this aspect of the life of the philosopher would have helped to make this film subject 'acceptable ideologically for the leadership'.[227] Bruno also believed that God existed in everything and in everyone.[228] This was one of the ideas that Eisenstein liked in his classes with Bogori the Second. It was this type of thinking, considered heretical, which brought Bruno into conflict again and again with both the academic and the ecclesiastical authorities of his time. However in the context of Stalin's atheistic state, this should not have posed an ideological problem, especially as there was also a link in influence from Bruno to Hegel to Marx.[229]

Synaesthesia, the 'imprecise sciences', and the universal language of audiovisual cinema

Eisenstein, as mentioned earlier, acquired an extensive collection of books about the occult and hermetic traditions, what he called the 'imprecise sciences'. In the 1930s this section on his shelves was augmented when he was doing extensive research on Catholicism and its relation to religious frenzy, religious ecstacy, and other related mental states.[230] Though he did not drink alcohol or smoke, he did sometimes experiment with these drugs, as part of his research for his work. Seton mentions Eisenstein drinking beer on a 'pub crawl' in London's Whitechapel district, as part of his study of English working class life, and drinking multiple coffees and chain smoking in a Lyon's teashop in Holborn.[231] Once, inspired by the example of Balzac's working habits, he spent a whole winter working only at night 'draining cup after cup of black coffee'. He acknowledged that this type of empirical knowledge was part of his artistic method. In Mexico it is likely that he tried out '...that wondrous marijuana, which Mexican soldiers stun themselves with'.[232] He also mentions having spent 'many days within the sacred fraternity of the *danzantes*,' the descendants of ancient Mesoamerican dancers.[233]

Eisenstein believed that apart from a direct and unexpected shock, there were three basic techniques which could be used to bring oneself into a range of various highly subjective psychic states:

- the rhythmic repetition of movement (as in Dervish dances),
- the following of a strictly regulated set of exercises (like the Spiritual Exercises of Ignatius Loyola), which use the same principle of rhythmic repetition but in a psychic form, and
- the taking of narcotic drugs.[234]

We have seen how Baudelaire's experiments with hashish produced in him an impression analogous to the effect of Eisenstein's use of the close-up, where an everyday object, in the poet's words 'becomes a symbol with meaning'. In his series of texts, *Les Paradis artificiels*, Baudelaire mentions another personal impression which he experienced as a result of his intoxication through hashish. At a certain stage he noticed how 'sounds take on the appearance of colours, and colours become music.'[235]

Baudelaire explains that such 'analogies' are easily conceived by the poetic mind in its normal and healthy state, but he is at pains to underline the intensity of these experiences under the influence of hashish:

> at this point these analogies take on an unusually vivid quality; they penetrate, they invade, they overwhelm your spirit with their despotic nature. Musical notes become numbers, and, if you have a certain aptitude in mathematics, the melody and harmony which is being heard, while at the same time retaining its voluptuous and sensual character, transforms itself into a vast arithmetical operation.[236]

What Baudelaire describes as 'analogies' in this text would later be called synaesthesia.

In his case, Rimbaud deliberately used drugs, alcohol, hunger, thirst and fatigue to disorientate his senses for the purpose of reaching areas of involuntary subconscious thought so that he could write his poetry. He believed that poets could not compose their work unless they were in some form of a possessed state. He had read and been inspired by ancient Greek texts about the nature of poetic creation, like Plato's description of the act of creating poetry, which Starkie believes Rimbaud would have known: '(poets) ... when falling under the power of music and metre ... are inspired and possessed ... for the poet is a light and winged and holy thing, and there is no invention in him until he has been inspired and is out of his senses, and the mind is no longer in him.' Rimbaud believed that a new language had to be found to transmit the visions he experienced, and he echoes Schopenhauer when he writes that 'every word being an idea, the time for a universal language will come.'[237]

As was noted in the chapter *Audiovisual Counterpoint*, a preoccupation with the concept of a universal language was common to many artists in the early twentieth century, including the Dadaists during the First World War. In *Ulysses*, Joyce has the character of Stephen Daedalus mention the idea of universal language, in the context of Symbolist concerns with the creation of an ideal synthesis of the senses in art:

> *Stephen.* (Looks behind.) So that gesture, not music, not odours, would be a universal language, the gift of tongues rendering visible not the lay sense but the first entelechy, the structural rhythm.[238]

The 'gift of tongues' refers to communication which takes place during a state of ecstatic inspiration and possession. Eisenstein uses this quote as

an epigraph to his text *A Course in Treatment*, written for his classes in
direction, at the State Cinema Institute in Moscow in 1932.

This concept of a universal language was what Eisenstein and other
filmmakers had hoped *cinema* would be. To maintain the silent film's
international and universal language at the dawn of the sound film was
one of the main reasons for the 1928 *Statement on Sound*. In 1932
Eisenstein stated that 'only the sound-film is capable of reconstructing all
phases and all specifics of the course of thought.'[239] Remembering his
unrealised sound film ideas, he imagined a new form of audiovisual
montage in which all elements played an equally important part, each at
the appropriate moment; a form which would involve both a mixing and a
separation of sound and vision, at times rhythmically evoking a heightened
awareness, an ecstatic state:

> What wonderful sketches those montage lists were! Like thought,
> they would sometimes proceed with visual images. With sound.
> Synchronised or non-synchronised. Then as sounds. Formless. Or
> with sound-images: with objectively representational sounds. ...
> Then suddenly, definite intellectually formulated words – as
> 'intellectual' and dispassionate as pronounced words. With a black
> screen, a rushing imageless visuality. Then in passionate
> disconnected speech. Nothing but nouns. Or nothing but verbs.
> Then interjections. With zigzags of aimless shapes, whirling along
> with these in synchronisation. Then racing visual images over
> complete silence. Then linked with polyphonic sounds. Then
> polyphonic images. Then both at once.[240]

An extensive variety of combinations of images and sounds appear in this
evocation of audiovisual montage. Different kinds of synaesthesia are
explored: sounds which are synchronised and non-synchronised, 'sound-
images', 'polyphonic' images, words which stimulate 'a rushing imageless
visuality' against a black screen, 'racing visual images' which would be
'heard' in silence. In addition various levels of abstraction and disassociation are mentioned both in sound and image: words which have
recognisable meanings, disconnected speech, sets of nouns, of verbs, of
interjections, recognisable sounds, formless sounds, polyphonic sounds,
abstract 'zigzags of aimless shapes,' recognisable visual images. Here
Eisenstein is attempting a recreation of the conscious mind and the
subconscious, of voluntary and involuntary thought. He believes that
audiovisual montage should in its structure be 'a reconstruction of the
laws of the thought process'.[241] Part of this thought process is the

phenomenon of synaesthesia, various types of reflex responses, metaphorical thought, conceptual synaesthesia, association and disassociation,
all of which can be reconstructed in audiovisual montage, to produce a
complete range of emotional and sensual thought.

Beyond imagination

This chapter has revealed a bewildering array of audiovisual ideas and
methods relating to synaesthesia in its various forms, not least the ways in
which Eisenstein (and Prokofiev) used this phenomenon to work audiovisually in cinema. So it is not surprising that Eisenstein, when addressing
his film direction students in 1947, admitted that the process of making an
audiovisual film in colour was 'as complex as hell' as 'you have to handle
extraordinarily large numbers of correspondences'.[242]

We have seen some examples of the range and complexity of these
correspondences, from Eisenstein's vastly detailed analysis of the audiovisual process in the sequence of twelve relatively still shots he selected
from *Alexander Nevsky*, his first collaboration with Prokofiev and his first
completed audiovisual film. At the end of his lengthy analysis he confronts
his readers, as he is aware that at this stage they shall ask him how he
could possibly have been in control of such a complex creative process:
"did you know all that *in advance?* Did you really have all that in mind
before you *started?* Had you really worked all that out *beforehand?*"
Eisenstein admits that during the audiovisual creative process he rarely
'*formulates* all those "hows" and "whys"' which result in the selection of a
'correspondence'. He goes on to explain that the conscious mind, during
the period of working on an audiovisual film, does not stop in order to
explain these intentions and choices.[243]

By what Eisenstein calls '*direct action,*' the consciousness of the audiovisual filmmaker 'hurries on *towards completion of the structure*'.[244] In this
comment the word 'hurries' is vitally important. It perfectly describes the
moment when someone is working on a complex task beyond the
capacities of the individual imagination, and senses that the ideas which
come rushing forwards, vying for attention all at once, have to be captured
as rapidly as possible in case they disappear and are forgotten. Because this
mental process is followed by an emotionally climactic moment, one
which appears after a period of working 'beyond imagination,' it is likely
that some form of synaesthesia will occur at this point. For Eisenstein it is
the moment where the audiovisual correspondences reach the stage at
which their combination 'begins to sing out'.[245] This moment of audiovisual
unity is transformed synaesthetically: the audiovisual corresponddences
dissolve and turn instantaneously into audiovisual music.

Notes

Introduction

1 S. M. Eisenstein, *Beyond The Stars: The Memoirs of Sergei Eisenstein*, ed. Richard Taylor, trans. William Powell, vol. 4, *S. M. Eisenstein: Selected Works* (London: BFI, Calcutta: Seagull Books, 1995), 794. Undated.

2 S. M. Eisenstein, *Beyond The Stars*, 14, xii, xv, 647. 1946.

3 Ibid. Eisenstein had planned to write *My Art in Life*. His title was a jocular reference to Stanislavsky's book *My Life in Art*, (Oksana Bulgakowa, *Sergei Eisenstein, A Biography*, trans. Anne Dwyer (Berlin: Potemkin Press, 2001), 72. The Bauhaus series (1925–29) included artist's textbooks by Gropius, Klee, Malevich and Kandinsky.

4 For example: 'audiovisual counterpoint, the sine qua non of audiovisual cinema'. in S. M. Eisenstein, *Beyond The Stars*, 657. 1946. And 'The audiovisual image is the extreme limit of self-revelation outside the basic motivating themes and ideas of creative work' in S. M. Eisenstein, *Immoral Memories: An Autobiography*, trans. Herbert Marshall (London: Peter Owen limited, 1985), 235. 1946.

5 Yon Barna, *Eisenstein: The Growth of a Cinematic Genius* (Bloomington: Indiana University Press, 1973); the five volumes of Eisenstein's writings published by the BFI; and the nine volumes of Eisenstein's works, published by Christian Bourgois in his Union Générale d'Editions.

6 Richard Taylor and Ian Christie, *The Film Factory: Russian and Soviet Cinema in Documents, 1896–1939* (Routledge & Kegan Paul Ltd., 1988), 87. 1923. Vlada Petrić, *Constructivism in Film, The Man with the Movie Camera: A Cinematic Analysis* (Cambridge: Cambridge University Press, 1987), 11. In this study all use of italics in quotes are to be found in the original text.

7 S. M. Eisenstein, *Writings, 1922–34*, ed. and trans. Richard Taylor, vol. 1, *S. M. Eisenstein: Selected Works* (London: BFI Publishing, 1988), 39. 1924.

8 S. M. Eisenstein, *Writings, 1934–47*, ed. Richard Taylor, trans. William Powell, vol. 3, *S. M. Eisenstein: Selected Works* (London: BFI Publishing, 1996), 86. 1936. M. Cole and S. Cole, eds, *The Making of Mind: The Autobiography of A.R. Luria* (Cambridge, Mass.: Harvard University Press, 1979), 207.

9 Richard Taylor and Ian Christie, *The Film Factory*, 88, 89. 1923. S. M. Eisenstein, *Nonindifferent Nature*, trans. Herbert Marshall (Cambridge: Cambridge University Press, 1976), 15. 1939.

10 Richard Taylor and Ian Christie, *The Film Factory*, 88. 1923.

11 Ibid. S. M. Eisenstein, *Que Viva Mexico!* (New York: Arno Press, 1972), 10. 1931.

12 Vlada Petrić, *Constructivism in Film,* 11, 33–41. S. M. Eisenstein, *Writings, 1922–34,* 161. 1929.

13 Petrić, *Constructivism in Film,* 25, 221–2.

14 Richard Taylor and Ian Christie, *The Film Factory,* 90–1, 93. 1923.

15 Alma Law and Mel Gordon, *Meyerhold, Eisenstein and Biomechanics: Actor Training in Revolutionary Russia* (Jefferson, NC, and London: McFarland & Company, Inc., Publishers, 1996), 208. 1935.

16 Richard Taylor and Ian Christie, *The Film Factory,* 93. 1923.

17 Luda Schnitzer, *Cinema in Revolution: the Heroic Era of the Soviet Film,* eds Luda and Jean Schnitzer and Marcel Martin, trans. and with additional material by David Robinson (London: Secker and Warburg, 1973), 70–1. Richard Taylor and Ian Christie, *The Film Factory,* 92–3. 1923.

18 Richard Taylor and Ian Christie, *The Film Factory,* 88, 92–3. 1923.

19 Ibid., 69, 71. 1922. 93–4. 1923.

20 Ibid., 87–8. 1923.

21 Luda Schnitzer, *Cinema in Revolution,* 126, 128.

22 For example Eisenstein explains how at the end of *The Strike* he avoids depicting the expected chain of events when people are being shot: 'the gun is cocked – the shot fired – the bullet strikes – the victim falls.' Instead we see 'the fall – the shot – the cocking – the raising of the wounded', which is more shocking and subjective, as it is closer to what someone in the crowd being shot at might see. S. M. Eisenstein, *Writings, 1922–34,* 41. 1924.

23 V. I. Pudovkin, *Film Technique and Film Acting,* trans. and ed. Ivor Montagu (London: Vision: Mayflower, 1958), 75. 1926.

24 S. M. Eisenstein, *Writings, 1922–34,* 143, 144. 1929.

25 Richard Taylor and Ian Christie, *The Film Factory,* 88. 1923.

26 S. M. Eisenstein, *Writings, 1922–34,* vi.

27 S. M. Eisenstein, *Towards a Theory of Montage,* revised ed., ed. Richard Taylor, ed. and trans. Michael Glenny, vol. 2, *S. M. Eisenstein: Selected Works* (London: BFI, 1994), viii.

28 Following Richard Taylor's advice, whenever I refer to Eisenstein's writings, I give the date of composition of his text at the end of my reference.

29 S. M. Eisenstein, *Beyond The Stars,* xi-xxi.

30 For example, in S. M. Eisenstein, *Beyond The Stars:* 'If I mention here also that I once spent an entire winter working only by night, always wearing a dressing gown, and draining cup after cup of black coffee, all because my imagination had been fired by the similar behaviour of … Balzac, then that is one more characteristic trait which defined my route to art.' (36). Probably 1944. And 'that wondrous marijuana, which Mexican soldiers stun themselves with'. (241). 1946.

31 Ibid., 206, 247n. Nesbet quotes from the Eisenstein archive: fond 1923, dated 17 November 1947.

Audiovisual Counterpoint

1   S. M. Eisenstein, *Beyond the Stars: The Memoirs of Sergei Eisenstein*, ed. Richard
     Taylor, trans. William Powell, vol. 4, *S. M. Eisenstein: Selected Works* (London:
     BFI, Calcutta: Seagull Books, 1995), 657, 869n. 1946.

2   Ibid., 100–1, 706–7. 1946. Yon Barna, *Eisenstein: The Growth of a Cinematic
     Genius* (Boston, Toronto: Little, Brown and Company, 1975), 34.

3   S. M. Eisenstein, *Beyond the Stars*, 73, 75, 77, 657. 1946.

4   Vsevolod Meyerhold, *Meyerhold on Theatre*, revised ed., and trans. Edward
     Braun (London: Methuen and Co Ltd., 1991), 76.

5   S. M. Eisenstein, *Beyond the Stars*, 814.

6   Grigori Kozintsev, *The Space of Tragedy* (Berkeley and Los Angeles: University
     of California Press, 1977), 5.

7   S. M. Eisenstein, *Towards a Theory of Montage*, revised ed., ed. Richard Taylor,
     ed. and trans. Michael Glenny, vol. 2, S. M. Eisenstein: *Selected Works*
     (London: BFI, 1994), 350. 1940.

8   Wassily Kandinsky and Franz Marc, eds, *The Blaue Reiter Almanac*, ed., Klaus
     Lankheit, trans., Henning Falkenstein (London: Macmillan, 1974), 29, 42–3.

9   S. M. Eisenstein, *Towards a Theory of Montage*, 350–2. 1940.

10   Examples of other artists at this time who used the fugue in their work were
     the painter composer Mikaloj Konstantinas Ciurlionis, and the painters
     Wassily Kandinsky, Marsden Hartley, Frantisek Kupka, Robert Delaunay:
     Karin V. Maur, *The Sound of Painting: Music in Modern Art*, 26, 31, 44, 46, 54,
     56.

11   Paul Vogt, *The Blue Rider* (London and Woodbury NY: Barron's Educational
     Series, Inc., 1980), 8.

12   Peter Vergo, *Abstraction: Towards a New Art; Painting, 1910–1920* (London:
     Tate Gallery, 1980), 76, 79. Karin v. Maur, *The Sound of Painting: Music in
     Modern Art*, 38–9.

13   Hajo Düchting, *Paul Klee: Painting Music* (Munich, London, New York:
     Prestel, 2002), 9, 14, 20.

14   Paul Klee, *The Diaries of Paul Klee, 1898–1918*, ed. Felix Klee, (Berkeley, Los
     Angeles, London: University of California Press, 1964), 374.

15   Düchting, *Paul Klee: Painting Music*, 27. This painting is reproduced in Maur's
     The Sound of Painting: Music in Modern Art, 55. It is also reproduced on the
     Internet.

16   Ibid., 28.

17   Ibid., 28, 39. See also Maur, 116.

18   Dorothy C. Miller, ed., *Lyonel Feininger – Marsden Hartley* (New York: The
     Museum of Modern Art, 1944), unpaginated.

19   S. M. Eisenstein, *Nonindifferent Nature*, trans. Herbert Marshall (Cambridge:
     Cambridge University Press, 1987), 285. 1945.

20   Düchting, *Paul Klee*, 108n.

21   Hans Richter, *Dada: Art and Anti-Art* (London: Thames and Hudson, 1997),
     62.

22   Hans Richter, *Hans Richter by Hans Richter, Pioneer of Dada and the Experimental Film*, ed. Cleve Gray (London: Thames and Hudson Limited, 1971), 20, 38. Peter Wollen, 'Lund Celebrates a Dada Child,' Pix 2 (1997): 146.

23   Hans Richter, *Dada: Art and Anti-Art*, 13–14, 27–8, 33.

24   Richter, *Dada: Art and Anti-Art*, 26–7.

25   Richter, *Hans Richter by Hans Richter*, 67–8, 86. See also Richter, *Dada: Art and Anti-Art*, 63.

26   Ibid., 35, 37, 80.

27   Ibid., 68.

28   Ibid., 86.

29   S. M. Eisenstein, *Nonindifferent Nature*, 285. 1945.

30   Richter, Hans Richter by Hans Richter, 20.

31   Vlada Petrić. *Constructivism in Film: The Man with the Movie Camera, A Cinematic Analysis* (Cambridge: Cambridge University Press, 1987), 5–12.

32   Peter Wollen, 'Lund Celebrates a Dada Child,' 149–50.

33   Ibid.

34   Wassily Kandinsky and Franz Marc, eds, *The Blaue Reiter Almanac*, 38, 262, 112, 170. Goethe's quote is from a conversation with Friedrich Wilhelm Riemer in 1807, (Franz Deibel and Friedrich Gundelfinger, eds, *Goethe im Gespräch*, 3rd enlarged edition (Leipzig: Insel-Verlag, 1907, 94)).

35   Peter Wollen, 'Lund Celebrates a Dada Child', 149.

36   Ibid., 150.

37   Tamara Levitz, *Teaching New Classicality: Ferruccio Busoni's Master Class in Composition*, vol. 152, European University Studies (Frankfurt a.M.: Peter Lang, 1996), 127.

38   Wollen, 'Lund Celebrates a Dada Child', 150–1.

39   Richter, *Dada: Art and Anti-Art*, 62.

40   Richter *Hans Richter by Hans Richter*, 112.

41   Richter, *Dada: Art and Anti-Art*, 63–4.

42   Richter *Hans Richter by Hans Richter*, 112.

43   Ibid., 20, 86. Richter, *Dada: Art and Anti-Art*, 62.

44   Richter *Hans Richter by Hans Richter,* 113–14, 130. For a reproduction of Richter's *Fugue* scroll (1920) analysed here, see *Hans Richter by Hans Richter,* 87.

45   Ibid., 41.

46   Quoted in Wollen, 'Lund Celebrates a Dada Child', 154.

47   Richter, *Hans Richter by Hans Richter*, 130.

48   Wollen, 'Lund Celebrates a Dada Child', 151.

49   Richter, Hans Richter by Hans Richter, 131.

50   Ibid.

51   Wollen, 'Lund Celebrates a Dada Child', 155.

52   Richter, *Hans Richter by Hans Richter*, 130, 131.

53   Ibid.

54   Ibid., 57, 150.

55   Eisenstein, *Beyond the Stars*, 336, 841n. 1946.

56   Richter, *Hans Richter by Hans Richter*, 57, 145.

57   Eisenstein, *Nonindifferent Nature*, 289. 1945.

58   Eisenstein, *Beyond the Stars*, 336. 1946.

59   Richter, *Hans Richter by Hans Richter*, 67.

60   Eisenstein, *Towards a Theory of Montage*, 232–3, (1946) 26, 155. 1937–40.

61   Richard Ellmann, *James Joyce* (Oxford: Oxford University Press, 1959), 422.

62   Eisenstein, *Beyond the Stars*, 5. Unless otherwise noted, all emphases in quotations are in the original source. 1946.

63   Jay Leyda and Zina Voynow, eds, *Eisenstein at Work* (London: Methuen London Ltd., 1985), 37.

64   S. M. Eisenstein, *Writings, 1922–34*, ed. and trans. Richard Taylor, vol.1, *S. M. Eisenstein: Selected Works* (London: BFI; Bloomington and Indianapolis: Indiana University Press, 1988), 113. 1928.

65   Ibid.

66   Leyda and Voynow, *Eisenstein at Work*, 37. 1928.

67   Eisenstein, *Immoral Memories*, 214. 1946.

68   Ellmann, *James Joyce*, 666n.

69   James Joyce, *Ulysses* (Harmondsworth UK: Penguin Books Ltd., 1971), 256–257, 267.

70   Ibid., 255.

71   Eisenstein, *Immoral Memories*, 214. 1946.

72   Ibid.

73   Richter, *Hans Richter by Hans Richter*, 169.

74   Richter, *Dada: Art and Anti-Art*, 30.

75   Wollen, 'Lund Celebrates a Dada Child', 152.

76   Richter, *Dada: Art and Anti-Art*, 169.

77   Eisenstein, *Towards a Theory of Montage*, 233. 1946.

78   Eisenstein, *Immoral Memories*, 215. 1946.

79   Ibid.

80   James Joyce, *Finnegans Wake*, 4th ed. (London: Faber and Faber Limited, 1975), 215.

81   Ibid. 215–16.

82   Quoted in Wollen, 'Lund Celebrates a Dada Child', 152.

83   S. M. Eisenstein, *Writings, 1922–34*, 114. 1928.

84   Eisenstein, *Towards a Theory of Montage*, 194n., 195. 1937–40.

85   Eisenstein, *Beyond the Stars*, 663, 869n. 1946.

86   Gilbert, *James Joyce's Ulysses: A Study* (London: Faber & Faber, 1930, reprinted 1969), 212.

87   Eisenstein, *Beyond the Stars*, 663. 1946.

88   Ibid., 663, 869–870n. 1946. Eisenstein, *Nonindifferent Nature*, 324. 1945.

89   S. M. Eisenstein, *Writings, 1922–34*, 114. 1928.

90   Eisenstein, *Beyond the Stars*, 667. 1946.

91   Ibid., 668. 1946.

92   Richter, *Hans Richter by Hans Richter*, 37.

93   E. K. Rozenov quoted in Eisenstein's *Nonindifferent Nature*, 4. 1939.

94 Eisenstein, *Beyond the Stars*, 666–667. 1946.
95 Gilbert, *James Joyce's Ulysses*, 224.
96 Arthur Power, ed. Clive Hart, *Conversations with James Joyce*, (London: Millington Books Ltd., 1978), 97.
97 Gilbert, *James Joyce's Ulysses*, 213.
98 Joyce, *Ulysses*, 254.
99 Eisenstein, *Towards a Theory of Montage*, 194. 1937–40.
100 Ibid., 194–5.
101 Neil Cornwell, *James Joyce and the Russians* (Basingstoke and London: Macmillan, 1992), 83.
102 Eisenstein, *Nonindifferent Nature*, 249. 1945.
103 Joyce, *Ulysses*, 669.
104 Donald Jay Grout, *A History of Western Music* (New York: W.W. Norton & Company Inc., 1960), 391.
105 Sergei M. Eisenstein, *Film Form: Essays in Film Theory*, trans. and ed. Jay Leyda (San Diego, New York, London: Harcourt Brace & Company, 1977), 105–6. 1932.
106 Eisenstein, *Nonindifferent Nature*, 250. 1945.
107 Richter, *Hans Richter by Hans Richter*, 113.
108 Eisenstein, *Nonindifferent Nature*, 231. 1945.
109 Ibid.
110 Ibid., 233. 1945.
111 Ibid. 230. 1945.
112 S. M. Eisenstein, *Writings, 1922–34*, 114. 1928.
113 Sergei M. Eisenstein, *The Film Sense*, 2nd edition, trans. and ed. Jay Leyda (London: Faber and Faber Limited, 1968), 67. 1940.
114 Ibid.
115 Eisenstein, *The Film Sense*, 64–65, 67. 1940.
116 Ibid., 67, 73. 1940.
117 Richter, *Hans Richter by Hans Richter*, 86.
118 Eisenstein, *Nonindifferent Nature*, 279. 1945.
119 Richter, *Hans Richter by Hans Richter*, 38, 113.
120 Eisenstein, *Beyond the Stars*, 214. 1946.
121 Richter, *Dada: Art and Anti-Art*, 62.
122 Eisenstein, *Nonindifferent Nature*, 239. 1945.
123 S. M. Eisenstein, *Writings, 1922–34*, 114. 1928.

Organic Unity

1 S. M. Eisenstein, *Film Form: Essays in Film Theory*, trans. and ed. Jay Leyda (San Diego, New York, London: Harcourt & Company, 1949). 1939.
2 S. M. Eisenstein, *Immoral Memories: An Autobiography*, trans. Herbert Marshall (London: Peter Owen Limited, 1985), 75. 1943.
3 Ibid., 130.

4   S. M. Eisenstein, *Beyond the Stars: The Memoirs of Sergei Eisenstein*, ed. Richard
     Taylor, trans. William Powell, vol. 4, *S. M. Eisenstein: Selected Works* (London:
     BFI Publishing and Calcutta: Seagull Books, 1995), 448. 1936.

5   Vsevolod Meyerhold, *Meyerhold on Theatre*, revised ed., ed. and trans. Edward
     Braun (London: Methuen and Co Ltd., 1991), 311.

6   S. M. Eisenstein, *Writings, 1934–47*, ed. Richard Taylor, trans. William
     Powell, vol. 3, *S. M. Eisenstein: Selected Works* (London: BFI Publishing, 1996),
     284.

7   Alma Law and Mel Gordon, *Meyerhold, Eisenstein and Biomechanics: Actor
     Training in Revolutionary Russia* (Jefferson, NC, and London: McFarland &
     Company, Inc., Publishers, 1996), 75–76.

8   Yon Barna, *Eisenstein: The Growth of a Cinematic Genius* (Bloomington: Indiana
     University Press, 1973), 40.

9   Law and Gordon, *Meyerhold, Eisenstein and Biomechanics*, 76–7.

10   Eisenstein, *Beyond the Stars*, 449. 1946.

11   Law and Gordon, *Meyerhold, Eisenstein and Biomechanics*, 78, 80, 166.

12   S. M. Eisenstein, *Writings, 1922–34*, ed. and trans. Richard Taylor, vol. 1,
     S. M. Eisenstein: Selected Works, (London: BFI Publishing, 1988), 33–8. 1923.

13   Law and Gordon, *Meyerhold, Eisenstein and Biomechanics*, 82–3, 84, 87–8.

14   Aleksandr Gladkov, *Meyerhold Speaks, Meyerhold Rehearses*, ed. and trans. Alma
     Law (Amsterdam: Harwood Academic Publishers, 1997), 180.

15   Law and Gordon, *Meyerhold, Eisenstein and Biomechanics*, 89–91.

16   Aleksandr Gladkov, *Meyerhold Speaks, Meyerhold Rehearses*, 49.

17   Law and Gordon, *Meyerhold, Eisenstein and Biomechanics*, 79, 91.

18   Ibid., 15–16.

19   Norman Swallow, *Eisenstein: A Documentary Portrait* (London: George Allen &
     Unwin Ltd., 1976), 22–4.

20   Law and Gordon, *Meyerhold, Eisenstein and Biomechanics*, 16.

21   Béatrice Picon-Vallin, *Meyerhold* (Paris: Editions du Centre National de la
     Recherche Scientifique, 1990), 368.

22   Law and Gordon, *Meyerhold, Eisenstein and Biomechanics*, 18–20.

23   Ibid., 20–2.

24   Ibid., 20–1.

25   Picon-Vallin, *Meyerhold*, 40.

26   Ibid., 400–1.

27   Gladkov, *Meyerhold Speaks*, 12.

28   Meyerhold, *Meyerhold on Theatre*, 246.

29   Ibid., 76, 247.

30   Meyerhold, *Ecrits sur le théâtre*, Tome IV, *1936–1940* (Lausanne: L'Age
     d'Homme, 1992), 217.

31   Picon-Vallin, *Meyerhold*, 378.

32   Aleksandr Gladkov, *Meyerhold Speaks, Meyerhold Rehearses*, 115.

33   Gladkov, *Meyerhold Speaks*, 124.

34   Modulation in music is a change of key, achieved by harmonic means, which
     has significance both in terms of formal change and continuity in a piece of

music. Modulations connect what has already been performed with what is to happen next, and are thus vital in providing the unity and organic form of a musical work.

35 Meyerhold, *Ecrits sur le théâtre*, 94, 95.

36 Ibid., 95–6. Meyerhold's emphasis.

37 Picon-Vallin, *Meyerhold*, 56.

38 Meyerhold, *Ecrits sur le théâtre*, 95–7.

39 Gladkov, *Meyerhold Speaks*, 135–6.

40 Ibid., 117–18.

41 Ibid., 124.

42 Picon-Vallin, *Meyerhold*, 252–3, 259.

43 Ibid., 251.

44 Ibid., 250–2.

45 Ibid 252, 260.

46 Ibid., 375–7.

47 Nikolai V. Gogol, *The Government Inspector*, trans. D.J. Campbell (London: Heinemann Educational Books, 1947), 22.

48 Picon-Vallin, *Meyerhold*, 265–266.

49 Law and Gordon, 88.

50 S. M. Eisenstein, *Writings, 1922–34*, 116. 1928.

51 Picon-Vallin, *Meyerhold*, 161, 299, 401.

52 Claudine Amiard-Chevrel, ed., *Théâtre et cinéma années vingt*, vol. 1, *Théâtre années vingt* (Lausanne: L'Age d'Homme, 1990), 244.

53 Picon-Vallin, *Meyerhold*, 298–301.

54 Ibid., 271, 296, 306, 308–10, 327, 333, 338–9, 356. A reproduction of Dürer's *Jesus Among the Doctors* can be found on the Internet.

55 Meyerhold, *Meyerhold on Theatre*, 97.

56 Eisenstein, *Film Form*, 41. 1929.

57 Picon-Vallin, *Meyerhold*, 285, 292, 300, 309, 321, 333.

58 Ibid., 304, 343. Gladkov, *Meyerhold Speaks*, 97, 166–7.

59 S. M. Eisenstein, *Beyond the Stars*, 299–306. Undated, probably 1946.

60 S. M. Eisenstein, *Towards a Theory of Montage*, ed. Michael Glenny and Richard Taylor, trans. Michael Glenny, vol. 2, *S. M. Eisenstein: Selected Works* (London: BFI Publishing, 1991), 29–30. 1937.

61 S. M. Eisenstein, *Nonindifferent Nature*, trans. Herbert Marshall (Cambridge: Cambridge University Press, 1987), 230–3. 1945.

62 Picon-Vallin, *Meyerhold*, 344.

63 Ibid., 265n., 297.

64 Ibid., 285, 313–14, 347, 350, 353, 355, 362.

65 Ibid., 332, 336, 346, 347–8, 353.

66 Ibid., 311–312, 351–353, 352n.

67 Ibid., 307.

68 Meyerhold, *Ecrits sur le théâtre*, 380.

69 Picon-Vallin, *Meyerhold*, 307, 378.

70 Law and Gordon, *Meyerhold, Eisenstein and Biomechanics*, 22.

71   Picon-Vallin, *Meyerhold*, 368–369.

72   Law and Gordon, *Meyerhold, Eisenstein and Biomechanics*, 24.

73   Ibid., 28–9.

74   Picon-Vallin, *Meyerhold*, 379.

75   Meyerhold, *Ecrits sur le théâtre*, 26.

76   Law and Gordon, *Meyerhold, Eisenstein and Biomechanics*, 39–41.

77   Ibid. 78.

78   Ibid., 75. Part of Meyerhold's Biomechanics study programme involved what was described as 'Movement and musical background'. This involved the 'construction of a score of movements in relation to a given musical score according to the laws of counterpoint, or the construction of a musical score in relation to a given movement score according to the same laws.' (Ibid., 126). Here is a foreshadowing of the interchangeability of roles in Eisenstein's future collaboration with Sergei Prokofiev, described in the chapter on synaesthesia.

79   Ibid., 206, 210, 212.

80   Ibid., 208, 213–214.

81   Ibid., 22–23.

82   S. M. Eisenstein, *Beyond the Stars*, ed. Richard Taylor, trans. William Powell, vol 4, *S. M. Eisenstein: Selected Works* (London: BFI Publishing, and Calcutta: Seagull Books), 1995, 28. Picon-Vallin, *Meyerhold*, 45–47. Probably 1944.

83   Law and Gordon, *Meyerhold, Eisenstein and Biomechanics*, 89.

84   Eisenstein, *Writings, 1934–47*, 164.

85   Bergan, *Sergei Eisenstein*, 317.

86   S. M. Eisenstein, *Writings, 1934–47*, 164. 1940.

87   Ibid., 165.

88   Jay Leyda and Zina Voynow, eds, *Eisenstein at Work* (London: Methuen London Ltd., 1985), 91. 1935–37.

89   Marie Seton, *Sergei M. Eisenstein: A Biography* (New York: A.A. Wyn, Inc., 1952), 356. 1935–37. Seton quotes her source as being from an unpublished production diary kept by Jay Leyda.

90   Ivor Montagu, *With Eisenstein in Hollywood* (Berlin: Seven Seas Publishers, 1968), 185. 1930.

91   Ivor Montagu, *With Eisenstein in Hollywood*, 186.

92   Ibid., 188.

93   Picon-Vallin, *Meyerhold*, 381.

94   Nicoletta Misler, 'MOTO-BIO – The Russian Art of Movement: Dance, Gesture, and Gymnastics, 1910–1930', *Experiment/эксперимент, 2* (1996): 170–1.

95   S. M. Eisenstein, *Nonindifferent Nature*, trans. Herbert Marshall (Cambridge: Cambridge University Press, 1976), 19, 21–2. 1939.

96   However Eisenstein was aware of the limitations of a non-organic use of the golden mean principle. See S. M. Eisenstein, *Writings, 1922–34*, 213–14. 1930.

97   Meyerhold, *Meyerhold on Theatre*, 297–8.

98   Picon-Vallin, *Meyerhold*, 251.
99   S. M. Eisenstein, *Nonindifferent Nature*, 14. 1939.
100   Picon-Vallin, *Meyerhold*, 260.
101   Eisenstein, *Writings*, 1922–34, 114. 1928.
102   Meyerhold, *Meyerhold on Theatre*, 309–10.
103   Eisenstein, *Film Form*, 20. 1928.
104   Ibid., 21, 24.
105   Eisenstein, *Towards a Theory of Montage*, 331–2. 1940.
106   Eisenstein, *The Film Sense*, ed. and trans. Jay Leyda (London: Faber and Faber, 1968), 67. 1940.
107   Eisenstein, *Film Form*, 24. 1928.
108   Marie Seton, *Sergei M. Eisenstein*, 246. Seton quotes her source as being from an interview of Eisenstein by Lotte Eisner in the *Film Kurier*, Berlin, 28 April, 1932.
109   Yon Barna, *Eisenstein: The Growth of a Cinematic Genius*, 195, 211.
110   Leyda and Voynow, *Eisenstein at Work*, 83.
111   Eisenstein, *Writings, 1934–47*, 56, 59. 1935.
112   S. M. Eisenstein, *Towards a Theory of Montage*, revised ed., ed. Richard Taylor, ed. and trans. Michael Glenny, vol. 2, *S. M. Eisenstein: Selected Works* (London: BFI Publishing, 1994), 279–80. 1937–40.

Nonindifferent Nature

1   S. M. Eisenstein, *Immoral Memories: An Autobiography*, trans. Herbert Marshall (London: Peter Owen Limited, 1985), 235. 1946.
2   Marie Seton, *Sergei M. Eisenstein: A Biography* (New York: A.A. Wyn, Inc., 1952), 145.
3   Aleksandr Gladkov, *Meyerhold Speaks, Meyerhold Rehearses*, ed. and trans. Alma Law (Amsterdam: Harwood Academic Publishers, 1997), 101.
4   Marie Seton, *Sergei M. Eisenstein: A Biography*, 164–165. For another account of Eisenstein in Chicago, see Yon Barna, *Eisenstein: The Growth of a Cinematic Genius*, 153–4.
5   S. M. Eisenstein, *Writings, 1934–47*, ed. Richard Taylor, trans. William Powell, vol. 3, *S. M. Eisenstein: Selected Works* (London: BFI Publishing, 1996), 194. 1942.
6   S. M. Eisenstein, *The Film Sense*, ed. and trans. Jay Leyda (London: Faber and Faber, 1968), 83. 1940.
7   Ibid., 81–2.
8   Ibid., 82. Stuart Davis' *Swing Landscape* is reproduced on the Internet. Check it out, it's a wonderful painting.
9   S. M. Eisenstein, *Beyond the Stars: The Memoirs of Sergei Eisenstein*, ed. Richard Taylor, trans. William Powell, vol. 4, *S. M. Eisenstein: Selected Works* (London: BFI, Calcutta: Seagull Books, 1995), 194–5. 1946.
10   Sergei Eisenstein and Upton Sinclair, *The Making and Unmaking of Que Viva Mexico!* Harry M. Geduld and Ronald Gottesman, eds (London: Thames and Hudson Ltd., 1970), 10–11.

11   S. M. Eisenstein, *Nonindifferent Nature*, trans. Herbert Marshall (Cambridge: Cambridge University Press, 1976), 379. 1945.
12   Ibid.
13   S. M. Eisenstein, *Writings, 1934–47*, ed., Richard Taylor, trans., William Powell, vol.3, *S. M. Eisenstein: Selected Works* (London: BFI Publishing, 1996), 194. 1942.
14   Sergei Eisenstein and Upton Sinclair, *The Making and Unmaking of Que Viva Mexico!*, 12–14.
15   S. M. Eisenstein, *Nonindifferent Nature*, 379–383. 1945.
16   Inga Karetnikova and Leon Steinmetz, *Mexico According to Eisenstein* (Albuquerque: University of New Mexico Press, 1991), 5–6.
17   Ibid., 8, 13, 15.
18   Marie Seton, *Sergei M. Eisenstein: A Biography*, 257. Seton quotes from a letter from Eisenstein. 1932.
19   S. M. Eisenstein, *Beyond the Stars: The Memoirs of Sergei Eisenstein*, ed. Richard Taylor, trans. William Powell, vol. 4, *S. M. Eisenstein: Selected Works* (London: BFI, Calcutta: Seagull Books, 1995), 361. 1946.
20   Karetnikova and Steinmetz, *Mexico According to Eisenstein*, 12–13.
21   Ibid., 10–12, 15, 18–19, 22, 28.
22   S. M. Eisenstein, *Que Viva Mexico!* (New York: Arno Press, 1972), 27. 1931.
23   Sergei Eisenstein and Upton Sinclair, *The Making and Unmaking of Que Viva Mexico!* Harry M. Geduld and Ronald Gottesman, eds (London: Thames and Hudson Ltd., 1970), 25, 212, 277.
24   S. M. Eisenstein, *Que Viva Mexico!* (New York: Arno Press, 1972), 22–23.
25   S. M. Eisenstein, *Eisenstein on Disney*, ed. Jay Leyda, trans. Alan Upchurch (London: Methuen Ltd., 1988), 3–4. 1941.
26   S. M. Eisenstein, *Beyond the Stars: The Memoirs of Sergei Eisenstein*, 413. No date.
27   Ibid., 413–14, no date. 417, 1943.
28   S. M. Eisenstein, *Nonindifferent Nature*, 382. 1945.
29   S. M. Eisenstein, *Beyond the Stars*, 11, 1946. 417–18, 1943.
30   S. M. Eisenstein, *Nonindifferent Nature*, 380–381. 1945.
31   Ibid., 376–8, 382–3. 1945.
32   Karetnikova, 39–40.
33   S. M. Eisenstein, *Que Viva Mexico!* (New York: Arno Press, 1972), 27–8, 33. Karetnikova and Steinmetz, *Mexico According to Eisenstein*, 42.
34   S. M. Eisenstein, *Beyond the Stars*, 471.
35   Karetnikova, 40,43. 1931.
36   A. N. Lavrentiev, *Rodchenko* (Moscow: Iskusstvo, 1992), 90.
37   Miguel Covarrubias, *Mexico South: The Isthmus of Tehuantepec* (London: Cassell and Company Limited, 1947), 323, 326.
38   Karetnikova, 29, 54–7, 61, 63, 69.
39   S. M. Eisenstein, *The Film Sense*, 198, 200. 1931. Karetnikova, 65.
40   S. M. Eisenstein, *Beyond the Stars*, 419.
41   Karetnikova, 75–9.
42   Ibid., 79, 91.

43   Ibid., 95–98.

44   S. M. Eisenstein, *Beyond the Stars*, 419. Part of MS not yet dated. 1943.

45   Karetnikova, 95–6, 98.

46   Ibid., 128–32.

47   Ibid., 137–8, 149.

48   Marie Seton, *Sergei M. Eisenstein: A Biography*, 509, 511. From an introduction by Eisenstein to his scenario for *Que Viva Mexico!* 1947.

49   S. M. Eisenstein, *Writings, 1934–47*, ed., Richard Taylor, trans., William Powell, vol. 3, *S. M. Eisenstein: Selected Works* (London: BFI Publishing, 1996), 69. 1935.

50   Karetnikova, 37.

51   Ibid., 40.

52   Miguel Covarrubias, *Mexico South: The Isthmus of Tehuantepec*, 326.

53   Karetnikova, 54.

54   Ibid., 76, 78–9.

55   Ibid., 96–8.

56   Ibid., 128–32. 1947.

57   Seton, 504, 510.

58   S. M. Eisenstein, *Beyond the Stars*, 632–633. 1946.

59   Seton, 510. 1947.

60   S. M. Eisenstein, *Beyond the Stars*, 632–634. 1946.

61   Karetnikova, 170. 1946.

62   Seton, 510–11. 1947. Sergei Eisenstein and Upton Sinclair, *The Making and Unmaking of Que Viva Mexico!*, 117, 150. 1931.

63   Karetnikova, 40, 53–4, 57, 78–9, 96–7. 1931.

64   Ibid., 128–9.

65   Ibid., 130–2.

66   Ibid., 137–8.

67   Ronald Bergan, *Sergei Eisenstein: A Life in Conflict*, 220. Bergan's source regarding Eisenstein's artistic freedom on his Mexican project is the Upton Sinclair Archive in Bloomington, Indiana. Sinclair also refers to the same idea regarding Eisenstein's artistic independence in Mexico, in a letter to L.I. Monosson of Amkino, the Soviet film authority in the United States (Sergei Eisenstein and Upton Sinclair, *The Making and Unmaking of Que Viva Mexico!*, 38. 1931.

68   S. M. Eisenstein, *Eisenstein on Disney*, 27. 1940.

69   John Ruskin, *Modern Painters*, Vol. III (Orpington: George Allen, 1897), 205.

70   Karetnikova, 2, 15.

71   Ibid., 11–12. This episode is also documented in Sergei Eisenstein and Upton Sinclair, *The Making and Unmaking of Que Viva Mexico!*, 44. 1931.

72   S. M. Eisenstein, *Beyond the Stars*, 414. No date, and 1943.

73   Karetnikova, 45–6, 58, 67, 145.

74   S. M. Eisenstein, *Beyond the Stars*, 418. No date, and 1943.

75   See Herbert Marshall's translation of *Immoral Memories*: an unpaginated plate, between pages 132 and 133. Marshall attributes this drawing to Eisenstein.

76   Karetnikova, 38, 51–2, 72, 114, 136, 150, 180. 1931. S. M. Eisenstein, *Writings, 1922–34*, ed. and trans. Richard Taylor, vol.1, *S. M. Eisenstein: Selected Works* (London: BFI Publishing, and Bloomington and Indianapolis: Indiana University Press 1988), 319. 1931.

77   S. M. Eisenstein, *Immoral Memories*, 211–12. 1946.

78   S. M. Eisenstein, *Towards a Theory of Montage*, ed. Michael Glenny and Richard Taylor, trans. Michael Glenny, Vol. 2, *S. M. Eisenstein: Selected Works* (London BFI Publishing, 1991), 43. 1937.

79   S. M. Eisenstein, *Beyond the Stars*, 379. 1946.

80   Ibid., 348. 1944.

81   Elie Faure, *Mon périple: Voyage autour du monde, 1931–1932* (Paris: Editions Seghers, 1987), 362. My translation.

82   Ibid., 63, 67.

83   Elie Faure, *Fonction du Cinéma : De la cinéplastique à son destin social* (Lausanne : Editions Gonthier, 1964), 24. Originally published in *L'Arbre d'Eden*, ed. Jean-Marie Tremblay (Paris: Crès, 1922). My translation.

84   Nicoletta Misler, 'MOTO-BIO – The Russian Art of Movement: Dance, Gesture, and Gymnastics, 1910–1930', in *Experiment/эксперимент, 2* (1996), 169–170, 184.

85   Elie Faure, *Fonction du Cinéma*, 24–25. My translation.

86   Abraham Segal, *The Complete Films of Eisenstein* (London: Weidenfeld and Nicolson, 1974), 99.

87   Karetnikova, 37.

88   Elie Faure, *Fonction du Cinéma*, 35. My translation.

89   S. M. Eisenstein, *Que Viva Mexico!*, 10. 1931.

90   S. M. Eisenstein, *Towards a Theory of Montage*, 266n–267n. 1940.

91   S. M. Eisenstein, *Beyond the Stars*, 414–15. No date, and 1943.

92   Ibid., 413–15.

93   Seton, 213.

94   S. M. Eisenstein, *Beyond the Stars*, 471. 1931.

95   Karetnikova, 63, 65, 88, 90, 111.

96   S. M. Eisenstein, *Que Viva Mexico!*, 4, 49, 65.

97   S. M. Eisenstein, *Beyond the Stars*, 92. 1946.

98   Karetnikova, 86, 112, 122, 139. S. M. Eisenstein, *Que Viva Mexico!*, 89.

99   Karetnikova, 121, 140.

100   Ibid., 41,43, 45, 46, 58, 59, 61, 62, 65, 69, 70, 71, 102, 104, 110, 123, 147, 149.

101   S. M. Eisenstein, *Beyond the Stars*, 412. No date, and 1943.

102   Karetnikova, 6.

103   S. M. Eisenstein, *Beyond the Stars*, 575, 863n.11.

104   Karetnikova, 123–5.

105   S. M. Eisenstein, *Beyond the Stars*, 579. 1946.

106   Ibid., 576.

107   Ibid., 578, 581. 1946.

108   S. M. Eisenstein, *Que Viva Mexico!*, 51, 55.

109   S. M. Eisenstein, *Beyond the Stars*, 581. 1946.

110 Ibid., 415. No date, and 1943.

111 S. M. Eisenstein, *Que Viva Mexico!* 51, 55.

112 Alexei Metchenko et al., *Vladimir Mayakovsky: Innovator*, trans. Alex Miller (Moscow: Progress Publishers, 1976), 159.

113 S. M. Eisenstein, *Beyond the Stars*, 415. No date, and 1943.

114 Ibid., 463. 1946.

115 Ibid., 377. 1931.

116 S. M. Eisenstein, *Nonindifferent Nature*, 46–8. 1939.

117 S. M. Eisenstein, *Beyond the Stars*, 463. 1946.

118 Karetnikova, 94, 104.

119 S. M. Eisenstein, *Beyond the Stars*, 463–4. 1946.

120 Ibid., 417–18. No date, and 1943.

121 Ibid., 418.

122 Ibid.

123 Ibid., 418–19.

124 Elie Faure, *Fonction du cinéma*, 23.

125 Ibid., 25, 34. My translation.

126 S. M. Eisenstein, *Beyond the Stars*, 413, 419.

127 Ibid., 418, 420. No date, and 1943. 241. 1946.

128 S. M. Eisenstein, *Nonindifferent Nature*, 141–143. 1946–7.

129 Ibid., 142–3.

130 S. M. Eisenstein, *Beyond the Stars*, 92–93. 1946.

131 Karetnikova, 112.

132 S. M. Eisenstein, *Beyond the Stars*, 92–93. 1946.

133 Ibid., 92.

134 Ibid., 208–209, 211, 699, 820n. 1946.

135 Sainte Thérèse de l'Enfant Jésus, *Manuscrits autobiographiques*, ed. Andreas Jacquemin, Episcopus Bajocencis et Lexoviensis (Lisieux: Office Central de Lisieux, 1957), 131.

136 S. M. Eisenstein, *Beyond the Stars*, 699. 1946.

137 Ibid., 210–211.

138 John Frederick Nims, *The Poems of St John of the Cross* (New York: Grove Press, 1959), vii, 7, 119, 120. My translation.

139 Ibid., 121.

140 S. M. Eisenstein, *Nonindifferent Nature*, 380–381. 1945.

141 John Frederick Nims, *The Poems of St John of the Cross*, 27. My translation.

142 S. M. Eisenstein, *Beyond the Stars*, 92, 210. 1946.

143 S. M. Eisenstein, *Nonindifferent Nature*, 27–9. 1939.

144 S. M. Eisenstein, *Beyond the Stars*, 743–4. 1946.

145 Karetnikova, 57, 78, 97.

146 S. M. Eisenstein, *The Film Sense*, 83. 1940.

147 S. M. Eisenstein, *Beyond the Stars*, 209. 1946.

148 S. M. Eisenstein, *Nonindifferent Nature*, 177.

149 Seton, 509–11. 1947.

150 S. M. Eisenstein, *Beyond the Stars*, 416. 1931. Karetnikova, 142. 1931.

151   D. H.Lawrence, *The Plumed Serpent* (Ware, Hertfordshire: Wordsworth Editions Ltd., 1995) 9, 12.

152   Karetnikova, 120.

153   S. M. Eisenstein, *Nonindifferent Nature*, 27. 1939.

154   Karetnikova, 115.

155   According to Barthélemy Amengual, Eisenstein studied the models for the scene designs for Mayakovsky's *Mystery-Bouffe* in 1918: Barthélemy Amengual, *Que viva Eisenstein!* (Lausanne: Editions l'Age d'Homme, 1980), 630.

156   Herbert Marshall, *Mayakovsky and His Poetry* (London: Pilot Press, 1942), 40. Marshall's source is taken from G.R. Noyes, *Masterpieces of the Russian Drama* (New York, London: Appleton & Co., 1933).

157   Alma Law and Mel Gordon, *Meyerhold, Eisenstein and Biomechanics: Actor Training in Revolutionary Russia* (Jefferson, North Carolina, and London: McFarland & Company, Inc., Publishers, 1996), 77.

158   John Bowlt and Nancy Van Norman Baer: *Theatre in Revolution: Russian Avant-garde Stage Design, 1913–1935* (San Francisco: Thames and Hudson and The Fine Arts Museums of San Francisco, 1991),188.

159   Herbert Marshall, *Mayakovsky and His Poetry*, 40.

160   Vsevolod Meyerhold, *Meyerhold on Theatre*, revised ed., ed. and trans. Edward Braun (London: Methuen and Co Ltd., 1991), 161.

161   Karetnikova, 101–3.

162   Picon-Vallin, *Meyerhold*, 34–5, 84.

163   Vsevolod Meyerhold, *Meyerhold on Theatre*, 141.

164   S. M. Eisenstein, *Beyond the Stars*, 451. 1946.

165   Ibid., 830n.

166   Karetnikova, 148.

167   Picon-Vallin, *Meyerhold*, 38.

168   Timothy C. Westphalen, ed. and trans., *Aleksandr Blok's Trilogy of Lyric Dramas* (London and New York: Routledge, 2003), 32.

169   Karetnikova, 80.

170   S. M. Eisenstein, *Beyond the Stars*, 316. 1943–44.

171   Timothy C. Westphalen, *Aleksandr Blok's Trilogy of Lyric Dramas*, 26.

172   Karetnikova, 136.

173   S. M. Eisenstein, *Beyond the Stars*, 263, 265. 1943. 426. 1946.

174   Ibid., 376, 538. 1946.

175   Timothy C. Westphalen, *Aleksandr Blok's Trilogy of Lyric Dramas*, 30.

176   Picon-Vallin, *Meyerhold*, 400–1.

177   Ibid., 35.

178   S. M. Eisenstein, *Beyond the Stars*, 413–14. No date, and 1943. 500. 1946.

179   Ibid., 266. 1943.

180   Ibid., 498. 1946.

181   S. M. Eisenstein, *Nonindifferent Nature*, 28. 1939.

182   S. M. Eisenstein, *Beyond the Stars*, 129. Probably 1946.

183   Edgar Allan Poe, *Selected Stories and Poems* (New York: Airmont Publishing Co., Inc., 1962), 163.

184   S. M. Eisenstein, *Que Viva Mexico!*, 10. 1931.

185   S. M. Eisenstein, *Beyond the Stars*, 478, 497–498. 1946.

186   Ibid., 478. Cf. Kasimir Malevich in *The Non-Objective World*, *The Manifesto of Suprematism* (Mineola, New York: Dover Publications, Inc., 2003. Original edition published by Albert Langen in Munich, 1927, as vol. 11 in the Bauhaus Books series), 9, 40: 'Every work of art – every picture – is the reproduction, so to speak, of a subjective state of mind – the representation of a phenomenon seen through a subjective prism (the prism of the brain).'

187   Ibid.

188   Ibid., 614. 1946.

189   S. M. Eisenstein, *Immoral Memories*, 211. 1946.

190   Karetnikova, 164–165. 1935.

191   Olier Mordrel, *Rivera, les fresques de Mexico* (Paris: Editions Atlas, 1984), 21, 22, 27, 30, 32. S. M. Eisenstein, *Que Viva Mexico!*, 37, 45, 67. Karetnikova, 87.

192   Karetnikova, 162. 1935.

193   Ibid., 165.

194   Ibid., 160, 162.

195   Ibid., 166. For a black and white reproduction of this painting by Siqueiros, see Jay Leyda and Zina Voynow, *Eisenstein at Work* (London: Methuen London Ltd., 1985), 64.

196   S. M. Eisenstein, *Beyond the Stars*, 415. No date, and 1943. 632–634. 1946. Karetnikova, 139.

197   S. M. Eisenstein, *Que Viva Mexico!*, 12.

198   S. M. Eisenstein, *Writings, 1934–47*, 375n. 1939. 136. 1940.

199   Ibid.

200   S. M. Eisenstein, *Nonindifferent Nature*, 307–308. 1945.

201   Ibid., 308.

202   Ibid., 227, 229–31, 236–7.

203   S. M. Eisenstein, *Beyond the Stars*, 412. Undated.

204   S. M. Eisenstein, *The Film Sense*, 197. 1931.

205   S. M. Eisenstein, *Nonindifferent Nature*, 253. 1945.

206   'My heart cannot distinguish between an objective image and an image in my imagination.' Eisenstein wrote this observation in his diary at a moment of strong emotion, just after his mother's death, in August 1946. He was recalling another highly charged moment when he realised that his film *Que Viva Mexico!* would probably never be realised. S. M. Eisenstein, *Beyond the Stars*, 728, 876. 1946.

207   Ibid., 174–6, 178–9. 1939.

208   Ibid., 178–9.

209   S. M. Eisenstein, *Beyond the Stars*, 412. Undated.

210   S. M. Eisenstein, *Nonindifferent Nature*, 216. 1945.

211   However Eisenstein *does* see the process of creating legend and myth as part of his use of nonindifferent nature, in the audiovisual synthesis of landscape and 'emotion, music, action, light and colour' in his production of Wagner's music-drama, *Die Walküre*, in 1940 (Eisenstein, *Writings, 1934–47*, 161). 1940.

212   S. M. Eisenstein, *Nonindifferent Nature*, 216–17. 1945.
213   Ibid., 396. 1945–7.

Synaesthesia

1   S. M. Eisenstein, *Beyond the Stars: The Memoirs of Sergei Eisenstein*, ed. Richard
     Taylor, trans. William Powell, vol. 4, *S. M. Eisenstein: Selected Works* (London:
     BFI, Calcutta: Seagull Books, 1995), 678. 1946.
2   Sergei Eisenstein, *Notes of a Film Director* (New York: Dover Publications,
     Inc., 1970), 38. 1939.
3   Tatiana K. Egorova, *Soviet Film Music: an Historical Survey*, trans., Tatiana A.
     Ganf and Natalia A. Egunova (Amsterdam: Harwood Academic Publishers,
     1997), 62–3.
4   S. M. Eisenstein, *The Film Sense*, ed. and trans. Jay Leyda (London: Faber and
     Faber, 1968), 124. 1940.
5   Donald Jay Grout, *A History of Western Music*, (New York: W.W. Norton &
     Company Inc., 1960) 11.
6   S. M. Eisenstein, *The Film Sense*, 124–5. 1940.
7   Ibid., 69
8   S. M. Eisenstein, *Writings, 1922–34*, ed. and trans. Richard Taylor, vol. 1,
     S. M. Eisenstein: Selected Works (London: BFI; Bloomington and Indianapolis:
     Indiana University Press, 1988), 114.
9   David Bordwell and Kristin Thompson, *Film Art: An Introduction* (New York:
     McGraw Hill, 2001), 2.
10   S. M. Eisenstein, *The Film Sense*, 68. 1940.
11   Sergei Eisenstein, *Notes of a Film Director*, 115–116. 1940.
12   S. M. Eisenstein, *Beyond the Stars*, 474. 1946.
13   S. M. Eisenstein, *The Film Sense*, 119. 1940.
14   S. M. Eisenstein, *Nonindifferent Nature*, trans. Herbert Marshall (Cambridge:
     Cambridge University Press, 1976), 297. 1945–47.
15   Sergei Eisenstein, *Notes of a Film Director*, 116. 1940.
16   S. M. Eisenstein, *Nonindifferent Nature*, 296. 1945–47.
17   S. M. Eisenstein, *Towards a Theory of Montage*, ed. Michael Glenny and Richard
     Taylor, trans. Michael Glenny, Vol. 2, *S. M. Eisenstein: Selected Works*
     (London: BFI Publishing, 1991), 259. 1940.
18   Ibid.
19   Ibid.
20   Ibid., 260. 1940.
21   Cole, M., and Cole, S., editors, *The Making of Mind. The Autobiography of A.R.
     Luria* (Cambridge, Mass.: Harvard University Press, 1979), 207.
22   S. M. Eisenstein, *The Film Sense*, 118–119. 1940.
23   S. M. Eisenstein, *Towards a Theory of Montage*, 256–258. 1940.
24   Wassily Kandinsky and Franz Marc, eds, *The Blaue Reiter Almanac*, ed., Klaus
     Lankheit, trans., Henning Falkenstein (London: Macmillan, 1974), 130–131.
25   S. M. Eisenstein, *Beyond the Stars*, 614. 1946.
26   Wassily Kandinsky and Franz Marc, eds, *The Blaue Reiter Almanac*, 127.

27   S. M. Eisenstein, *Nonindifferent Nature*, 386. 1945–47.
28   S. M. Eisenstein, *Towards a Theory of Montage*, 121, 337, 257. 1940.
29   S. M. Eisenstein, *Notes of a Film Director*, 156. 1946.
30   Egorova, *Soviet Film Music*, 67.
31   S. M. Eisenstein, *Nonindifferent Nature*, 332. 1945.
32   Ibid., 333
33   Ibid.
34   Ibid.
35   Ibid.
36   S. M. Eisenstein, *Towards a Theory of Montage*, 259. 1940.
37   S. M. Eisenstein, *Nonindifferent Nature*, 333. 1945.
38   Ibid., 333, 335–6.
39   Ibid., 336–7.
40   Ibid., 337–8.
41   S. M. Eisenstein, *Writings, 1934–47*, 320. 1946–47.
42   S. M. Eisenstein, *Nonindifferent Nature*, 338. 1945.
43   Ibid., 337–8.
44   S. M. Eisenstein, *Writings, 1934–47*, 320. 1946–47.
45   Sergei Eisenstein, *Notes of a Film Director*, 163. 1946.
46   Ibid., 157–8.
47   Egorova, *Soviet Film Music*, 91.
48   Ibid.
49   S. M. Eisenstein, *Nonindifferent Nature*, 333. 1945.
50   S. M. Eisenstein, *The Film Sense*, 136. 1940.
51   S. M. Eisenstein, *Writings, 1922–34*, 117–118. 1928.
52   Ibid., 121.
53   Ibid., 118.
54   S. M. Eisenstein, *The Film Sense*, 60. 1940.
55   S. M. Eisenstein, *Writings, 1922–34*, 118. 1928.
56   Ibid.
57   S. M. Eisenstein, *The Film Sense*, 76–77. 1940.
58   S. M. Eisenstein, *The Film Sense*, 78. 1940. Lafcadio Hearn (1850–1905) was a
     writer of Irish-Greek origin who greatly admired Japanese culture, which he
     introduced to the West in a series of studies and translations into English.
59   S. M. Eisenstein, *Towards a Theory of Montage*, 260. 1940.
60   A. R. Luria, *The Mind of a Mnemonist*, trans. Lynn Solotaroff (Harmondsworth,
     Middlesex: Penguin Books Ltd., 1975), 26.
61   Sergei Eisenstein, *Notes of a Film Director*, 114. 1940.
62   On the Eureka Films label.
63   Eisenstein, *Notes of a Film Director*, 116–17. 1940.
64   S. M. Eisenstein, *The Film Sense*, 72.
65   Ibid., 71.
66   S. M. Eisenstein, *Towards a Theory of Montage*, 229, and footnote. 1937.
67   S. M. Eisenstein, *Writings, 1922–34*, 182–3. 1929.
68   Ibid., 182–3, 185.

69   S. M. Eisenstein, *Towards a Theory of Montage*, 402n. 1937.
70   S. M. Eisenstein, *Writings, 1922–34*, 185. 1929.
71   Ibid., 186.
72   Ibid.
73   Sergei Eisenstein, *Notes of a Film Director*, 118. 1940.
74   S. M. Eisenstein, *Nonindifferent Nature*, 4. 1939.
75   Denis Diderot, *Le Neveu de Rameau* (Paris : Librairie Générale Française, 1972), 91–2, 96–8.
76   Boris de Schloezer, *Alexandre Scriabine* (Paris: Librairie des Cinq Continents, 1975), 176–7, 185–6. De Schloezer also mentions how Scriabin was aiming in his *Mystery* to achieve a counterpoint of different arts and senses (de Schloezer, 177, 179). This concept resembles the idea of cross-media counterpoint, mentioned in the chapter on organic unity.
77   S. M. Eisenstein, *Writings, 1934–47*, 142–147. 1940.
78   Ibid., 328. 1946–47.
79   S. M. Eisenstein, *Beyond the Stars*, 874n.1. No date.
80   Ibid., 712–723.
81   Ibid., 674. 1946.
82   This invasion in black also provided Eisenstein with a transition back to black and white film.
83   S. M. Eisenstein, *The Film Sense*, 124. 1940.
84   Ibid.
85   Ibid., 120.
86   S. M. Eisenstein, *Beyond the Stars*, 678. 1946.
87   S. M. Eisenstein, *The Film Sense*, 120. 1940.
88   Ibid., 120–121.
89   S. M. Eisenstein, *Writings, 1922–34*, 114. 1928.
90   S. M. Eisenstein, *The Film Sense*, 122. 1940.
91   S. M. Eisenstein, *Writings, 1934–47*, 322. 1946–47.
92   Ibid.
93   Ibid., 323.
94   Sergei Eisenstein, *Notes of a Film Director*, 125. 1948.
95   Ibid.
96   S. M. Eisenstein, *Writings, 1934–47*, 326. 1946–47.
97   James Joyce, *Ulysses* (Harmondsworth, Middlesex: Penguin Books Ltd., 1971. First published in Paris, 1922), 254.
98   S. M. Eisenstein, *Beyond the Stars*, 670. 1946.
99   S. M. Eisenstein, *Writings, 1934–47*, 326. 1946–47.
100 Kenneth C. Lindsay and Peter Vergo, eds, *Kandinsky: Complete Writings on Art*, Vol. 1, 1901–1921 (London: Faber and Faber, 1982), 149, 364.
101 S. M. Eisenstein, *Writings, 1934–47*, 326. 1946–47.
102 Ibid., 328.
103 Ibid., 327.
104 S. M. Eisenstein, *The Film Sense*, 93. 1940.
105 Sergei Eisenstein, *Notes of a Film Director*, 128. 1948.

106   S. M. Eisenstein, *Writings, 1934–47*, 320. 1946–47.

107   S. M. Eisenstein, *Beyond the Stars*, 658, 660. 1946.

108   S. M. Eisenstein, *Beyond the Stars*, 660.

109   Ibid.

110   S. M. Eisenstein, *The Film Sense*, 93. 1940.

111   Ibid., 93–5.

112   S. M. Eisenstein, *Beyond the Stars*, 660, 661. 1946.

113   Nicoletta Misler, 'A Choreological Laboratory', *Experiment/эксперимент*, 2 (1996), 170, 172.

114   S. M. Eisenstein, *Beyond the Stars*, 583. 1946.

115   S. M. Eisenstein, *Writings, 1934–47*, 333. 1945–47.

116   Ibid.

117   Guy Cogeval, *Vuillard: Le temps detourné* (Paris: Gallimard-Réunion des Musées Nationaux, 1993), 25.

118   Sergei Eisenstein, *Notes of a Film Director*, 122, 126–127. 1948.

119   S. M. Eisenstein, *Writings, 1934–47*, 334. 1946–47.

120   Ibid., 335–6, 338.

121   S. M. Eisenstein, *Nonindifferent Nature*, 389–91. 1945–47.

122   Ibid., 333.

123   S. M. Eisenstein, *Writings, 1934–47*, 331. 1946–47.

124   S. M. Eisenstein, *Nonindifferent Nature*, 320–1. 1945.

125   S. M. Eisenstein, *Writings, 1934–47*, 317–19. 1946–47.

126   S. M. Eisenstein, *Writings, 1922–34*, 114. 1928.

127   S. M. Eisenstein, *Writings, 1934–47*, 324–5. 1946–47.

128   S. M. Eisenstein, *The Film Sense*, 136–7, 140–1. 1940.

129   Ibid., 146–7.

130   Ibid., 139.

131   S. M. Eisenstein, *Writings, 1934–47*, 332. 1946–47.

132   S. M. Eisenstein, *The Film Sense*, 138–139. 1940.

133   Ibid., 138.

134   Russell Merritt points out that the musicians who played Prokofiev's score were under-rehearsed. In addition, Stalin's peremptory request to view the film before it was actually completed may have meant that the recording (already of poor quality) may not have been the one intended by Eisenstein and Prokofiev to go with the finished film (Russell Merritt, 'Recharging Alexander Nevsky – Tracking the Eisenstein-Prokofiev War Horse', *Film Quarterly*, Vol. 48, Number 2, Winter 1994–95), 44, 45. In Prokofiev's cantata, *Alexander Nevsky*, which he drew from his music for the film, the four G#s are also absent.

135   S. M. Eisenstein, *The Film Sense*, 161–162. 1940.

136   Sergei Eisenstein, *Notes of a Film Director*, 114. 1940.

137   S. M. Eisenstein, *The Film Sense*, 161–164. 1940.

138   Eisenstein describes how he used the piano to check his audiovisual analysis of another part of this sequence, in a class at the State Institute of Cinematography (*The Film Sense*, 137). 1940.

139   S. M. Eisenstein, *Writings, 1934–47*, 320. 1946–47.

140   S. M. Eisenstein, *The Film Sense*, 133, 138, 141–145, 152–153. 1940.

141   S. M. Eisenstein, *Writings, 1922–34*, 185. 1929.

142   S. M. Eisenstein, *The Film Sense*, 151–152. 1940.

143   Ibid., 124, 133–136, 150, 165–167.

144   S. M. Eisenstein, *Nonindifferent Nature*, 228. 1945.

145   In the Eureka edition of the film, this progression from mist to increasing
      clarity is confused, as the montage differs considerably from the director's
      account of it. For example, we see Vakulinchuk with the flickering candle
      both before and after the mists sequence, thereby removing the sense of
      climax implied in Eisenstein's description of his montage for this sequence.
      The shots he mentions are in the sequence, but not in the order that he
      presents them in his text.

146   S. M. Eisenstein, *Nonindifferent Nature*, 228–9. 1945.

147   S. M. Eisenstein, *Towards a Theory of Montage*, 293–4. Undated.

148   Sergei Eisenstein, *Notes of a Film Director*, 118. 1940. 120–1. 1948.

149   S. M. Eisenstein, *The Film Sense*, 41, 44. 1940.

150   Ibid., 46.

151   Ibid.

152   Ibid., 44.

153   Egorova, *Soviet Film Music*, 61–2.

154   Ibid., 62.

155   S. M. Eisenstein, *Writings, 1934–47*, 327. 1946–47.

156   Sergei Eisenstein, *Notes of a Film Director*, 119–120. 1948.

157   Ibid., 122.

158   Ibid., 121, 123. 1948.

159   Egorova, *Soviet Film Music*, 95–96.

160   Sergei Eisenstein, *Notes of a Film Director*, 128. 1948.

161   S. M. Eisenstein, *Writings, 1934–47*, 333. 1946–47.

162   S. M. Eisenstein, *The Film Sense*, 129. 1940.

163   Sergei Eisenstein, *Notes of a Film Director*, 124. 1948.

164   S. M. Eisenstein, *Beyond the Stars*, 636. 1946.

165   Ibid.

166   Ibid.

167   Ibid., 637. 1946. Also see page 95 in Frank Lloyd Wright's *An American
      Architecture*: 'Colors; in paste or crayon, pencil; always a thrill. To this day I
      love to hold a handful of many-colored pencils and open my hand to see
      them lying close upon my palm, in the light.'

168   Ibid.

169   Ibid.

170   Ibid.

171   Ibid., 487. 1946.

172   S. M. Eisenstein, *Nonindifferent Nature*, 394–5. 1945–47. My translation from
      the original text in French.

173   Ibid.

174   Sergei Eisenstein, *Film Form: Essays in Film Theory*, ed. and trans. Jay Leyda
        (San Diego: Harcourt Brace & Company, 1977), 186. 1939.

175   Guy Cogeval, *Vuillard*, 37.

176   Sergei Eisenstein, *Film Form*, 189. 1939.

177   Ibid., 186–187.

178   Ibid.

179   S. M. Eisenstein, *Nonindifferent Nature*, 238. 1945.

180   Karin v. Maur, *The Sound of Painting: Music in Modern Art*, trans. John W.
        Gabriel (Munich: Prestel Verlag, 1999), 13–14.

181   S. M. Eisenstein, *Nonindifferent Nature*, 220–1, 238. 1945.

182   S. M. Eisenstein, *Beyond the Stars*, 8. 1946. 29, 31. 1944.

183   John E. Atwell, *Schopenhauer on the Character of the World: The Metaphysics of Will*
        (Berkeley: University of California Press, 1995), 101.

184   Arthur Schopenhauer, *The World as Will and Idea*, trans. R.B. Haldane and J.
        Kemp (London: Kegan Paul, Trench, Trubner & Co. Ltd., 1883), 333.

185   As was shown in the *Organic Unity* chapter, Meyerhold was also a significant
        influence on Eisenstein with regard to the use of musical ideas in his work.

186   Arthur Schopenhauer, *The World as Will and Idea*, 333.

187   Lovgren, Hakan, *Eisenstein's Labyrinth: Aspects of a Cinematic Synthesis of the Arts*,
        Acta Universitatis Stockholmiensis, Stockholm Studies in Russian Literature, Vol. 31
        (Stockholm: Almqvist & Wiksell International, 1996), 87.

188   S. M. Eisenstein, *Beyond the Stars*, 78, 80–82. 1946.

189   S. M. Eisenstein, *Beyond the Stars*, 82–83. 1946. Eliphas Levi, pseudonym of
        Alphonse Louis Constant (1810–75), was an influential historian of the
        occult traditions.

190   Kenneth C. Lindsay and Peter Vergo, *Kandinsky: Complete Writings on Art*, Vol.
        1, 117.

191   S. M. Eisenstein, *The Film Sense*, 74–75. 1940. Karl von Eckartshausen (1752–
        1803) was a German writer and specialist in magic and the occult traditions.

192   Ibid., 74. 1940.

193   Ibid., 75.

194   Ibid.

195   S. M. Eisenstein, *Towards a Theory of Montage*, 258. 1940.

196   S. M. Eisenstein, *The Film Sense*, 76. 1940. My translation from the original in
        French.

197   Enid Starkie, *Arthur Rimbaud* (London: Hamish Hamilton, 1947. First edition
        published by Faber & Faber in 1938), 118.

198   Enid Starkie, *Baudelaire* (Harmondsworth, Middlesex: Penguin Books Ltd.,
        1971), 12.

199   Francis Scarfe, ed., *Baudelaire* (Harmondsworth, Middlesex: Penguin Books
        Ltd., 1972), 36–7. My translation.

200   Ibid.

201   Leonid Sabaneiev (Scriabin's biographer) describes the composer's aim in his
        Mystery whereby a synthesis of the arts would be 'united in one work, whose
        ambiance conveys such a great exaltation that it must absolutely be followed

by an authentic ecstasy, an authentic vision of higher realities.'(Wassily Kandinsky, Franz Marc eds, *The Blaue Reiter Almanac*, 130–1).

202   S. M. Eisenstein, *Beyond the Stars*, 614. 1946.

203   Enid Starkie, *Baudelaire*, 260–4.

204   Emanuel Swedenborg, *Heaven and Its Wonders and Hell: From Things Heard and Seen* (London: The Swedenborg Society, 1989), 60–1.

205   F.-F. Gautier, ed., *Oeuvres complètes de Charles Baudelaire* (Paris: Editions de la Nouvelle Revue Française, 1921, reprint of original 1869 edition), 236. My translation.

206   S. M. Eisenstein, *Beyond the Stars*, 478. 1946.

207   Ibid., 30. 1944.

208   Ibid., 30, 35–36. 1944.

209   Ibid., 30.

210   Ibid., 30–31. 1944.

211   S. M. Eisenstein, *Writings, 1934–47*, 7–12. 1934.

212   S. M. Eisenstein, *Writings, 1922–34*, 56–57. 1924.

213   S. M. Eisenstein, *Writings, 1934–47*, 19. 1935.

214   S. M. Eisenstein, *Beyond the Stars*, 663. 1946. For this diagram see Stuart Gilbert's study, *James Joyce's Ulysses*, 38.

215   S. M. Eisenstein, *Towards a Theory of Montage*, 195. 1937–40.

216   Enid Starkie, *Arthur Rimbaud*, 129.

217   S. M. Eisenstein, *Towards a Theory of Montage*, 198. 1937–40.

218   Ibid., 258, 364–365.

219   In the fourth verse of *Le Sonnet des voyelles*, Rimbaud associates 'U' with 'Lines printed by alchemy on the great brows of the wise'. (*The Film Sense*, 76). 1940.

220   Enid Starkie, *Arthur Rimbaud*, 133–135.

221   James Joyce, *Ulysses* (Harmondsworth, Middlesex: Penguin Books Ltd., 1971), 299–300.

222   S. M. Eisenstein, *Beyond the Stars*, 83.

223   Richard Ellmann, *James Joyce* (Oxford: Oxford University Press, 1965), 61, 144.

224   Hilary Gatti, *Giordano Bruno and Renaissance Science* (Ithaca and London: Cornell University Press, 1999), 191–193, 195, 200, 203.

225   Richard Ellmann, *James Joyce*, 61.

226   Ibid., 671, 870n.

227   Ibid.

228   Hilary Gatti, *Giordano Bruno and Renaissance Science*, 113, 142.

229   Ibid., 114.

230   S. M. Eisenstein, *Beyond the Stars*, 82–83, 208–209. 1946.

231   Marie Seton, *Sergei M. Eisenstein: A Biography* (New York: A.A. Wyn, Inc., 1952), 145–6.

232   S. M. Eisenstein, *Beyond the Stars*, 36. 1944. 241. 1946.

233   S. M. Eisenstein, *Immoral Memories*, 211. 1946.

234   S. M. Eisenstein, *Nonindifferent Nature*, 177. 1945–47.

235   F.-F. Gautier, ed., *Oeuvres complètes de Charles Baudelaire*, 218. My translation.

236   Ibid., 218–19.

237   Enid Starkie, *Arthur Rimbaud*, 126, 219, 131.

238   Sergei Eisenstein, *Film Form*, 84. 1932.

239   Ibid., 105. 1932.

240   Ibid.

241   Ibid., 106. 1932.

242   S. M. Eisenstein, *Writings, 1934–47*, 322. 1946–47.

243   S. M. Eisenstein, *The Film Sense*, 167–168. 1940.

244   Ibid. 245 S. M. Eisenstein, *Writings, 1934–47*, 322. 1946–47.

Bibliography

Amiard-Chevrel, Claudine ed. *Théâtre et cinéma années vingt*. Vol.1. *Théâtre années vingt*. Lausanne: L'Age d'Homme, 1990.

Atwell, John E. *Schopenhauer on the Character of the World: The Metaphysics of Will*. Berkeley: University of California Press, 1995.

Barna, Yon. *Eisenstein: The Growth of a Cinematic Genius*. Bloomington: Indiana University Press, 1973.

Baudelaire, Charles. *Oeuvres complètes de Charles Baudelaire*. Gautier, F.-F. ed. Paris : Editions de la Nouvelle Revue Française, 1921. Reprint of original 1869 edition.

Bergan, Ronald. *Sergei Eisenstein: A Life in Conflict*. Woodstock, NY: The Overlook Press, 1999.

Bordwell, David. *The Cinema of Eisenstein*. New York: Routledge, 2005.

Bowlt, John, and Nancy Van Norman Baer. *Theatre in Revolution: Russian Avant-garde Stage Design, 1913–1935*. San Francisco: Thames and Hudson and The Fine Arts Museums of San Francisco, exhibition catalogue, 1991.

Bulgakowa, Oksana. *Sergei Eisenstein: A Biography*. Anne Dwyer, trans. Berlin: Potemkin Press, 2001.

Christie, Ian and David Elliott, eds *Eisenstein at Ninety*. Oxford: Museum of Modern Art, 1988.

Christie, Ian and Richard Taylor, eds *Eisenstein Rediscovered*. London and New York: Routledge, 1998.

Cogeval, Guy. *Vuillard: le temps detourné*. Paris: Gallimard-Réunion des Musées Nationaux, 1993.

Cornwell, Neil. *James Joyce and the Russians*. Basingstoke and London: The Macmillan Press Ltd, 1992.

Covarrubias, Miguel. *Mexico South: The Isthmus of Tehuantepec*. London: Cassell and Company Limited, 1947.

Diderot, Denis. *Le Neveu de Rameau*. Paris: Librairie Générale Française, 1972. First published in German, Leipzig, 1805. Johann Wolfgang von Goethe, trans.

Düchting, Hajo. *Paul Klee: Painting Music*. Munich, London, New York: Prestel, 2002.

Egorova, Tatiana K. *Soviet Film Music: An Historical Survey*. Tatiana A. Ganf and Natalia A. Egunova, trans. Amsterdam: Harwood Academic Publishers, 1997.

Eisenstein, S. M. *Beyond the Stars: The Memoirs of Sergei Eisenstein*. Vol. 4. *Selected Works*. Richard Taylor, ed. and William Powell, trans. London: BFI, Calcutta: Seagull Books, 1995.

Eisenstein, S. M. *Eisenstein on Disney*. Jay Leyda, ed. and Alan Upchurch, trans. London: Methuen Ltd., 1988.

Eisenstein, S. M. *Film Form: Essays in Film Theory*. Jay Leyda, ed. and trans. San Diego, New York, London: Harcourt Brace & Company, 1977.

Eisenstein, S. M. *Immoral Memories: An Autobiography*. Herbert Marshall, trans. London: Peter Owen Limited, 1985.

Eisenstein, S. M. *Nonindifferent Nature*. Herbert Marshall, trans. Cambridge: Cambridge University Press, 1987.

Eisenstein, S. M. *Notes of a Film Director*. X. Danko, trans. New York: Dover Publications, Inc., 1970.

Eisenstein, S. M. *Que viva Mexico!* New York: Arno Press, 1972.

Eisenstein, S. M. *The Film Sense*. Jay Leyda, ed. and trans. London: Faber and Faber, 1970. First published 1943.

Eisenstein, S. M. *Towards a Theory of Montage*. Vol.2. *Selected Works*. Michael Glenny and Richard Taylor, eds, Michael Glenny, trans. London: BFI Publishing, 1991. Revised ed., 1994.

Eisenstein, S. M. *Writings, 1922–34*. Vol. 1. *Selected Works*. Richard Taylor, ed. and trans. London: BFI Publishing, 1988.

Eisenstein, S. M. *Writings, 1934–47*. Vol. 3. *Selected Works*. Richard Taylor, ed., and William Powell, trans. London: BFI Publishing, 1996.

Eisenstein, Sergei M. *The Complete Films of Eisenstein, Together with an Unpublished Essay by Eisenstein*. John Hetherington, trans. London: Weidenfeld and Nicolson, 1974.

Eisenstein, Sergei. *Film Essays and a Lecture*. Jay Leyda, ed. New York and Washington: Praeger Publishers, 1970.

Ellmann, Richard. *James Joyce*. Oxford: Oxford University Press, 1965.

Faure, Elie. *Fonction du Cinéma: De la cinéplastique à son destin social*. Lausanne: Editions Gonthier, 1964.

Faure, Elie. *Mon périple: Voyage autour du monde, 1931–1932*. Paris: Editions Seghers, 1987.

François Albera, *Eisenstein et le Constructivisme Russe*. Lausanne: Editions l'Age d'Homme, 1990.

Gatti, Hilary. *Giordano Bruno and Renaissance Science*. Ithaca and London: Cornell University Press, 1999.

Geduld, Harry M. *Sergei Eisenstein and Upton Sinclair: The Making and Unmaking of Que Viva Mexico!* Harry M. Geduld & Ronald Gottesman, eds Bloomington, Indiana University Press, 1970.

Gilbert, Stuart. *James Joyce's Ulysses, A Study.* Harmondsworth, UK: Peregrine Books, 1969.

Gladkov, Aleksandr. *Meyerhold Speaks, Meyerhold Rehearses.* Alma Law, ed. and trans. Amsterdam: Harwood Academic Publishers, 1997.

Gogol, Nikolai V. *The Government Inspector.* D.J. Campbell, trans. London: Heinemann Educational Books, 1947.

Gray, Cleve, ed. *Hans Richter by Hans Richter, Pioneer of Dada and the Experimental Film.* London: Thames and Hudson Limited, 1971.

Grout, Donald Jay. *A History of Western Music.* New York: W.W. Norton & Company Inc., 1960.

Joyce, James, *Ulysses.* Harmondsworth, UK: Penguin Books Ltd., 1971. First published in Paris, 1922.

Joyce, James. *Finnegans Wake.* London: Faber and Faber Limited, 1975. First published simultaneously in London and New York, 1939.

Kandinsky, Wassily, and Franz Marc, eds *The Blaue Reiter Almanac.* Klaus Lankheit, ed., and Henning Falkenstein, trans. London: Macmillan, 1974.

Kandinsky, Wassily. *Kandinsky: Complete Writings on Art.* Vol. 1, 1901–1921. Kenneth C. Lindsay and Peter Vergo, eds London: Faber and Faber, 1982.

Karetnikova, Inga. *Mexico According to Eisenstein.* Inga Karetnikova, in collaboration with Leon Steinmetz. Albuquerque: University of New Mexico Press, 1991.

Klee, Paul. *The Diaries of Paul Klee, 1898–1918.* Klee, Felix, ed. Berkeley, Los Angeles, London: University of California Press, 1964.

Kozintsev, Grigori. *The Space of Tragedy.* Berkeley and Los Angeles: University of California Press, 1977.

La Valley, Al and Barry P. Scherr. *Eisenstein at 100.* New Brunswick and London: Rutgers University Press, 2001.

Lavrentiev, A. N. *Rodchenko.* Moscow: Iskusstvo, 1992.

Law, Alma and Mel Gordon. *Meyerhold, Eisenstein and Biomechanics: Actor Training in Revolutionary Russia.* Jefferson, NC and London: McFarland & Company, Inc., Publishers, 1996.

Lawrence, D. H. *The Plumed Serpent.* Ware, Hertfordshire: Wordsworth Editions Ltd., 1995. First published 1926.

Levitz, Tamara. *Teaching New Classicality: Ferruccio Busoni's Master Class in Composition.* Vol. 152. European University Studies. Frankfurt a.M.: Peter Lang, 1996.

Leyda, Jay and Zina Voynow. *Eisenstein at Work.* London: Methuen London Ltd., 1985.

Lovgren, Hakan. *Eisenstein's Labyrinth: Aspects of a Cinematic Synthesis of the Arts.* Vol. 31. Acta Universitatis Stockholmiensis, Stockholm Studies in Russian Literature. Stockholm: Almqvist & Wiksell International, 1996.

Luria, A.R. *The Mind of a Mnemonist.* Lynn Solotaroff, trans. Harmondsworth, Middlesex: Penguin Books Ltd., 1975.

Luria, A.R. *The Making of Mind; The Autobiography of A.R. Luria.* M. Cole and S. Cole, eds Cambridge, Mass.: Harvard University Press, 1979.

Marshall, Herbert. *Mayakovsky and His Poetry.* London: Pilot Press, 1942.

Maur, Karin v. *The Sound of Painting: Music in Modern Art.* John W. Gabriel, trans. Munich: Prestel Verlag, 1999.

Merritt, Russell. 'Recharging "Alexander Nevsky"; Tracking the Eisenstein-Prokofiev War Horse'. *Film Quarterly.* Vol. 48, No 2 (Winter, 1994–5), 34–45.

Metchenko, Alexei, et al. *Vladimir Mayakovsky: Innovator.* Alex Miller, trans. Moscow : Progress Publishers, 1976.

Meyerhold, Vsevolod. *Ecrits sur le théâtre, 1936–1940.* Béatrice Picon-Vallin, ed. and trans. Lausanne: L'Age d'Homme, 1992.

Meyerhold, Vsevolod. *Meyerhold on Theatre.* Edward Braun, ed. and trans. London: Methuen and Co Ltd., 1969. Revised ed., 1991.

Miller, Dorothy C., ed. *Lyonel Feininger – Marsden Hartley.* New York: The Museum of Modern Art, 1944.

Misler, Nicoletta. 'A Choreological Laboratory' in *Experiment/Ekcnepement.* Vol. 2. *MOTO-BIO – The Russian Art of Movement: Dance, Gesture, and Gymnastics, 1910–1930.* Natalia Chernova, ed. Los Angeles: University of Southern California, 1996, 169–99.

Montagu, Ivor. *With Eisenstein in Hollywood.* Berlin: Seven Seas Publishers, 1968.

Mordrel, Olier. *Rivera, les fresques de Mexico.* Paris: Editions Atlas, 1984.

Nesbet, Anne. *Savage Junctures: Sergei Eisenstein and the Shape of Thinking.* London, New York: I.B.Tauris, 2003.

Nims, John Frederick. *The Poems of St John of the Cross.* New York: Grove Press, 1959.

Picon-Vallin, Béatrice. *Meyerhold.* Paris: Editions du Centre National de la Recherche Scientifique, 1990.

Pimenov, Yuri, et al. *S. Eisenstein: Drawings.* Moscow: Iskusstvo, 1961.

Poe, Edgar Allan. *Selected Stories and Poems.* New York: Airmont Publishing Co., Inc., 1962.

Power, Arthur, and Clive Hart, ed. *Conversations with James Joyce.* London: Millington Books Ltd., 1978.

Richter, Hans. *Dada: Art and Anti-Art*. London: Thames and Hudson, 1997.

Ruskin, John. *Modern Painters*. Vol. 3. Orpington: George Allen, 1897.

Scarfe, Francis ed. and trans. *Baudelaire*. Harmondsworth, Middlesex: Penguin Books Ltd., 1972.

Schloezer, Boris de. *Alexandre Scriabine*. Paris: Librairie des Cinq Continents, 1975.

Schopenhauer, Arthur. *The World as Will and Idea*. R.B. Haldane and J. Kemp, trans. London: Kegan Paul, Trench, Trubner & Co. Ltd., 1883.

Seton, Marie. *Sergei M. Eisenstein: A Biography*. New York: A.A. Wyn, Inc., 1952.

Starkie, Enid. *Arthur Rimbaud*. London: Hamish Hamilton, 1947.

Starkie, Enid. *Baudelaire*. Harmondsworth, Middlesex: Penguin Books Ltd., 1971.

Swallow, Norman. *Eisenstein: A Documentary Portrait*. London: George Allen & Unwin Ltd., 1976.

Swedenborg, Emanuel. *Heaven and Its Wonders and Hell: From Things Heard and Seen*. London: The Swedenborg Society, 1989. First published in Latin, London, 1758.

Taylor, Richard, and Ian Christie. *The Film Factory: Russian and Soviet Cinema in Documents, 1896–1939*. London and New York: Routledge, 1994.

Taylor, Richard. *The Battleship Potemkin: The Film Companion*. London: I.B.Tauris, 2000.

Thérèse de l'Enfant Jesus, Sainte. *Manuscrits autobiographiques*. Andreas Jacquemin, Episcopus Bajocencis et Lexoviensis, ed. Lisieux: Office Central de Lisieux, 1957.

Vergo, Peter. 'Hoelzel and Itten' in *Abstraction: Towards a New Art; Painting, 1910–1920*. London: Tate Gallery, exhibition catalogue, 1980, 76–9.

Vogt, Paul. *The Blue Rider*. London and Woodbury NY: Barron's Educational Series, Inc., 1980.

Westphalen, Timothy C. ed. and trans. *Aleksandr Blok's Trilogy of Lyric Dramas*. London and New York: Routledge, 2003.

Wollen, Peter, 'Lund Celebrates a Dada Child' in *Pix,* Vol. 2, 1997, 146–56.

Wollen, Peter. *Signs and Meaning in the Cinema*. London: Secker and Warburg, 3rd ed., 1972.

Note Regarding Versions of Eisenstein's Films

To avoid confusion regarding the various versions of Eisenstein's films, here are the editions to which I refer in my text:

For *The Strike* (herein titled *Strike*), *The Battleship Potemkin*, *October* (herein *October 1917*): the *Russia in Revolt* collection. Eureka Video. 2002.

For *Que viva Mexico!* reconstructed by Grigory Alexandrov and Nikita Orlov (1931/1979), Kino on Video. 1998.

For *Alexander Nevsky, Ivan the Terrible, Parts 1 and 2*:
Eisenstein, the Sound Years. The Criterion Collection. DVD. 2002.

The film stills and other illustrations reproduced in this book that are not from Richard Taylor's edition of Eisenstein's *Selected Works* are from the author's private collection.

Index